WALKING THE ROAD

Race, Diversity, and Social Justice in Teacher Education

MARILYN COCHRAN-SMITH

TEACHERS
COLLEGE
PRESS

Teachers College, Columbia Univers
New York and London

Antonio Machado's poem, "Caminando," is reprinted by permission of the publisher from *Antonio Machado: Selected Poems*, translated by Alan S. Trueblood, p. 143, Cambridge, Mass.: Harvard University Press, Copyright © 1982 by the President and Fellows of Harvard College.

The author is grateful to the following organizations and publishers for granting her permission to present revised versions of the following articles and book chapters that she authored:

Harvard University Press for: Learning to teach against the grain. *Harvard Educational Review*, 1991, 51(3): 279–310. By permission of Harvard University Press.

American Educational Research Association for: Color blindness and basket making are not the answers: Confronting the dilemmas of race, culture, and language diversity in teacher education. *American Educational Research Journal*, 1995, 32(3): 493–522. Copyright 1995 by the American Educational Research Association. Adapted with the permission of the publisher.

National Society for the Study of Education for: Learning to teach for social justice. In G. Griffin (Ed.), *Ninety-eighth Yearbook of the National Society for the Study of Education* (pp. 114–144). Chicago: University of Chicago Press, 1999. By permission of NSSE.

Harvard University Press for: Blind vision. *Harvard Educational Review*, 2000, 70(2): 151–190. By permission of Harvard University Press.

Elsevier Science for: The outcomes question in teacher education. *Teaching and Teacher Education*, 2001, 17: 527–546. Copyright 2001, with permission of Elsevier Science.

American Educational Research Association for: Sticks, stones, and ideology: The discourse of reform in teacher education. *Educational Researcher*, 2001, 30(8): 3–15. Copyright 2001 by the American Educational Research Association. Adapted with the permission of the publisher.

Caddo Gap Press for: The multiple meanings of multicultural education: A conceptual framework. *Teacher Education Quarterly*, 2003, Spring: 7–26. By permission of Caddo Gap Press.

Published by Teachers College Press, 1234 Amsterdam Avenue, New York, NY 10027

Copyright © 2004 by Teachers College, Columbia University

Library of Congress Cataloging-in-Publication Data

Cochran-Smith, Marilyn. 1949-
　　Walking the road : race, diversity, and social justice in teacher education / Marilyn Cochran-Smith.
　　　p. cm. — (Multicultural education series)
　　Includes bibliographical references (p.) and index.
　　ISBN 0-8077-4434-4 (cloth : alk. paper) — ISBN 0-8077-4433-6 (pbk : alk. paper)
　　1. Teachers—Training of—Social aspects—United States.　2. Discrimination in education—United States.　3. Multicultural education—United States.　4. Critical pedagogy—United States.　I. Title.　II. Multicultural education series (New York, N.Y.)
　　LB1715.C59 2004
　　370'.71'1—dc22

2003066284

ISBN 0-8077-4433-6 (paper)
ISBN 0-8077-4434-4 (cloth)

Printed on acid-free paper
Manufactured in the United States of America

11　10　09　08　07　06　05　04　　　8　7　6　5　4　3　2　1

Contents

Series Foreword

The nation's deepening ethnic texture, interracial tension and conflict, and increasing percentage of students who speak a first language other than English make multicultural education imperative in the 21st century. The U.S. Census Bureau (2000) estimated that people of color made up 28% of the nation's population in 2000, and predicted that they would make up 38% in 2025, and 47% in 2050.

American classrooms are experiencing the largest influx of immigrant students since the beginning of the 20th century. About a million immigrants are making the United States their home each year (Martin & Midgley, 1999). More than seven and one-half million legal immigrants settled in the United States between 1991 and 1998, most of whom came from nations in Latin America and Asia (Riche, 2000). A large but undetermined number of undocumented immigrants also enter the United States each year. The influence of an increasingly ethnically diverse population on the nation's schools, colleges, and universities is and will continue to be enormous.

Forty percent of the students enrolled in the nation's schools in 2001 were students of color. This percentage is increasing each year, primarily because of the growth in the percentage of Latino students (Martinez & Curry, 1999). In some of the nation's largest cities and metropolitan areas, such as Chicago, Los Angeles, Washington, D.C., New York, Seattle, and San Francisco, half or more of the public school students are students of color. During the 1998–1999 school year, students of color made up 63.1% of the student population in the public schools of California, the nation's largest state (California State Department of Education, 2000).

Language and religious diversity is also increasing among the nation's student population. In 2000, about 20% of the school-age population spoke a language at home other than English (U.S. Census Bureau, 2000). Harvard professor Diana L. Eck (2001) calls the United States the "most religiously diverse nation on earth" (p. 4). Most teachers now in the classroom and in teacher education programs are likely to have students from diverse ethnic, racial, language, and religious groups in their classrooms during their careers. This is true for both inner-city and suburban teachers.

An important goal of multicultural education is to improve race relations and to help all students acquire the knowledge, attitudes, and skills needed to participate in cross-cultural interactions and in personal, social, and civic action that will help make our nation more democratic and just. Multicultural education is consequently as important for middle-class White suburban students as it is for students of color who live in the inner city. Multicultural education fosters the public good and the overarching goals of the commonwealth.

The major purpose of the *Multicultural Education Series* is to provide preservice educators, practicing educators, graduate students, scholars, and policy makers with an interrelated and comprehensive set of books that summarizes and analyzes important research, theory, and practice related to the education of ethnic, racial, cultural, and language groups in the United States and the education of mainstream students about diversity. The books in the *Series* provide research, theoretical, and practical knowledge about the behaviors and learning characteristics of students of color, language minority students, and low-income students. They also provide knowledge about ways to improve academic achievement and race relations in educational settings.

The definition of multicultural education in the *Handbook of Research on Multicultural Education* (Banks & Banks, 2004) is used in the *Series*: Multicultural education is "a field of study designed to increase educational equity for all students that incorporates, for this purpose, content, concepts, principles, theories, and paradigms from history, the social and behavioral sciences, and particularly from ethnic studies and women's studies" (p. xii). In the *Series*, as in the *Handbook*, multicultural education is considered a "metadiscipline."

The dimensions of multicultural education, developed by Banks (2004) and described in the *Handbook of Research on Multicultural Education*, provide the conceptual framework for the development of the books in the *Series*. They are: *content integration, the knowledge construction process, prejudice reduction, an equity pedagogy,* and *an empowering school culture and social structure.* To implement multicultural education effectively, teachers and administrators must attend to each of the five dimensions of multicultural education. They should use content from diverse groups when teaching concepts and skills; help students to understand how knowledge in the various disciplines is constructed; help students to develop positive intergroup attitudes and behaviors; and modify their teaching strategies so that students from different racial, cultural, language, and social-class groups will experience equal educational opportunities. The total environment and culture of the school must also be transformed so that students from diverse groups will experience equal status in the culture and life of the school.

Although the five dimensions of multicultural education are highly interrelated, each requires deliberate attention and focus. Each book in the *Series* focuses on one or more of the dimensions, although each book deals with all of them to some extent because of the highly interrelated characteristics of the dimensions.

This informative and engaging book by one of the nation's most influential, insightful, and compassionate teacher educators is both timely and needed. Teacher education is now at the crossroads. An intense political battle is taking place within the 50 states and at the national level between teachers educators and those outside the profession who have conflicting visions and ideologies about educating teachers in a diverse democratic society. The conservative agenda to produce "highly qualified teachers," codified in the No Child Left Behind Act of 2001 and by Secretary of Education Rod Paige's report, *Meeting the Highly Qualified Teacher Challenge* (U.S. Department of Education, 2002), is designed to circumvent professional teacher education within schools and colleges of education. As Cochran-Smith documents in this skillfully written and incisive book, the current federal agenda for teacher education poses serious problems and challenges for educating reflective and creative teachers who are committed to social justice and to low-income and minority students who have historically been underserved and left behind.

Cochran-Smith describes the major problems faced by the teaching profession today and identifies the characteristics of effective teacher education programs that produce teachers who can and will teach for social justice. She also specifies actions that teacher educators can take to strengthen teacher education programs and to respond to the difficult social and political contexts in which teacher education now takes place. A unique strength of this book is that Cochran-Smith helps readers to reconceptualize the problems in teacher education. She presents convincing evidence to support her argument that teaching quality is not a technical problem of testing and training. Rather, it is a learning problem and a political problem related to social justice and educational equality.

The rich texture and thick descriptions in this engrossing book result from the author's deep and thoughtful participation in teacher education programs for two decades and from her efforts to reconstruct her knowledge and actions as she "walked" the teacher education road. Cochran-Smith's use of the "walking" metaphor conveys the significant ways in which teacher education for social justice—for professors, students, and school participants in teacher education— is a complex and lifelong process that should be conceptualized, constructed, and reconstructed as it is undertaken. I hope this book will encourage teacher educators to make social justice a priority in their work and to develop their own ideas and programs for educating teachers for social justice by "walking." They will find the guideposts in this discerning book helpful, hopeful, and inspiring.

James A. Banks
Series Editor

REFERENCES

Banks, J. A. (2004). Multicultural education: Historical development, dimensions, and practice. In J. A. Banks & C. A. M. Banks (Eds.). *Handbook of research on multicultural education* (2nd ed.; pp. 3–29). San Francisco: Jossey-Bass.

Banks, J. A., & Banks, C. A. M. (Eds.). (2004). *Handbook of research on multicultural education* (2nd ed.). San Francisco: Jossey-Bass.

California State Department of Education (2000). On-line: http://data1.cde.ca.gov/ dataquest

Eck, D. L. (2001). *A new religious America: How a "Christian country" has become the world's most religiously diverse nation*. New York: HarperSanFrancisco.

Martin, P., & Midgley, E. (1999). Immigration to the United States. *Population Bulletin, 54*(2), pp. 1–44. Washington, DC: Population Reference Bureau.

Martinez, G. M., & Curry, A. E. (1999, September). *Current population reports: School enrollment—Social and economic characteristics of students* (update). Washington, DC: U.S. Census Bureau.

Riche, M. F. (2000). America's diversity and growth: Signposts for the 21st century. *Population Bulletin, 55*(2), pp. 1–43. Washington, DC: Population Reference Bureau.

U.S. Census Bureau. (2000). *Statistical abstract of the United States* (120th edition). Washington, DC: U.S. Government Printing Office.

U.S. Department of Education. (2002). *Meeting the highly qualified teachers challenge: Secretary's annual report on teacher quality*. Washington, DC: U.S. Department of Education, Office of Postsecondary Education.

Foreword

Marilyn Cochran-Smith brilliantly uses the metaphor of "walking the road" to describe the long, complex, difficult, and seemingly endless journey that teachers, teacher educators, researchers, and policy makers embark upon as they seek to discover the various meanings and different paths associated with educating teachers for diversity and social justice. As she explains, traveling the road for social justice requires skilled and committed sojourners who are capable of maneuvering the current political climate that shortsightedly pits the goals of high standards, accountability, and teacher quality against equity and equal opportunity for all students. Finding one's way through this quagmire demands a close examination of multifaceted questions and concerns. Cochran-Smith's analysis of this problem is instructive on several points related to predispositions, directions, outcomes, agendas, and support systems.

When educators attempt to implement practice consistent with social justice, they discover the influence of teachers' predispositions acquired through previous and recent experiences, particularly experiences with "the cultural other." I discovered in my work with teachers, both pre- and in-service, that those who have close association with diverse populations have fewer difficulties and less hesitation in embracing cultural differences. Most notably, teachers who grew up or presently live in integrated neighborhoods, attended integrated schools, or participated in study abroad exchanges were more likely to be risk takers and strong advocates of children, reflective and complex thinkers, more persistent, open-minded, and more willing to examine assumptions about racism and prejudice.

As educators start their journey for social justice, these predispostions and experiences inform the maps that educators choose to direct the trip. Our unique biographies, values, and beliefs profoundly influence the mission and "stance" we adopt. The directions we choose and the agendas we endorse lead to different junctures and require different decisions, choices, courses of action, and eventually different outcomes. Cochran-Smith emphasizes that the outcomes issues (such as teacher learning, student learning, professional practice) are dependent on the political context and the measures we use to assess them. Unfortunately social justice and equity have been rarely included in these discussions. In fact, using social justice as an outcome for both teachers and their students is perceived by some as antithetical to issues of student and teacher learning.

A commitment to social justice, advocacy for change, and critical inquiry requires diverse personal and profession support systems because the questions raised about race make the walk less safe and leave educators vulnerable and lonely. Teachers often find that their colleagues and administrators prefer not to associate with them when they act as change agents. Little wonder few faculty and students of education venture into this uncertain territory. Transforming teachers into critical inquirers and culturally responsive pedagogists becomes less demanding and more powerful when teachers build meaningful networks and collaborations that include mentors, supporters, professional colleagues, and students' families and communities.

Although attention to predispositions, directions, outcomes, agendas, and support systems are promising strategies to employ while "walking the road" to social justice, these strategies have to be situated within the history of teacher education. The field of teacher education has not taken seriously its role to prepare teachers as activists and advocates of social justice. Some teacher educators and their pre- and in-service teachers discover that discussions of race and ethnicity produce discomfort, guilt, anger, and ultimately denial. Too many in the profession appear to be not only colorblind but "color deaf" and "color mute" when it comes to issues of race—that is, unable or unwilling to see, hear, or speak about instances of individual or institutional racism in their personal and professional lives. I agree with Lee Bell's (2002) conclusion that white teachers' colorblind beliefs are rooted in a "sincere yet dangerous fiction" that prevents them from self-reflection about domination and privilege.

However difficult the collective struggle, educators must engage in frequent and honest dialogue and debate about the value of diversity and social activism in the curriculum. As teacher educators, we cannot shy away from unpleasant and uncertain conversations because the failure and unwillingness to look, listen, and learn about diversity, oppression, and the experiences of the cultural other significantly interfere with the ability to critique and problematize schooling or "teach against the grain."

Cochran-Smith points out that "teaching against the grain" contradicts simplistic, generic, decontextualized, and overly prescriptive teacher education programs that fail to produce thoughtful activist-teachers, particularly in urban schools. Teaching is clearly a complex act involving some person teaching something to some student somewhere. Context is the operative word here. Social reconstructivists understand context and the complexity of teaching and do not use a set of rigid pedagogical principles in their classrooms. Instead, they modify what they have learned in teacher education, recognizing that mastery of pedagogical principles and subject matter content are necessary but not sufficient conditions for effective teaching. Activists for social justice recognize that they do not instruct culturally homogenized, standardized students. Teachers armed with such generic teaching skills often find themselves ineffective and ill-prepared when faced with a classroom of diverse learners. These unprepared teachers soon leave the profession.

I believe the implications of Cochran-Smith's compelling work is that teacher educators should concentrate on institutional programs and individual classroom pedagogy as well as other critical factors such as the students we admit into our programs; the larger institutional context where we teach; and the articulation of our political ideology related to social justice.

One sobering finding in teacher education that keeps surfacing in the literature is that our programs and courses may have some short term effect on changing our students' beliefs and attitudes about diversity, but our long-term influence is minimal. We should look more closely at the predispositions and beliefs systems that students bring into the teacher education program. Preservice teachers' beliefs are unlikely to be replaced unless they prove unsatisfactory, and they are not likely to prove unsatisfactory unless teacher educators and peers challenge them.

The institutional context makes a difference. Efficacious teachers committed to social justice do not come out of racist institutions and teacher education programs—no matter how competent, persuasive, or hardworking each of us might be. A few maverick activist teacher educators who advocate for social justice and change usually do not change an institution's culture and climate. Culture and climate changes are most evident when teacher education programs are successful in providing a model of cultural diversity on their own campuses. If colleges of education are not able to recruit and retain faculty and students of color, how will they provide examples of cultural diversity for their teacher education students? If teacher educators have limited experiences with diverse populations, how will preservice teachers acquire positive personal and professional attitudes and skills to teach culturally diverse students? Clearly, deans, directors, and chairs must provide the leadership necessary to develop an organizational climate that values diversity and provides opportunities for professional development for faculty who have limited experiences and knowledge about diversity and the social justice agenda.

Finally, faculty in colleges of education have to model inquiry and social justice in their own teaching, making explicit to teacher education students how and why they know what they know. Professors have political ideologies and views about racism, inequality, and oppression. But too often we hesitate out of fear or rejection to share our ideologies and political stances.

We can no longer delay "walking the road." The profession is at a critical crossroad burdened with political landmines, circuitous routes, and unpredictable and uncertain detours. We must accept Cochran-Smith's challenge to speak loudly and articulately for social justice and democracy. Could our society face a more urgent or compelling issue?

Jacqueline Jordan Irvine
Emory University

REFERENCE

Bell, L. A. (2002). Sincere fictions: The pedagogical challenges of preparing White teachers for multicultural classrooms. *Equity and Excellence in Education*, *35*(3), 236–244.

Acknowledgments

This book would not have been possible without the many professional colleagues, friends, and graduate students at the University of Pennsylvania, Boston College, and the larger educational community who have helped to sustain my work over the last 15 years. Their companionship, ideas, and commitments have supported my efforts to put into practice locally and theorize more publicly a commitment to teacher education for social justice. In particular, I am indebted to the student teachers, teachers, supervisors' group, and university faculty who were part of the Project START inquiry community during the decade in which it emerged and thrived.

I am especially grateful to my long-time friend, colleague, and coauthor Susan L. Lytle, who walked much of the road with me and whose intelligence, warmth, and shared beliefs about inquiry, knowledge, and teaching for social justice helped make the journey possible. As noted throughout this text, many of the ideas about the role of inquiry in learning to teach that are fundamental to this book were developed collaboratively with Susan and with our colleagues in a number of inquiry communities.

Many thanks also to my good colleague and friend James A. Banks, who invited me to collect and revise the many essays and articles I had written about teacher education for social justice over the years. His encouragement and suggestions about how to shape 15 years' worth of articles into a coherent book were invaluable.

Finally I want to acknowledge and thank my husband, Larry H. Ludlow. Although his own academic field is worlds apart from mine, his confidence in my abilities as a writer and his belief in the importance of my work in teacher education have been unfailing. His willingness to read every one of my articles, editorials, and manuscripts for the last 8 years and to comment on each of them critically but respectfully has been a great gift.

CALMINANTE
ANTONIO MACHADO

Caminante, son tus huellas
el camino, y nada mas;

caminante, no hay camino
se hace camino al andar.
Al andar se hace camino,
y al volver la vista astras
se ve la senda que nunca
se ha de volver a pisar.
Caminante, no hay camino
sino estelas en el mar.

TRAVELER

Traveler, your footsteps
Make the path and nothing more;

Traveler, there is no path
You make it as you go along.
In walking the path is made,
And as you turn around
You see the path that
You will never pass again.
Traveler there is no path
Only wakes on the sea

Preface

For more than 2 decades, I have been actively involved in preservice teacher education programs while also researching and writing about teacher education practice, policy, and research at local and larger levels. During the roughly 15-year period from the mid to late 1980s until the early years of the 2000s, I worked as a teacher educator in two different urban teacher education programs, one at the University of Pennsylvania and one at Boston College. I also wrote dozens of papers, presentations, chapters, articles, and editorials related to race, diversity, and social justice in teacher education, many of which were published in well-known education journals, books, and yearbooks. I have selected seven of these essays and collected them, along with two new ones, into this book.

WALKING THE ROAD

This collection of essays serves two purposes. First, when read chronologically, it tells a story about what it means to pay serious attention over a long time to race, diversity, and social justice in teacher education—a story I have called "Walking the Road." This phrase is taken from Miles Horton and Paulo Freire's book, *We Make the Road by Walking: Conversations on Education and Social Change* (Bell, Gaventa, & Peters, 1990). Their title, in turn, is derived from the words of the poet Antonio Machado, and his adaptation of the Spanish proverb *"se hace camino al andar."* This line in Machado's poem, entitled *Calminante* (Traveler), has been translated as, "in walking, the path is made," "you make the way as you go," or "you make it as you go along." Horton and Freire used the phrase "we make the road by walking," as they began to "talk their book" about participatory education as an instrument for social change. Their talk over many days—later transcribed and edited—focused on how each of them had struggled in quite different (but also similar) circumstances to link theory and practice in their lives and work. For Horton, this work was at Highlander in the Cumberland Plateau in Tennessee, particularly in the citizenship schools there that taught some 100,000 Blacks to read and write and thus contributed significantly to the Civil Rights Movement. For Freire, it was the adult literacy programs in northeastern Brazil intended not only to educate but also to emancipate thousands of rural peasants by enabling them to participate in the political process.

Humbly I borrow and transform Machado's phrase into "walking the road" as the title for my own modest story, which unfolds in the essays in this book. The story is about what it means to put into practice locally and theorize more publicly a commitment to teacher education that meets the needs of the increasingly racially and culturally diverse population and is committed to equity and social justice. My title is intended to emphasize the journey metaphor—walking, a road that goes on and on, traversing a long route over a long time—a metaphor that is central to what it means to conceptualize and live out in practice the notion of teaching and teacher education for social justice. This book makes the case that doing teacher education for social justice is an ongoing, over-the-long-haul kind of process for prospective teachers as well as for teacher education practitioners, researchers, and policy analysts.

My title is also intended to convey an image of uncertainty—the idea that there is no path already there and that the traveler must make the path while going along, although never passing over the same path again. This idea is central to understanding both the daily work and the lifetime commitment of teaching and learning to teach for social justice. When Horton and Freire agreed to "make the road by walking," they were agreeing that in order to start their book together, they would, simply, have to start. In short, they agreed that they would begin by talking about their lives and work, rather than attempting to theorize or outline in advance all of the larger ideas that would eventually be part of the book. Along these lines, I use the term "walking the road" to signify the organic link, rather than the dichotomy, between acting and theorizing, practice and scholarship, and between doing teacher education and doing scholarly work about teacher education.

Over the years, my own experiences as practitioner and scholar have served as both the context and the content of my writing, with the yeasty stuff of day-to-day work with prospective teachers, school- and university-based educators, and policy makers and administrators shaping but also being shaped by the theories, policy analyses, and studies of practice circulating in the field. There is a sense, then, in which writing this book has also been a way of "writing my life" as a teacher educator. Although emphasized differently in different chapters, the larger story of what it means to make and walk the road is woven throughout and across the essays.

THE "PROBLEM" OF TEACHER PREPARATION

The second purpose of this collection of essays is to offer an alternative way of conceptualizing the problem of teacher preparation that contrasts sharply with the view that prevails within the acutely conservative political climate that dominates the early 21st century. Regardless of the fact that many teacher education practitioners and scholars find it wrongheaded and even retrograde, the prevalent view is that enhancing teaching quality and providing a "highly qualified teacher" for every classroom is, by and large, a technical problem of testing and training and an implementation problem of getting to scale with policies that specify the qualifications and practices of teachers "proven effective" in producing pupil outcomes. *Walking the Road* presents a markedly different conceptualization of the problem of teacher preparation. Reading across the essays in this book, one can see that teacher preparation needs to be understood as both a learning problem (rather than a training-and-testing problem) and a political problem related to issues of equity and social justice (rather than simply a policy implementation problem). These two ideas, which are tightly braided and mutually supportive of one another, are threaded throughout the essays of this book. This overall conceptualization of the problem of teacher preparation is developed and spelled out in detail in the first chapter of this book and then elaborated in the chapters that follow.

Although each of the chapters in this book reflects both of the key premises above about how the problem of teacher education should be conceptualized, some of them concentrate primarily on teacher education as a learning problem, while others concentrate primarily on teacher education as a political problem. Chapters 2 through 5 emphasize that teacher education is a learning problem and that there is a reciprocal relationship in learning to teach for social justice among the learning of student teachers, the learning of their more experienced mentors, and the learning of the pupils they teach. These chapters examine various aspects of learning in one inquiry community that existed for a decade and that included multiple nested contexts wherein prospective teachers, school-based cooperating teachers, and university supervisors and faculty inquired individually and collectively about teaching for social justice. Chapters 2 through 5 explore how prospective teachers in one urban teacher education program came to understand race, diversity, and multicultural issues as part of the larger process of learning to teach during the preservice period. These essays explore the kinds of questions prospective teachers posed about teaching diverse populations as well as how they constructed and puzzled over the dilemmas of teaching in urban schools. The essays also describe and analyze the social, intellectual, and organizational contexts that support prospective teachers' learning, particularly the ways that inquiry functioned as both an emerging stance on teaching and a vehicle for asking questions, challenging assumptions, collecting classroom data, and constructing interpretive and action frameworks. These chapters suggest that, for prospective teachers, learning to teach for social justice is as much a process of learning to make certain kinds of decisions as it is a process of learning to make sense of and think across those decisions.

Chapters 2 through 5 also explore the learning of teaching mentors, including both the mentors who are experienced school-based teachers and the mentors who are university-based teacher educators. By concentrating on inquiry group conversations as well as looking closely at the changes one group of university-based teacher educators made in response to concerns that were raised about race and diversity issues by students themselves, these chapters reveal teacher educators' questions about race and diversity as well as what it means, on a concrete level, to do teacher education for social justice. The chapters show that teacher educators' learning, like that of student teachers, is a long road with "unlearning" a rugged but unavoidable part of a journey during which people double back, turn around, start and stop, reach dead ends, and yet, sometimes, forge on.

Chapters 6 through 8 are quite different from those in the first part of this book. They emphasize that teacher preparation for social justice needs to be understood as a political problem by offering frameworks for understanding and critiquing some of the larger issues in teacher education. These chapters explore how teacher education for social justice is shaped by but also shapes larger policy contexts and agendas. Chapters 6 through 8 explore the broader project of teacher education for social justice by synthesizing some of the scholarly work in the area, offering conceptual frameworks, and linking pressing policy mandates for teacher education to issues of social justice. The notion of "policy" in these chapters is broad. At the very least, it includes the governmental policies at the local, regional, and federal levels that directly or indirectly control funding, program approval, teacher certification and licensure; the nongovernmental policies and standards that guide accreditation, program development, curriculum, assessment, and professional recognition; and the local and larger political agendas, reform strategies, and funding opportunities that are forwarded by philanthropic foundations, professional organizations, business concerns, and advocacy groups that directly and indirectly have an impact on teacher education.

Taken together, the chapters that concentrate on teacher preparation as a learning problem and those that concentrate on teacher preparation as a political problem make the case that those who would forward the larger enterprise of teacher education for social justice must work simultaneously on several projects. The first is helping prospective teachers begin the lifelong process of learning to teach for social justice. The second is taking our own professional work as educators as a research site and learning by systematically investigating our own practice and interpretive frameworks in ways that are critical, rigorous, and intended to generate both local knowledge and knowledge that is useful in more public spheres. And the third is analyzing and interrogating all of the policies and political agendas that have an impact on teacher education from the lenses of social justice, race, and diversity.

ABOUT THIS BOOK

This book includes nine chapters that address the general topic of teacher education for social justice. While the first and last of these are broad framing chapters written especially for this collection, Chapters 2 through 8 of the book are edited versions of articles that were researched, written, and published at different points in time over a 15-year period. For example, *Against the Grain* (Chapter 2), which was first written as an American Educational Research Association paper in 1989 and published in 1991, draws on program material and data collected between 1986 and 1988. *Multiple Meanings* (Chapter 8), on the other hand, which was written in 2002 and published in 2003, is the final version of a framework for understanding multicultural teacher education that metamorphosed from earlier iterations in 1997, 1998, and 2000, but also draws on policy examples from as recently as 2002 and 2003. Like the two just mentioned, many of the chapters in this book developed over time, reflecting a continuous process of thinking and rethinking the deep tensions and issues underlying the very idea of teacher education for social justice. Although Chapters 2 through 8 are edited versions of previously published essays, it is worth noting that they were edited primarily for length and redundancy rather than to make them all uniform and update them all to the present time. The time perspective that is reflected in the writing style of these chapters has not been altered; this was done in order to preserve the integrity of the chapters as research on practice and also to convey the sense of work over time. Finally, because they were written at different points during a period of time that saw extraordinary changes in the ways we thought about teacher education, the articles on which the different chapters are based reflect different kinds of concerns and issues that mirror to a certain extent the issues that were prevalent in the field. (These issues and some of the changes that occurred over this period are discussed in detail in Chapter 1.)

In Chapter 1, I lay the foundation for all of the chapters in this book. This chapter provides historical and conceptual background and also elaborates the argument that teacher education for social justice is both a learning problem and a political problem. In Chapter 2, I ask whether prospective teachers can learn to be both educators and activists—to think of themselves as agents for change and understand reform as an integral part of teaching. The chapter answers this question in the affirmative, pointing out, however, that it is neither the university nor the school that is the site for this work. Instead this chapter argues that it is the synergy and collaboration of participants from both sites that create a powerful new learning space—the inquiry community wherein prospective teachers learn in the company of experienced teachers and teacher educators who see themselves as learners and are themselves struggling to teach against the grain in their own classrooms, schools, and programs.

In Chapters 3 and 4, I look more closely at prospective teachers learning to teach for social justice supported by social and intellectual contexts that bridge university and school. In Chapter 3, I suggest that prospective teachers learn to teach for social justice when they are initiated into the discourses of teaching and learning through generative inquiry-based processes that invite them to link the specifics of particular students and classrooms to bigger educational ideas and frameworks rather than through scripted lessons and activities that require them to fit their students and classrooms into predetermined slots. In Chapter 4, I look closely at school practice. Specifically, I examine how prospective teachers attempt to put principles of social justice into practice in actual urban schools and classrooms once they have taken on the responsibilities of full-time student teaching and are faced with the immediacy of classroom life. The chapter also reveals how prospective teachers make sense of their practice and their interactions with others, thus demonstrating the inseparability of the intellectual and the practical work of teaching and teacher education for social justice. In Chapter 5, I concentrate on the learning of teacher educators themselves, confirming that there is a mutually constitutive relationship involved in the learning of prospective teachers, mentor teachers, and teacher educators. I also point out that teacher education for social justice requires structures and contexts that support the ongoing learning of all of those who are engaged in the larger enterprise.

In Chapter 6, I focus on the "outcomes question" in teacher education, which drove many teacher education reforms during the last 5 years or so of the 20th century. In this chapter I ask what impacts teacher education should be expected to have on teacher learning, professional practice, and student learning. I also analyze debates about how, by whom, and for what purposes outcomes should be documented, demonstrated, and/or measured. The chapter makes it clear that questions about the outcomes of teacher education are closely and critically related to issues of social justice and equity. Chapter 7, coauthored with Kim Fries, suggests that many highly politicized debates about reforming teacher education are embedded within two larger national agendas: the agenda to professionalize teaching and teacher education and the movement to deregulate teacher preparation. Drawing on public documents from each side and using the language and arguments of the advocates themselves, we argue that, despite very different agendas, the discourse of both deregulation and professionalization revolves rhetorically around the establishment of the same three warrants—evidentiary, political, and accountability—each of which has important implications for equity and social justice. In Chapter 8 I argue that there are dramatically different approaches to "multicultural teacher education" research and practice as well as major discrepancies among policies conceived in the name of equity. This chapter offers a conceptual framework for understanding and sorting out the multiple meanings of concepts that are related to multicultural and social justice teacher education policy, such as access, diversity, culture, equity, teacher quality, school success, and educational reform.

Chapter 9 is a brief epilogue on teacher education for social justice. In this chapter I suggest that in the early years of the 21st century, teacher education stands at a crossroads with the federal government's version of producing "highly qualified teachers" in stark contrast to the idea of educating teachers to work for social justice. This chapter comments on the current scene, speculates about the future, and forwards a call for action by educators committed to equity and rich learning opportunities for all the nation's schoolchildren.

CHAPTER 1

Teacher Education for Social Justice: A Learning Problem and a Political Problem

Since the 1970s, disparities among racial, cultural, and linguistic groups in school achievement, high school completion rates, poverty levels, and educational resources have been identified as matters of urgent national importance. Since the mid-1990s, matters related to teacher preparation and teaching quality have captured the attention of policy makers, researchers, and teacher educators as well as private interest groups and the public at large. Unfortunately, in the early years of the 21st century, these two sets of issues—which are related to one another but also different and separate in important ways—have been almost completely conflated. That is, concerns about educational equity and the achievement gap, on the one hand, and concerns about teaching quality and preparing highly qualified teachers, on the other, have been melded into one another and have also converged with state and federal policy makers' preoccupation with high-stakes testing and accountability.

The result is threefold. Educational equity is increasingly being conceptualized as opportunities for all students to be held equally accountable to the same high-stakes tests, despite unequal resources and opportunities to learn. Teacher preparation is increasingly being conceptualized as a training and testing problem to ensure that all teachers have basic subject matter knowledge and the technical skills to work in schools devoted to bringing pupils' test scores to certain minimum thresholds. And preparing young people to live in a democratic society is increasingly being conceptualized as efficiently assimilating all schoolchildren into mainstream values, language, and knowledge perspectives so they can enter the nation's workforce, contribute to the economy, and preserve the place of the United States as the dominant power in a global society.

Walking the Road is based on a different conception of the problem of teacher preparation. Taken together, the nine chapters in this book argue that teacher education needs to be conceptualized as both a learning prob-

1

lem and a political problem aimed at social justice. The first part of this argument is that teacher education is, in large part, a learning problem rather than a training-and-testing problem or a problem of large-scale implementation of particular teaching technologies. This point is based on the premise that teaching itself is an intellectual, cultural, and contextually local activity rather than one that is primarily technical, neutral in terms of values and perspectives, and universal in terms of causes and effects. The second part of the argument is that teacher education is a political problem connected to issues of social justice rather than simply a policy problem. This point is based on the premise that all arrangements and regulations related to the preparation of teachers for the nation's schoolchildren reflect broader political issues and are embedded in larger political purposes and agendas that cannot be reduced simply to cost-benefit analyses or value-added accountability systems. Policies regarding teacher preparation do not come about as the result of simple common sense or expediency alone, nor are they disconnected from existing systems of power and privilege. Taken as a whole, the chapters in *Walking the Road* represent an attempt to work out and work through the ideas involved in these two premises about teacher preparation and also to provide an example of what it means when the work of teacher education is guided by these assumptions over time.

WORKING THE DIALECTIC

Taken together, the two premises that unite the chapters of this book—that teacher preparation is a learning problem and a political problem—suggest the outlines of a theoretical framework for understanding and analyzing teacher education for social justice. It is important to note, however, that this framework did not precede or predate the program work described in Chapters 2 through 5 or the policy analyses presented in Chapters 6 through 8. In other words, the work of teacher education that is represented here was not an attempt to put a grand theory of teacher education into practice in a particular local context or to try out a fully developed theoretical position by applying it to a set of policy issues that were central at a given point in time. Rather the practice of teacher education in one program over time, the critique of a set of policies related to teacher preparation that emerged during a particular period in time, and the theoretical framework or set of premises regarding teacher education for social justice that underlie the ideas in this book stand in a dialectic and recursive relation to one another. They emerged and developed together over time, mutually enriching and playing off each other but also troubling each other and exposing discrepancies, shortcomings, and failures.

Elsewhere I have used the term "working the dialectic" to refer to the process of simultaneously theorizing the practice of teacher education and "practicizeing" a theory of teacher education, thereby generating local knowledge that is useful for an immediate context but may also be useful and relevant beyond the local context (Cochran-Smith & Lytle, in press). As my colleague Susan Lytle and I have suggested in our writing about teacher inquiry, knowledge, and practice, "working the dialectic" is a distinctly nonlinear process:

> For us, it has been more like improvising a dance than climbing a set of stairs. As we theorized the relationships of inquiry, knowledge and practice based on critical analysis of others' work as well as systematic inquiry into our own practice, we saw many ways to reinvent practice, which prompted further nuances in our theoretical frameworks and posed new questions to analyze; these, in turn, suggested new interpretive frameworks and strategies.

As university faculty members who took seriously the premises of teacher research, we found that "working the dialectic" was an especially productive way to invent and direct teacher education and professional development projects based on inquiry and, at the same time, theorize and analyze many aspects of those projects. In each of the conceptual essays we wrote about teacher research over many years, we addressed a particular question or set of questions that had been problematic in our daily work as teachers, teacher educators, and researchers. Thus, in a very real sense, the contradictions in our own practice oriented our research as much as our reading of the wider literature related to teacher learning, inquiry, school change, and language and literacy did. At the same time, the distinctions about inquiry, knowledge, and practice that we made in our writing provided new lenses on practice and on our interpretation of the theoretical and empirical literature.

With regard to the theme and the larger project of this book—teacher education for social justice—"working the dialectic" is also an appropriate descriptive term. Over time, as both scholar and practitioner, I tried to understand the kinds of questions my teacher education students and colleagues asked about race, culture, equity, diversity, and justice as well as how all of us struggled to reconcile these with issues of high standards, content coverage, and accountability. At some points in time, I struggled to develop conceptual frameworks that would accommodate the reality and the rhetoric of working with new and experienced teachers and teacher educators committed to opening the unsettling discourse of race, teaching, and teacher education. At other times, I labored with my colleagues to rethink and alter the curriculum and policies of our program, informed by new awareness of unintended discrepancies between our intensions and what was actually enacted. The contradictions and difficulties in my daily work as a teacher educator

oriented my research as much as my reading of and contributing to the literature related to teacher learning, multicultural education, critical theory,
and social change did. Along the same lines, as I began to analyze formally
the professional discourse about teacher education reform and to critique
policies and regulations related to multicultural education, teacher education outcomes, and evidence-based educational practices and policies, I
grounded those critiques in the theoretical constructs that emerged from
intimate knowledge of local practice. Working the dialectic over 15 years
meant an intentional blurring of the roles of teacher education practitioner,
teacher education researcher, and critic/analyst of the policies, political agendas, and popular and professional discourses that directly or indirectly influence teacher education.

This chapter begins with a discussion of what has been referred to as the
demographic imperative in teaching and teacher education, which is part of
the rationale for conceptualizing teacher education as a social justice project.
This is followed by a discussion of the two premises that unify the various
chapters in this book—the idea that teacher education needs to be thought
about and acted upon as a learning problem and the idea that teacher education must also be regarded as a political problem related to social justice.

THE DEMOGRAPHIC IMPERATIVE

The phrase "the demographic imperative" (Banks, 1995; Dilworth,
1992) has been used to draw the conclusion—increasingly inescapable—
that the educational community must take action in order to alter the disparities deeply embedded in the American educational system. Documented
and disseminated over a number of years, evidence for the demographic
imperative includes statistics and other information in three areas—the
diverse student population, the homogeneous teaching force, and "the demographic divide" (Gay, 2000; Hodgkinson, 2001, 2002), or the marked
disparities in educational opportunities, resources, and achievement among
student groups that differ from one another racially, culturally, linguistically, and socioeconomically.

Drawing on information collected for Census 2000, noted educational
demographer Harold Hodgkinson (2001) points out that although some 40%
of the school population is now from racially and culturally diverse groups,
this varies dramatically (from 7% to 68%), depending on the state.
Hodgkinson (2002) explains anticipated demographic changes:

> Future population growth in the United States continues to be uneven—61%
> of the population increase in the next 20 years will be Hispanic and Asian,

about 40% Hispanic and 20% Asian; but then, as now, 10 states will contain 90% of the Hispanic population, 10 will contain 90% of the Asian population, and 7 will do both. Half of all Mexican Americans live in California! In fact, most of this increased diversity will be absorbed by only about 300 of our 3,000 [U.S.] counties. . . .

If we look at what changes America, it is 1 million immigrants a year, 4 million births, 2 million deaths, and 43 million people moving each year. Transience is a major factor in crime rates, poor health care, and poor-performing schools and states . . . The worst performing states in terms of the percentage of 19-year-olds who have both graduated from high school and been admitted to a college . . . also are the states with the most transience and the highest crime rates. (pp. 103–104)

If projections are accurate, children of color will constitute the statistical majority of the student population by 2035 and account for 57% by 2050 (U.S. Department of Education, 1996; Villegas & Lucas, 2002).

Meanwhile, due in part to declining enrollments among Asian, Black, and Hispanic students in teacher education programs with a proportionate increase in enrollments in business majors, the teaching force is becoming increasingly White European American (Hodgkinson, 2002). The most recent information available (as of 2002) on the nation's teaching force suggests a profile that is quite different from the student profile, with White teachers currently accounting for some 86% of the teaching force and teachers of color collectively accounting for only 14% (National Center for Education Statistics, 1997a). This pattern reflects a modest increase in the percentage of minority teachers since a low point of only 7% in 1986. Information about who is currently preparing to teach indicates a pattern that is generally similar to that of the current teaching force (American Association of Colleges for Teacher Education [AACTE], 1997, 1999; Dilworth, 1992; Howey, Arends, Yarger, & Zimpher, 1994), with White students representing the vast majority (80%–93%) of students enrolled in collegiate education programs, depending on institution and location. Hodgkinson (2002) and others have pointed out that declines since the 1960s in enrollments among African-American students in teacher education programs are related in part to proportionate increases in enrollments in business administration majors. Although there is some evidence that teacher education programs may be becoming somewhat more diverse (AACTE, 1999) and some alternate route programs are attracting more minority students (Lauer, 2001), it seems clear that the teaching force will remain primarily White European American for some time to come.

As has been pointed out, the demographic implications for education are far greater than the obvious differences in the numbers, proportionately, between student and teaching populations. There are also marked differences in the biographies and experiences of most teachers who are White European Americans from middle-class backgrounds who speak only English, on the one hand, and the many students who are people of color, and/or live in poverty, and/or speak a first language that is not English, on the other hand (Gay, 1993; Irvine, 1997). Teachers tend not to have the same cultural frames of reference and points of view as their students because, as Gay (1993) suggests, "they live in different existential worlds" (p. 287) and thus often have difficulty functioning as role models for students (Villegas & Lucas, 2002) or as cultural brokers and cultural agents (Gay, 1993; Goodwin, 2000) who help students bridge home-school differences. They also often have difficulty constructing curriculum, instruction, and interactional patterns that are culturally responsive (Irvine, 2001; Ladson-Billings, 1995b), which means that the students in the greatest academic need are least likely to have access to educational opportunities congruent with their life experiences. Perhaps most serious, many White middle-class teachers understand diversity as a deficit to be overcome and have low expectations and fears about students who are different from themselves, especially those in urban areas (Gay, 2000; Irvine, 1990; Valenzuela, 2002; Weiner, 1993; Yeo, 1997).

The third part of the demographic imperative has to do with the staggering disparities in educational outcomes and conditions for students with and without the advantages conferred by race, culture, language, and socioeconomic status. Villegas and Lucas (2002) offer an excellent but chilling discussion of these disparities based on standard sources of education statistics as well as original analyses. They point out that the United States has the highest rate of children living in poverty among advanced nations worldwide (Children's Defense Fund, 2000), and that the percentage of Black and Hispanic children living in poverty (42% and 40%, respectively) far exceeds the percentage of White children (16%) (Kilborn, 1996). Further, they note that the achievement levels of Black and Hispanic students on the National Assessment of Educational Progress (NAEP) mathematics and reading assessments are consistently and markedly lower than levels for White students (National Center for Education Statistics, 1997b, 1998, 1999), as are high school graduation rates (Educational Research Service, 1995; National Education Goals Panel, 1994). Villegas and Lucas conclude that "the consistent gap between racial/ethnic minority and poor students and their White, middle-class peers . . . is indicative of the inability of the educational system to effectively teach students of color as schools have traditionally been structured" (p. 9).

In addition to staggering disparities in educational outcomes, it has long been documented that there are major discrepancies in allocation of resources (e.g., equipment, supplies, physical facilities, books, access to computer technology, and class size) to urban, suburban, and rural schools (Darling-Hammond, 1995; Kozol, 1991). A pending California lawsuit filed in 2000 by the American Civil Liberties Union (ACLU) on behalf of public school-children in 18 California school districts demonstrates a continuation of this pattern. The suit charges that children who attend schools that lack basic learning tools such as books, materials, functioning toilet facilities, safe and infestation-free buildings and grounds, trained teachers, and enough seats for all students are deprived of fundamental educational opportunities. In the plaintiffs' schools, 96.4% of the student population is children of color, compared with 59% in the state overall (ACLU, 2000). Along these same lines, there is growing evidence that children of color and children who live in urban or poor areas are the most likely to have teachers who are not fully qualified or licensed to teach (Darling-Hammond, 2000a; Darling-Hammond & Sclan, 1996).

What does all this add up to? What is the demographic imperative for teacher education at the beginning of the 21st century? In short, it is the recognition that bridging the chasm between the school and life experiences of those with and without social, cultural, racial, and economic advantages requires fundamental changes in the ways teachers are educated. This does not mean that changing teacher education will in and of itself change the schools or fix what is wrong with American education. Weiner (1993) has argued cogently and persuasively that teacher preparation cannot change schools, despite some expectations to the contrary. (Also see Cochran-Smith, 2001b; Earley, 2000; Weiner, 1990, 1993, 2000; Yeo, 1997). Teachers can, however, join with others to work for change. This is not a new idea, of course, and many scholars have made this argument for years. Unfortunately, however, despite the fact that the demographic imperative is now widely acknowledged and meticulously documented, there is still great need. In the context of the current political climate, it is assumed that mandatory and widespread use of high-stakes tests of achievement will bridge the gaps be-tween groups. Now more than ever, we need pointed analyses of differential access to resources and learning opportunities as well as plans of action to remedy these disparities.

CONCEPTUALIZING TEACHER EDUCATION: THE TENSIONS UNDERLYING REFORM

As noted in the preface, the essays collected in this book were generated during the period from the mid to late 1980s until the early years of the 2000s. There were momentous changes at the national level during this period of time that greatly affected teacher education. These included shifting popu-lation patterns, major swings in the political pendulum, the growth of a com-plex global economy, and the ascendance (but also in some senses, the competition) of a number of educational and political movements—the standards movement, the accountability movement, initiatives to privatize education and other public as well as consumer services, and the press for market-based approaches to the reform of education, health, and other professional services.

Related to these larger movements and within roughly the same time span, but more specifically within the teacher education community itself, there were two sea changes in how the "problem" of teacher education was conceptualized. During the 1980s, there was a shift in teacher education away from the training approaches that had previously dominated. When the emphasis was on training, prospective teachers were taught to engage in specific classroom behaviors that had been shown to be effective through programs of research correlating classroom processes (i.e., teacher behaviors) with educational products (i.e., gain scores in pupil achievement) (Gage, 1978; McNergney, Lloyd, Mintz, & Moore, 1988; Rosenshine & Stevens, 1986). During the 1980s and in keeping with changes in how learning and cognition were coming to be understood more generally, the focus of teacher education shifted away from training and toward teacher thinking, teacher knowledge, and teacher learning (Barnes, 1989; Clark & Peterson, 1986; Shulman, 1987). From this perspective, the point of teacher education was to build the intellectual, organizational, and social contexts within which teachers could learn what they needed to know (and be able to do) in order to teach to high academic standards, adjust curriculum and instruction for local contexts, and contribute to the larger agenda to provide a professional teacher for every school child. By the mid to late 1990s, however, there was another sea change in teacher education. This was a shift away from assessing prospective teachers according to their knowledge and skill and assessing their teacher education programs according to their coherence and alignment with the knowledge base. The shift was toward performance-based accountability, particularly assessments of the demonstrated outcomes that teachers and programs produced (or not) in the learning of K–12 students (Cochran-Smith, 2001b; Schalock & Imig, 2000; Wise, 1998).

In the early years of the 21st century, there was intense political pressure for teacher education to be carried along by another sea change in how teaching and preparing to teach were conceptualized. Along with other political initiatives, the federal government began accelerating what Elmore (2002) referred to as "the worst trend of the current accountability movement: that performance-based accountability has come to mean testing alone" (p. 35). As discussed in the final chapter of this book, the defining feature of this trend, which was propelled by the incursion of the federal government into areas previously considered to be the purview of the states and/or the educational research and policy communities, was a singular and, some would say, relentless, focus on teaching as a technical activity and teacher preparation as a training and testing problem.

The preceding paragraphs are intended to underscore the point that the central issues that animate this book are not new issues in the history of teacher education, nor were they new issues during the 15-year span in which the essays collected here were written. The idea that teacher education must be conceptualized as a learning problem, rather than a training problem, is certainly not a new issue. Although the tensions between learning and training played out differently in the latter part of the 20th century from the way they did during earlier time periods, these issues reflected a long history of tensions between what Borrowman (1956; 1965) called "the liberal and the technical" in the history of teacher education in America and, along related but somewhat different lines, what Dewey (1904) referred to in his discussion of the relationship between theoretical insight and practical activity as "laboratory" versus "apprenticeship" approaches to learning to teach.

The second premise here is that teacher education needs to be understood as a political problem rather than a problem simply of determining policy on the basis of expediency and then efficiently and faithfully implementing that policy across settings and contexts. Like the learning aspects of teacher education, its political aspects also reflect a long history of tensions in education about the purposes of schooling in a democratic society and the role of teachers and teacher preparation in relation to those purposes. Indeed, Glazer (1997) has suggested that 20th-century issues related to multiculturalism date back at least to the 1840s and reflect what have become perennial disagreements between those who favor and oppose the full inclusiveness of deprived groups in American education. Along different but related lines, Pinar et al. and others (2002) have pointed out that political analyses of schooling, teaching, and curriculum have ebbed and flowed as issues animating curriculum, teaching, and teacher preparation. These first emerged in the 1920s, as exemplified by George Counts's (1926; 1932) critiques of the reproductive nature of teaching and curriculum. Political analyses then waned in the decades to come, but later reemerged in the 1970s and 1980s (e.g., Apple, 1986; Aronowitz & Giroux, 1985), heavily influenced by the work of Karl Marx and the European critical theorists.

Although this book is not an analysis of historical themes influencing teacher education, it is important to note the complexity and deep roots of the issues involved so as not to contribute to the amnesiac renderings of teacher education that are often prominent in the policy and research literature. What I want to emphasize in this book is that the fundamental tensions that drive teacher education—such as the tension between its technical and liberal aspects and the tension between its role in the reproduction or reconstruction of the larger social structure—emerge and reemerge periodically. Each time they do, they are threaded into and wound around the current intersections of educational and other kinds of research, practice, and policy. Thus, new incarnations of perennial issues may or may not appear on the surface to be different from previous incarnations, and, in fact, their historically iterative dimensions are often unacknowledged. Nevertheless, the tensions are both old and new. They are new in that they are woven into the tapestry of changed and changing political, social, and economic times and thus have a different set of implications each time they reemerge in prominence. But they are also old in that they represent enduring and deep disagreements in society about the purposes of schooling, the value of teaching, and the preparation of teachers.

TEACHER EDUCATION FOR SOCIAL JUSTICE AS A LEARNING PROBLEM

The next two sections of this chapter elaborate in some detail on the idea that teacher education for social justice needs to be conceptualized as both a learning problem and a political problem. Conceptualizing teacher education in terms of teachers', teacher educators', and students' learning is central to this book.

The "New" Teacher Education

The idea that teacher preparation is about learning rather than training was shaped by, but also helped to shape, what a number of people over the last decade have referred to as a "new image" of teacher learning, a "new model" of teacher education, and even a "new paradigm" of professional development (Cochran-Smith & Lytle, 1999; Darling-Hammond, 1994; Grimmett & Neufeld, 1994; Hawley & Valli, 1999; Lieberman & Miller, 1991; Little, 1993b; McLaughlin, 1993; Stein, Smith, & Silver, 1999). This new image supplanted the idea that teacher education was a one-time process of "training" wherein undergraduates were equipped with methods in the subject areas and then sent out to "practice" teaching. Similarly, for experienced teachers, this meant that teacher education was no longer seen as a process of periodic "staff development" wherein experienced teachers were congregated into auditoriums to receive the latest information from educational experts about the most effective teaching techniques. For teacher educators, this meant that they could no longer regard themselves or be regarded by others as the outside experts who transmitted knowledge to their students or injected knowledge into the schools in order to "fix" teachers and other educators.

These new images of teacher education were informed by research about how teachers thought about their work (Clark & Peterson, 1986) and by the emerging notion of "learning to teach" (Feiman-Nemser, 1983). As noted above, the emphasis shifted from what teachers did to what they knew, what their sources of knowledge were, and how those sources influenced their work in classrooms (Barnes, 1989; Cochran-Smith & Lytle, 1990; Lampert, 1990; Shulman, 1987).

The general orientation of this "new" approach to teacher education was more constructivist than transmission-oriented—the recognition that both prospective and experienced teachers (like all learners) brought prior knowledge and experience to all new learning situations, which are social and specific. In addition, there was growing recognition that teacher education took place over time rather than in isolated moments in time, and that active learning required opportunities to link previous knowledge with new understandings. During this time, it was widely acknowledged that professional development needed to be linked to educational reform (Loucks-Horsley, 1995) and needed to focus on "culture-building" rather than skills training (Lieberman & Miller, 1994). It was also generally agreed that teacher education and professional development that were linked to student learning and curricular reform had to be deeply embedded in the daily life of schools (Darling-Hammond, 1998; Elmore & Burney, 1997) and had to feature opportunities for teachers to inquire systematically about how teaching practice constructs rich learning opportunities for some students (Ball & Cohen, 1999; Little, 1993a) but also sometimes limits access and learning opportunities for others (Cochran-Smith & Lytle, 1993; Cone, 1990).

Very broadly speaking, this new image of teacher education came to be shared by many of those responsible for designing, implementing, and researching programs, projects, and other initiatives intended to promote teacher learning. Some people even suggested that a major new consensus had emerged about what it took for truly effective teacher education and professional development to occur and flourish (Hawley & Valli, 1999). As I have pointed out (Cochran-Smith & Lytle, 2001), however, the "new" teacher education was much less monolithic and consensual than some people proposed, and in fact, just beneath the surface, new visions of teacher education looked quite different from one another, depending on underlying assumptions and goals, including underlying images of teaching, teachers' roles in reform, knowledge for teaching, and how teachers learn. Some visions, much more than others, emphasized the idea that teacher education was a process of continual learning wherein everybody was a learner who brought different kinds of knowledge and experience, but also posed questions to which they did not already have the answers and constructed dilemmas for which there *were* no simple answers. Some, but by no means all, images of the new teacher education focused heavily on how teaching and teacher education either contributed to or challenged the status quo of the educational system (Cochran-Smith, 1991; Ginsburg & Lindsay, 1995b; Liston & Zeichner, 1991a; Zeichner & Liston, 1987), while others did not make these issues central.

In this book, the idea that teacher education is a learning problem is based on three key ideas that are developed in the chapters that follow and elsewhere: teacher education occurs in the context of inquiry communities wherein everybody is a learner and a researcher; inquiry is an intellectual and political stance rather than a project or time-bounded activity; and, as part of an inquiry stance, teacher research is a way to generate local knowledge of practice that is contextualized, cultural, and critical. These three ideas, which are threaded throughout the chapters, are introduced below.

The Role of Inquiry Communities

The idea that teacher education is a learning problem, rather than a training-and-testing problem, assumes both that learning to teach is a process that occurs across the professional life span and that beginning and experienced teachers need to engage in similar intellectual work over the life span. This means that teacher education for social justice is not simply a matter of training prospective teachers to do certain things in their classrooms because those actions are assumed to have predictable and uniform results for all students or because wise teachers advocate those actions. Nor is it a matter of helping prospective teachers develop certain kinds of knowledge about cultural groups or subject matter that can be tailored and applied in most classrooms. Rather, learning to teach for social justice is a matter of all the participants in teacher education (beginning and experienced teachers alike, school- and university-based educators alike) working together as teachers but also learners, and as educators but also activists, within inquiry communities that extend over the long haul and across the professional life span.

Neither the university nor the school is the site for this work. Instead, it is the synergy and collaboration of participants from across these sites that create a new and powerful learning space—the inquiry community. Inquiry communities provide some of the key intellectual, social, and organizational contexts within which prospective teachers can learn in the company of other educators who are also learning to teach for social justice. The discourse in inquiry communities is quite different from the usual supervisory discourse, which focuses on technical rather than substantive or critical aspects of teaching. In inquiry communities, experienced teachers do not function simply as authorities who pass along their expertise to novices—although they certainly do share knowledge and experience. By the same token, university-based supervisors do not function simply as evaluators who check to see how closely the novices are implementing the strategies of the experts. Rather, in inquiry communities, experienced teachers and university supervisors work along with prospective teachers to make their own struggles and their own ongoing learning visible and accessible to others and thus offer their own learning as grist for the learning of others.

In communities like these, beginning teachers have a chance to see and hear over time how their more experienced mentors construct problems, wrestle with uncertainty, change their minds about long-established practices or assumptions, gather evidence and examples for analysis and interpretation, connect pieces of information to one another, and develop interpretive frameworks for the daily work of teaching for social justice. The across the life span perspective that is central to the learning approach to teacher education makes salient the role of communities and their joint intellectual projects. In contrast, the expert-novice distinction that is implicit in the training-and-testing approach to teacher education serves to maintain the individual in-the-head model of professional development that highlights individual differences among teachers.

The learning perspective on teacher education suggests that there is a reciprocal and dialectical relationship between the learning of prospective teachers, on the one hand, and the learning of the mentors with whom they work, on the other. This means that it is not enough for teacher educators to pay close attention to what their own students—the prospective teachers in their programs—are learning. Rather, teacher education for social justice also requires the intellectual and organizational contexts that support the ongoing learning of teacher educators who are engaged in the larger enterprise of teaching for social justice. Many teacher educators themselves—perhaps even most teacher educators—have not had the transformative learning experiences necessary to interrupt the conservative assumptions underlying teacher education programs at many higher education institutions. In addition, few teacher education programs and departments have built into their ongoing operations the intellectual and organizational contexts that support teacher educators' learning about (and struggling with) issues of race, racism, diversity, and social justice in education. Part of what this means is that learning to teach for social justice is partly a process of "unlearning" racism and other problematic stances that are often buried in teacher education courses and curricula. To do so, all participants have to own their complicity in maintaining oppression and have to grapple with their own failures to produce the kinds of changes they may advocate.

Inquiry as Stance

When teacher education is regarded as a learning problem, inquiry is understood to be a stance on teaching, learning, and schooling that is critical and transformative, rather than a project or an activity in a course. In everyday language, "stance" is used to describe body postures, particularly with regard to the position of the feet, as in sports or dance, and also to describe political positions, particularly their consistency (or the lack thereof) over time. In the discourse of qualitative research, "stance" is used to make visible and problematic the various perspectives through which researchers frame their questions, observations, and interpretations of data. In my work with Susan Lytle over many years (Cochran-Smith & Lytle, 1999; Cochran-Smith & Lytle, 2001; Lytle & Cochran-Smith, 1995), we have developed the term *inquiry as stance* to describe the positions that teachers and others who work together in inquiry communities take toward knowledge, its relationships to practice, and the purposes of schooling. We have used the metaphor of stance to suggest both orientational and positional ideas, and to carry allusions to the physical placing of the body and to intellectual activities and perspectives over time. In this sense, the metaphor is intended to capture the ways we stand, the ways we see, and the lenses we see through as educators. Teaching is a complex activity that occurs within webs of social, historical, cultural, and political significance. Across the life span an inquiry stance provides a kind of grounding within the changing cultures of school reform and competing political agendas—a place to put one's feet, as it were, as well as a frame of mind.

Inquiry as stance is distinct from the more common notion of inquiry (or action research or teacher research) as time-bounded project within a teacher education program or one of a number of "proven-effective" strategies for staff development. Taking an inquiry stance means new and experienced teachers and teacher educators working within communities to generate local knowledge, envision and theorize their practice, and interpret and interrogate the theory and research of others. Fundamental to this notion is the idea that the work of inquiry communities is both social and political—that is, it involves making problematic the current arrangements of schooling; the ways knowledge is constructed, evaluated, and used; and teachers' individual and collective roles in bringing about change. To use *inquiry as stance* as a construct for understanding teacher education as a learning problem, we have argued (Cochran-Smith & Lytle, 2001) that a more nuanced conception of knowledge than that allowed by the traditional formal knowledge/practical knowledge distinction is needed as well as a more complex conception of practice than that suggested in the aphorism that practice is practical. As we have conceptualized it, inquiry as stance also carries with it a political and critical edge, intended to inform ongoing critiques of the larger purposes of school and the impact of particular practices and policies on pupils' life chances.

Any and all of the activities of teacher education—like the activities of K–12 teaching—can be made problematic and explored from an inquiry stance within the larger context of a learning community that is committed to social justice. The goal is building, interrogating, elaborating, and critiquing conceptual frameworks that link action and problem-posing to the immediate context as well as to larger social, cultural, and political issues.

Generating Local Knowledge

In communities where inquiry is a stance (not a project or strategy), groups of prospective and experienced teachers and teacher educators engage in joint construction of local knowledge through conversation and other forms of collaborative analysis and interpretation. Together, they construct problems of practice within particular local contexts and consider alternative approaches to those problems. They also raise new questions about students, subject matter, learning assessments, equity, and access. This involves framing certain educational issues as dilemmas rather than problems with clear solutions and deliberating thoughtfully about decisions that involve competing claims to justice. Much of this depends on reconsidering assumptions about teaching, learning, and schooling but also challenging common school practices and policies that perpetuate inequities. In all of this work, students' learning is central—participants gather and analyze data from classroom and school contexts, valuing students' cultural and linguistic resources and advocating for students and their families. Working in communities over time, participants come to learn that all educational issues are, at least in part, issues of equity, diversity, and social justice. Communities provide a context where individual efforts are conjoined with those of others involved in larger movements for social justice and social change.

When teacher education for social justice is understood as a learning problem, this means that prospective teachers are initiated into the discourses of teaching and learning through generative inquiry-based processes that invite them to link the specifics of particular students and classrooms to bigger educational ideas and frameworks rather than through scripted lessons and activities that require them to fit their students and classrooms into predetermined slots. With the former, an important part of the teacher's role is to raise questions, generate knowledge, make connections, and construct curriculum. With the latter, the teacher's role is more limited to the technical aspects of organizing and managing lessons, implementing prescribed curriculum, and presenting information uniformly. When teacher education is regarded as a learning problem, constructing local knowledge and understanding is emphasized as much as or more so than developing a repertoire of "best practices," or standard behaviors and techniques. In other words, the perspectives that are critical to dealing with the dilemmas of race, culture, and language diversity in today's classrooms are generative intellectual processes such as asking questions, making sense of disparate information, considering and reconsidering previous experience, gathering and interpreting multiple sources of information, appreciating more than one perspective, entertaining alternative solutions and approaches, building on experiential and cultural resources, and connecting specific experiences to larger conceptual frames as well as rethinking theories in light of particular experiences.

None of these intellectual activities leads directly or necessarily to specific practical strategies for the classroom. All of them, however, generate recommendations for curricular, instructional, and community practices depending on the particularities of school and classroom cultures and contexts. From the perspective of teacher education as a learning problem, the inseparability of the intellectual and practical work of teachers is assumed.

TEACHER EDUCATION FOR SOCIAL JUSTICE AS A POLITICAL PROBLEM

As indicated in the Preface, Chapters 6, 7, and 8 focus explicitly on policy issues in teacher education, analyzing and critiquing some of the highly visible and often controversial policies that shaped teacher education during the late 20th and early 21st centuries. These chapters emphasize that teacher education for social justice is a political problem rather than a policy problem.

The "New" Multiculturalism in Teacher Education

The idea that teacher education is a political problem and not simply a problem of policy implementation was influenced by and also had an influence on what I have referred to as "the new multiculturalism" in teacher education (Cochran-Smith, 2003b; Cochran-Smith, Davis, & Fries, 2003). Prompted and/or required by professional organizations such as AACTE and NCATE in the late 1970s and early 1980s, many teacher education programs across the country began to include multicultural and diversity issues in the curriculum. At many institutions, this meant the addition of a course (e.g., "the diversity course" or "the multicultural course"), which was often optional for students and peripheral to the core curriculum. By and large, however, most programs did not change very much, and critics consistently concluded that teachers continued to be prepared from a monocultural perspective that failed to acknowledge the pervasive impact on schooling of race, class, linguistic background, culture, gender, and ability, and emphasized instead a universal knowledge base and an assimilationist standpoint on curriculum, pedagogy, and assessment (Grant & Wieczorek, 2000; Ladson-Billings, 1999; Zeichner & Hoeft, 1996).

Interestingly, however, although much of teacher education practice over the last quarter century did appear to remain conservative, theories of teacher education did not. In fact, a substantial body of theory and critique emerged that was relatively consistent and that outlined the contours of a "new" teacher education (e.g., Cochran-Smith, 1995b; Fox & Gay, 1995; Gay, 1993; Gay, 2000; Ginsburg & Lindsay, 1995a; King & Castenell, 2001; Ladson-Billings, 1999, 2001; Oakes & Lipton, 1999; Sleeter, 1995, 1996; Villegas & Lucas, 2001; Zeichner, 1993). This new teacher education was more multicultural and more imbued with critical understandings of how race, class, gender, and culture structure the life chances and school experiences of both individual schoolchildren and large groups of people who are not part of the cultural, racial, language, and socioeconomic mainstream. Some of this theoretical work was developed by teacher education scholars who were also involved as practitioners in the day-to-day work of teacher preparation, and much of it was built on the critique that the "problem" of diversity in teacher preparation historically had been constructed from a deficit perspective about the education of minority students (Ladson-Billings, 1999; Villegas & Lucas, 2001), a perspective that needed to be interrupted if all pupils were to have rich educational opportunities and enhanced life chances.

The new multiculturalism underlined the point that the ideology that was often implicit in teacher education perpetuated the following erroneous and problematic assumptions: American schooling (and society) are meritocratic (Goodwin, 2001; Ladson-Billings, 1999; Weiner, 2000); racism and sexism are problems that have been solved (Gay & Howard, 2000); tracking systems and high-stakes tests are neutral ways of organizing for learning and assessing merit (Oakes, 1988); and the purpose of schooling is to assimilate all students into the mainstream and thus into the labor force in order to support the nation's place in the global economy (Apple, 2001). The new multiculturalism in teacher education is closely akin to the notion of teacher education for social justice in that it challenges all of these assumptions and prepares prospective teachers to construct curriculum, implement instruction, interact with students, and collaborate with colleagues and communities in ways that likewise challenge them. Conceptualizing teacher education as an enterprise committed to critical multiculturalism and social justice has been a powerful and galvanizing idea for a certain group of theorists and teacher education researchers and practitioners. However, it is important to note that this perspective seems to be shared by a minority of those involved in the teacher education community.

The notion of teaching and teacher education for social justice—at least in broad strokes—is consistent with other critical understandings of the social, historical, and political dynamics of teaching and schooling. These understandings are drawn from several different but interrelated political and intellectual movements, some more than a century old and others emerging more recently: European critical social and economic theory; the American Civil Rights Movement and subsequent efforts to develop pedagogy and curriculum that are multicultural, antiracist, and/or culturally relevant; struggles for liberatory education in Latin America, particularly as conceptualized in the literacy work of Paulo Freire (1970); North American critical educational theory; and studies of schooling and teaching based on critical race theory, critical ethnography, radical feminist theory and research, and critical participatory action research.

In this book, the idea that teacher education is a political problem revolves around three key ideas that have been shaped by the theories noted above and the work of teacher education practitioners over many years: teaching and teacher education are political and collective enterprises, rather than neutral and individual efforts; all teacher education policies, whether local or federal, whether governing practice in one program or influencing a much larger constituency, are driven by values and are, at least in part, ideological; and teaching and teacher preparation for social justice are vital elements of an educational system in and for a democratic society. These ideas, briefly elaborated here, are woven throughout this book.

Teaching as a Political Activity

The idea that teaching is a political activity is animated by several basic premises. Schools (and how "knowledge," "curriculum," "assessment," and "access" are constructed and understood in schools) are not neutral grounds but contested sites where power struggles are played out. The structural inequities embedded in the social, organizational, and financial arrangements of schools and schooling help to perpetuate dominance for dominant groups and oppression for oppressed groups. Power, privilege, and economic advantage and/or disadvantage play major roles in the school and home lives of students whether they are part of language, cultural, or gender majority groups or minority groups in our society. The history of racism and sexism in America and the ways in which "race" and "gender" have been constructed in schools and society are central, whether consciously or not, in the ways that students, families, and communities make meaning of school phenomena as well as how they interact with school designates. Curriculum and instruction are neither neutral nor obvious. Rather, the academic organization of information and inquiry reflects contested views about what and whose knowledge is of most value. In addition, influential parts of curriculum and instruction include what is present or absent, whose perspectives are central or marginalized, and whose interests are served or undermined. The social and organizational structures of instruction, including classroom and other discourse patterns, grouping strategies, behavioral expectations, and interpretive perspectives are most congruent with White mainstream patterns of language use and socialization and are more conducive to the achievement of boys than that of girls.

These premises are often associated with terms and concepts such as teaching and teacher education for "social justice," "social change," "social responsibility," and teaching and teacher education "to change the world." Although not synonymous, these bear a strong resemblance to one another and are often used more or less interchangeably. These terms signify the following general argument: Teachers cannot fix the problems of society by "teaching better," nor can teachers alone, whether through individual or group efforts, alter the life chances of the children they teach (Anyon, 1994; Weiner, 1993), particularly if the larger issues of structural and institutional racism and inequity are not addressed (McCarthy, 1993). However, while teachers cannot *substitute for* social movements aimed at the transformation of society's fundamental inequities (Aronowitz & Giroux, 1985; Zeichner, 1986), their work has the potential to *contribute to* those movements in essential ways by being part of collective projects and larger communities for social justice.

It is important to note that the recognition that teaching and teacher education are political activities does not mean that teacher educators try to persuade prospective teachers to adopt particular partisan viewpoints. Rather, the point is to help prospective teachers understand that it is impossible to teach in ways that are *not* political and value-laden. This can be a tricky distinction for prospective teachers as well as for experienced teachers and teacher educators. The goal is not to politicize teaching but to acknowledge, as Bruner (1996) suggested, "that it is already politicized and that its political side needs finally to be taken into account more explicitly, not simply as though it were 'public protest'" (p. 29). Part of conceptualizing teaching and teacher education as a political problem, then, is being part of community where the participants deliberately claim the role of educator as well as activist based on political consciousness and on ideological commitment to diminishing the inequities of American life.

Policy and Ideology

When teacher education is regarded as a political problem, all of the policies related to the preparation of teachers are problematized and interrogated, particularly with regard to ideology. This viewpoint is based on a broad notion of what "policy" itself constitutes—not only federal policies regarding teacher quality and state policies governing teacher certification and licensing, but also the local policies of college and university programs, the agendas of private foundations and professional associations, and educational reform platforms and positions more broadly.

All of the policies related to the preparation of teachers for the nation's schoolchildren are, *in part*, ideological and values-driven. They are never the result of "simple" common sense, "unbiased" analysis of the empirical evidence, or "disinterested" rational debates about how to expend resources. This is the case despite the fact that policy is often characterized as if it were the result of completely rational processes disconnected from values and from existing systems of power and privilege. When teacher education is regarded as a political problem, the assumption is that all versions of "common sense," all analyses of evidence, and all "rational" debates are shaped by cultural, social, and political values and ideals. In other words, it is understood that all policies take a stance, whether implicitly or explicitly, on the purposes of schooling for a democratic society, the current social structure of schools and society, and the distribution of resources and opportunities in that society.

Part of framing teacher education as a political problem, then, is interrogating and revealing the "politics of policies" related to teacher preparation from the lenses of social justice, race, diversity, and equity. For example, when teaching quality and teacher preparation emerge as matters of national importance as they did in the late 20th century and when new legislation greatly expands the role of the federal government in both precollegiate and collegiate education, as it did in the early 21st century, there are often markedly different courses of action advocated by different constituencies in the same name and in the same language of equity, accountability, and serving the citizenry. When teacher education is seen as a political problem, it becomes important to analyze policy mandates and competing agendas for the reform of teacher education in terms of their political positions and their attention (or lack of attention) to issues of social justice. This means trenchant critique of the teacher education outcomes that are demanded by various power brokers as well as critical analyses of whose interests are served, whose needs are met, and whose goals are forwarded by allegiance to those outcomes.

Critiquing teacher education policy in terms of ideology also means acknowledging that many highly politicized debates about reforming teacher education are embedded within larger national agendas, in particular the agenda to professionalize teaching and teacher education, which is linked to the K–12 standards movement, and the movement to deregulate teacher preparation, which aims to dismantle teacher education institutions, break up the monopoly of the profession, and discipline teacher preparation in the ways of the market. To accomplish this kind of analysis, it is important to look at how competing agendas are publicly constructed, critiqued, and debated, drawing on public documents from various sides and using the language and arguments of the advocates themselves to expose underlying values and goals.

Justice and Democracy

When teacher education is regarded as a political problem, the critical roles of teaching and teacher eduation in a democratic society are brought into sharp relief. Democratic societies depend for their existence upon a thoughtful citizenry that believes in democratic ideals and is willing and able to participate in the civic life of the nation. Although with different points of emphases and for somewhat different purposes, this argument was made by a number of early 20th-century philosophers and educators, including John Dewey, Lucy Sprague Mitchell, W. E. B. DuBois, and Carter Woodson. Each of these influential thinkers argued that education was essential for the survival of a democracy in which all individuals are able to participate freely and equally.

While generally consistent with these early ideas, contemporary theories of democratic education (Gutman, 1999; Oakes, Quartz, Ryan, & Lipton, 2000) move beyond earlier theories in order to accommodate the modern dilemmas and issues of our increasingly diverse society. Gutman (1999), for example, argues that the key to what she calls "deliberative democracy" is democratic education: "Deliberative democracy underscores the importance of publicly supported education that develops the capacity to deliberate among all children as future free and equal citizens" (p. xii). Inspired by Dewey and his notion that a democratic society should be adamantly committed to providing the best education not just for some, but for all of its children, Gutman nonetheless diverges from Dewey. She argues that societies *must not be compelled* to legislate for all children what any particular group wants for its own children, pointing out that different local communities may well want different things and different curricula for their own and others' children. At the same time, however, she also argues that democratic societies must be compelled *not to* put policies into place that foster discrimination or repression, which undermine and ultimately destroy democracy. She states:

> A democratic theory of education recognizes the importance of empowering citizens to make educational policy and also of constraining their choices among policies in accordance with those principles—of nonrepression and

nondiscrimination—that preserve the intellectual and social foundations of democratic deliberations. A society that empowers citizens to make educational policy, moderated by these two principled constraints, realizes the democratic ideal of education. (p. 14)

Gutman's theory of democratic education focuses on preparing all persons to engage in deliberations as free and equal citizens as long as their choices are not repressive or discriminatory. Most importantly, her theory capitalizes on and makes a virtue out of the inevitable disagreements about educational (and other) issues that arise among free and equal citizens. It emphasizes that all citizens must be prepared through an "adequate civic education" to develop the skills and dispositions of deliberative citizenship. It is the willingness (and the ability) to deliberate civilly about matters of mutual concern that sets democratic citizens apart from both self-interested citizens, who deliberate only in order to further their own best interests, and from passive citizens, who do not deliberate at all but simply defer to authority. Gutman points out that just decisions are much more likely to be reached by citizens who deliberate together in search of mutually defensible positions than by people who are uninterested in politics altogether or interested only for their own benefit.

If all free and equal citizens of a society are to have the benefit of a democratic education, all teachers must have the knowledge, skills, and dispositions to teach toward the democratic ideal. In particular, in today's rapidly changing and increasingly diverse society, all teachers need knowledge of the social and cultural contexts that shape education as well as knowledge of the role of culture and language in mediating learning.

TEACHER EDUCATION: A LEARNING PROBLEM
AND A POLITICAL PROBLEM

In the preceding pages, I have described a conceptualization of teacher education for social justice as both a learning problem and a political problem. As noted, these are the guiding principles that both shaped and were shaped by my work as a teacher education practitioner and scholar over a 15-year period during which there were major shifts in the research, policies, and politics of teacher preparation.

Although these two principles are discussed separately in this chapter, they are in actuality not separate at all, but are intrinsically linked. The links are integral to the larger conception of teacher education for social justice and in the ways they are instantiated in inquiry, practice, and policy analysis. Chapters 2–5 in this book closely examine teachers' learning in inquiry communities and thus support the case for conceptualizing teacher education as a learning problem. In addition, however, they contribute to the argument that teacher education must also be regarded as a political problem. In fact, threaded through each of these chapters is the assumption that teaching and teacher education are fundamentally political rather than neutral activities and that a goal of teacher education is to make it normative rather than exceptional for teachers and teacher educators to work as advocates for social justice. In addition, the focus in these chapters on teacher learning communities makes the point that teaching and teacher education for social justice are not individual but conjoined endeavors. In this sense, part of the learning that goes on in inquiry communities is learning how to work as part of a community of educators with larger political commitments and as part of larger social movements.

The chapters in the second part of this book focus primarily on analysis and critique of teacher preparation policy and reform proposals in the context of larger political agendas, ideologies, and debates. They thus forward the case for conceptualizing teacher education as a political problem. Underlying each of these policy analyses, however, is a sharply focused point of view about teachers' and pupils' learning (rather than training) that is complex, contextual, and cultural. These chapters caution against policies that assume narrow and linear views of teaching and learning and/or that measure learning only in terms of test results. Thus, the policy-related chapters help make the case that teacher education is a learning problem.

The power of conceptualizing and enacting teacher education for social justice as both a learning problem and a political problem resides in the relationship of learning and politics. This relationship, which is both symbiotic and dialectic, is elaborated in the remaining chapters of this book.

CHAPTER 2

Against the Grain

In an essay condemning political and social indifference in prewar Italy, Antonio Gramsci (1916/1977) forcefully argued that action was everyone's responsibility and that each individual, no matter how apparently powerless, was accountable for the role he played or failed to play in the larger political struggle. If we accept Gramsci's notion that indifference is often a mainspring of history, and if we substitute the word "teacher" for Gramsci's "man," we have a powerful statement about the accountability of individual educators for their efforts to reform U.S. schools:

> Every [teacher] must be asked to account for the manner in which he [sic] has fulfilled the task that life has set him and continues to set him day by day; he must be asked to account for what he has done, but especially for what he has not done. . . . It is time that events should be seen to be the intelligent work of [teachers] and not the products of chance or fatality. (p. 18)

I use Gramsci's clarion call for social accountability to reassert that teachers are decision makers and collaborators who must reclaim their roles in the shaping of practice by taking a stand as both educators and activists (Aronowitz & Giroux, 1985). I am not suggesting that teachers alone have the power or the responsibility to reform education by "teaching better," or that teaching can be understood in isolation from the cultures of schools and communities or the historical and political contexts of school and society. In fact, I argue in favor of inquiry communities where inexperienced and experienced teachers learn together and in favor of teachers joining others in larger social movements. However, teaching is fundamentally a political activity in which every teacher plays a part by design or by default (Ginsburg, 1988; Willis, 1978).

Prospective teachers need to know from the start that they are part of a larger struggle and that they have a responsibility to reform, not just replicate, standard school practices. I argue in this chapter, however, that working to reform teaching, or what can be thought of as *teaching against the grain*, is not a generic skill that can be learned at the university and then "applied" at the school. Teaching against the grain is embedded in the culture and history of teaching at individual schools and in the biographies of teachers and their collaborative efforts to alter curricula, raise questions about common practices, and resist inappropriate decisions. These relationships must be explored in schools in the company of experienced teachers who are themselves engaged in complex, situation-specific, and sometimes losing struggles to work against the grain.

In this chapter I briefly analyze two approaches to preparing preservice teachers to teach against the grain, *critical dissonance* and *collaborative resonance*. I argue that programs built on the collaborative resonance of university and school have the potential to provide student teachers with unusually rich learning opportunities. Next, I take readers into four urban schools in the Philadelphia area where student teachers work and talk with experienced teachers who, in a variety of ways, are working against the grain. Drawing on data from these four schools, I present an analysis of teachers' and student teachers' discourse during weekly school-site meetings, revealing the groups' efforts to pose questions, struggle with uncertainty, and build evidence for their reasoning. These conversations provide vivid descriptive evidence that regular school-site talk among experienced reforming teachers and inexperienced student teachers is an indispensable resource in the education of reform-minded teachers.

CRITICAL DISSONANCE AND COLLABORATIVE RESONANCE

Student-teaching programs specifically designed to foster critical inquiry and prepare prospective teachers to be reformers are part of a small minority of preservice programs across the country (Goodlad, 1990b; Grant & Secada, 1990; Zeichner, Liston, Mahlios, & Gomez, 1988). Within this small group of programs, however, two variations in theory and practice can be distinguished as the products of two different sets of assumptions about the power and knowledge relationships of the school and the university.

Critical Dissonance

One approach to preparing student teachers to work against the grain is to create *critical dissonance*, or *incongruity based on a critical perspective*, between what students learn about teaching and schooling at the university and what they already know and continue to learn about them in the schools. In student-teaching programs based on critical dissonance, the "problem of student teaching" is generally identified as its tendency to bolster utilitarian perspectives on teaching and ultimately to perpetuate existing practices (Beyer, 1984; Feiman-Nemser, 1983; Goodman, 1986a; Tabachnick & Zeichner, 1984; Zeichner, Tabachnick, & Densmore, 1987). The goal of these programs is to interrupt the potentially conservative influences of student teachers' school-based experiences and instead call into question the implications of standard school policy and practice. The strategies of programs intended to foster critical dissonance include methods courses that emphasize alternative teaching strategies, field experiences coupled with ethnographic studies of schooling, critical theory-based curriculum study, seminars and journals in which students reflect critically on their teaching experiences, and action research projects in schools (Beyer, 1984; Gitlin & Teitelbaum, 1983; Goodman, 1986a; Zeichner & Liston, 1987).

Programs that aim to create critical dissonance are intended to be transformative, to help students broaden their visions and interrogate their own perspectives. Unfortunately, these programs have had limited success. Critical reflection is difficult, especially because cooperating teachers who do not have reflective skills themselves often co-opt the effort (Calderhead, 1989). Further, the intentions of programs are not necessarily implemented, particularly in the interactions of students and their supervisors (Zeichner et al., 1988) and in methods and fieldwork courses (Beyer, 1984; Goodman, 1986a, 1986b). Over time, such programs encourage some critique, but actually alter students' outlooks very little (Feiman-Nemser, 1990; Zeichner & Liston, 1987).

Many educators would agree that preparing more liberally educated teachers to think and work critically is an essential goal for teacher preparation. However, there are several troubling messages implicit in programs that aim to provoke critical dissonance between university and school: the way to link theory and practice is to bring a critical perspective to bear upon the institutional and instructional arrangements of schooling; people outside of schools are the agents who have developed these critical perspectives and thus can liberalize and reform the people and activities inside; the "wisdom" of teachers' practice is a conservative point of view that has to be gotten around, exposed, or changed; and the language and conceptual frameworks for describing and critiquing teachers' work lives need not be familiar to teachers or articulated in their own voices or words. This means that the radical critique prompted by critical dissonance, which argues in the abstract for the knowledge, voices, and power of teachers themselves, may in reality "set up" school-based teachers to be exposed and criticized in university-led courses, and may inadvertently convey the message that teachers' lived experiences are unenlightened and even unimportant.

Collaborative Resonance

A second approach to preparing student teachers to work against the grain is to create *collaborative resonance*, or *intensification based on the joint work of learning communities*, by linking what student teachers learn from their university-based experiences with what they learn from their school-based experiences. In programs based on resonance, the "problem of student teaching" is its failure to provide student teachers with not only the analytical skills needed to critique standard procedures, but also the resources needed to function as reforming teachers throughout their teaching careers. The goal is to prolong and intensify the influences of university *and* school experiences, both of which are viewed as potentially liberalizing.

The strategies of programs intended to foster collaborative resonance, some of which are similar to strategies of programs intended to foster dissonance, include placement of student teachers in sites where reform and restructuring efforts are underway; action research and teacher research projects conducted cooperatively by student teachers and experienced teachers; curriculum and methods courses taught and critiqued in both university and school settings; collaborative inquiry at school-site meetings and university-site seminars; and joint program planning and assessment by teachers and teacher educators (Clift, Veal, Johnson, & Holland, 1990; Cochran-Smith & Lytle, 1993; Rochester City Schools/University of Rochester Ford Foundation Report, 1988–89; Ross, 1987).

Programs based on resonance share with programs intended to stimulate dissonance the view that, in and of themselves, the formal aspects of preservice preparation are largely incapable of altering students' perspectives (Zeichner, Tabachnick, & Densmore, 1987), while the less formal, experiential aspects of student teaching are potentially more powerful (Feiman-Nemser, 1983). But unlike programs intended to provoke dissonance, programs based on resonance simultaneously aim to capitalize on the potency of teaching cultures to alter students' perspectives by creating or tapping into contexts that support ongoing learning by student teachers in the company of experienced teachers who are themselves actively engaged in efforts to reform, research, or transform teaching (Evertson, 1990; Richardson-Koehler, 1988).

Taken as a whole, the messages embedded in programs based on collaborative resonance are significantly different from those in many other programs: self-critical and systematic inquiry is a primary way to link theory and practice; inquiry is most effective within a larger culture of collaboration wherein novices and experienced professionals alike learn from, interpret, and ultimately alter the day-to-day life of schools; power is shared among participants in the community, and knowledge about teaching is understood as fluid and socially constructed; the language and critique of school-based reforming teachers are as essential as are those of university-based educators and researchers; and, in the end, the power to reinvent teaching, learning, and schooling is located in neither the university nor the school but in the collaborative work of the two. Programs based on resonance attempt to bring people who have insider perspectives together with those who have perspectives on teaching against the grain that have developed outside of schools themselves. The purpose here is not to homogenize ideas but to intensify through joint work the opportunities student teachers have to learn to teach against the grain.

TEACHING AGAINST THE GRAIN

Teachers who work against the grain are in the minority. Often they must raise their voices against teaching and testing practices that have been "proven" effective by large-scale educational research and delivered to the doorsteps of their schools in slick packages. Often they must provide evidence that their students are making sufficient progress according to standard measures of learning, despite the fact that they place little stock in those measures and believe, to the contrary, that they work against the best interests of their children. It is not surprising that teachers who work against the grain are sometimes at odds with their administrators and evaluators.

To teach against the grain, teachers have to understand and work both *within* and *around* the culture of teaching and the politics of schooling at their particular schools and within their larger school systems and communities. Unlike researchers who remain outside the schools, teachers who are committed to working against the grain inside their schools are not at liberty to publicly announce brilliant but excoriating critiques of their colleagues and the bureaucracies in which they work. Their ultimate commitment is to the school lives and futures of the children with whom they live and work. They have to be astute observers of individual learners with the ability to pose and explore questions that transcend cultural attribution, institutional habit, and the alleged certainty of outside experts. They have to see beyond and through the conventional labels and practices that sustain the status quo by raising unanswerable questions. Perhaps most importantly, teachers who work against the grain must wrestle with their own doubts, fend off the fatigue of reform, and depend on the strength of their individual and collaborative convictions that their work ultimately makes a difference in the fabric of social responsibility.

Teaching against the grain is challenging and sometimes discouraging work. In most student-teaching placements, there are few opportunities for experienced teachers or student teachers to participate in thoughtful inquiry, reflect on their daily decisions, or collaborate with others (Goodlad, 1984; Little, 1987; Su, 1990). In most of their encounters with school and university supervisors, student teachers are encouraged to talk about "relevant" and technical rather than critical or epistemological aspects of teaching

(Hursh, 1988; Zeichner et al., 1988). Finally, in most of their preservice programs, the role of the teacher as an agent for change is not emphasized, and students are not deliberately socialized into assuming responsibility for school reform and renewal (Edmundsen, 1990; Goodlad, 1990a).

As this chapter illustrates, however, student teachers' relationships and collaborations with teachers who are themselves struggling to teach against the grain make for a different kind of experience. Working and talking regularly with experienced teachers who share the goal of teaching differently allow student teachers to participate in their ways of knowing and reforming teaching. Despite their inexperience, student teachers do learn about teaching against the grain when they talk with experienced teachers in learning communities where questions are urged, answers are not expected, and the tentative forays of beginners are supported.

To illustrate, I focus in the remainder of this chapter on data collected in urban elementary schools in the Philadelphia area where student teachers worked actively with both university mentors and school-based teachers engaged in the enterprise of reform. I explore the learning opportunities that were available to student teachers within the weekly teacher-researcher school-site meeting, which was one of the major contexts of this student-teaching program. This program was intended to build on the collaborative resonance of university and school experiences. Participants in the school-site meetings were student teachers, cooperating teachers, and university supervisors in Project START, a 5-year preservice program in elementary education at the University of Pennsylvania that existed from 1986 to 1996.

In Project START, all participants (students, as well as cooperating teachers, university supervisors, and course instructors) were encouraged to view themselves as researchers, reformers, and reflective professionals responsible for critiquing and creating curriculum, instruction, forms of assessment, and the institutional arrangements of schooling. The combination of several instructional and supervisory structures made the student-teaching portion of the program somewhat unusual. Twenty to 25 students progressed through the 12-month program as a cohort, participating together in study groups, seminars, courses, and teacher-research groups. Each student teacher simultaneously completed university coursework and a full year of student teaching in the same classroom with the same teacher (5 months of student teaching 2 days per week, 3 months of student teaching 5 days per week). Subcohorts of three or four student teachers were placed at specially selected elementary school sites with cooperating teachers who, in a variety of ways, were working against the grain. They were involved, for instance, in curricular redesign projects, teacher research and publication, alternative schools and programs, grassroots parent-teacher community groups, teacher networks and collaboratives, or other teaching- and school-reform efforts. Alternative methods courses emphasized critical issues in theory and practice and required projects that were implemented in student-teaching classrooms and critiqued in both university and school settings. All participants in the program were teachers, learners, and researchers. They had opportunities to participate in many varieties of teacher research through course assignments, school and university-site activities, in-house and regional publications and professional forums, and the larger professional community. Each subcohort of student teachers, cooperating teachers, and university supervisor met weekly in a school-site, teacher-researcher group meeting to reflect on their work. All cohorts met together monthly for a university-site seminar on teaching, learning, and learning to teach. University supervisors and program organizers met biweekly in a teacher-educator-as-researcher group to inquire about their own theories and practices of teacher education. Supervisors, program organizers, and cooperating teachers met twice yearly to assess and revise the program.

This chapter draws on examples from school-site meetings that occurred over the course of one student teaching year at four urban schools (names of schools are pseudonyms): Community Central, a small central Philadelphia independent school; Charles A. Beard, a small desegregated Philadelphia public school; Edgeview Elementary School, a public school in an urban area on the edge of Philadelphia; and Stephen R. Morris Elementary, a large Philadelphia public school. These four schools were selected to demonstrate some of the range and variation in urban school-site discussions. The small groups of student teachers assigned to these schools met weekly as teacher-researcher groups with their cooperating teachers and university supervisors to raise questions and reflect on issues of theory and practice. Over the course of the year, the four schools hosted more than 70 teacher-researcher meetings, ranging in length from 30 to 90 minutes.

COLLABORATION, INTELLECTUAL WORK, AND THE CULTURE OF REFORM

I use observational data to reveal some of the "intellectual work" of teaching against the grain that occurred in inquiry communities. By "intellectual work," I mean the patterns of thinking, talking, and knowing about teaching that were characteristic of teachers engaged in the enterprise of reform: the problems they posed about children, the dilemmas they found impossible to answer, the knowledge they made problematic, the evidence they sought in order to document and explore particular issues, the bodies of knowledge they brought to bear on particular situations, the ways they connected diverse experiences, and the themes they explored as central to understanding teaching. The conversations demonstrate why student teachers needed opportunities to live and work with reformers if they themselves were to embrace a reformer's stance on schooling.

Rethinking the Language of Teaching

At Community Central Lower School, the threads of progressive philosophy were woven tightly into long-standing traditions of peaceful Quaker education. At the core of the culture was a deep commitment to community, diversity, and self-critical inquiry. Teachers strove to educate the mind, body, and spirit of all students and to prepare them to live more fully in the present as well as the future. In an important sense, daily school life at Community Central itself represented a transformative vision of what is possible in education. But the habit at Community Central was also to question the school's own practices. One teacher commented that she had chosen to work at the school because it was never self-satisfied. She explicitly told the student teachers:

> Don't ever apologize for being a teacher and always talk about it in an intellectual way to really show that as a responsibility, you have to keep learning. . . . As a model for your peers and colleagues, there is a way to say that there aren't any easy answers. . . . Especially as a new teacher, in a way you are given permission to ask *why* as a new teacher. And as a colleague it's your responsibility to constantly say, "Well, that's *an* answer," or, "That's an easy answer and what we need to do is to take some time to *really* think about the issue, talk about all the ways we can get information to illuminate what's going on, and then talk about all the strategies we can use to strengthen the situation." And that's much more complicated. But you're still modeling being a thinking individual, which is what you want to do.

Within a culture of reform and reflection, the teacher-researcher group at Community Central raised questions about the assumptions underlying school policies and the consequences of their labeling practices. Borrowing from Giroux (1984), I regard this form of intellectual work as *rethinking the language of teaching*—a collaborative process of uncovering the values and assumptions implicit in language and then thinking through the nature of the relationships they legitimize.

In one teacher-researcher meeting at Community Central, for example, the group discussed the consequences of the school's long-standing practice of labeling some students "transition children," or children who completed kindergarten but were "not ready" for first grade and hence spent 2 years instead of one to make the transition between the end of kindergarten and the beginning of second grade. An excerpt from their conversation demonstrates what it means to do the intellectual work of rethinking the language and practices of teaching.

Sherry Watson-Gage, Cooperating Teacher, Grades 3/4: I do not believe
   in a transition class, or having it—period! As a parent [in this school],
   last January I got a letter from my child's teacher, actually in November, when she had spent a month and a half with him. She said to me,
   "He may be a candidate for transition." I said, "Why?" And she said,
   "It's not academic, it's emotional". . . . I think all of those discussions
   are very fuzzy and [I know] they have to be in November, but what it
   said to me was, "He's not all right"—not that he's not perfect
   because, goodness, I know that, but it was, "He's not all right. There
   is something wrong with him. And we're now going to lower our
   expectations for the amount of growth that he is going to go through
   because we're not thinking probably that he will go to first grade—
   he'll go to transition."
Shelia Jules-James, Cooperating Teacher, Grades 3/4: What would you
   do then with a child who was not ready?
Warson-Gage: See, that to me is a hard thing. What does it mean not
   to be ready? Because last year, I had children who were "not ready"
   for third grade, and they are great in fourth grade. Now how do
   you predict? And what does it mean? I have fourth grade children
   who [were] transition children [years ago], and it's still an issue
   for them. They still say, "I was a transition child." And so they
   are still carrying something around. And nobody ever said it with
   glee, "I was a transition child!" . . . But what is the experience?
   [What can we see by] following a transition kid through to see if it
   really does help?
[*The conversation continued during the group's teacher research group
meeting the following week.*]
Jules-James: I think transition is . . . not a situation that has any easy
   solution. And I think what works for one family may not work for
   another child or another family. I see there being children who need
   more attention or more time in some way and they need it for a
   variety of reasons, and how do we give it to them without damaging
   their self-esteem or damaging their families' self-esteem or the way
   their families feel about them?

Over the course of two lengthy school-site conversations, members of the
teacher research group helped one another begin to do the intellectual work
of rethinking the language of learning and development. Specifically, they

worked to make the labels, language, and practices of children's early growth problematic, an activity that Tom (1985) emphasizes is a "conscious attempt on the part of the teacher to suspend judgment about some aspect of the teaching situation and, instead, to consider alternatives to established practice" (p. 37). The conversation was dominated by the experienced teachers, but it really began at the start of the school year (and several weeks prior to the conversation quoted above) when one student teacher commented to her supervisor, "I'm just not really sure what those [transition] classes are all about and how they came to be set up like that and whose decision it was and which kids get placed in those classrooms and that kind of thing." This question was carried to the teacher research group where it prompted an experienced teacher to express dissatisfaction with the practice of establishing transition classes, which eventually led to the group's exploration of the issue and to repeated admissions that the question had no ready answer.

Tom (1985) has argued that critical theorists have sometimes failed to provide an adequate enough account of individual intention and human agency in their explanations of the development and evolution of culture, explanations that would help educators move beyond "deterministic thinking" and toward "intentionality" (1985, p. 38). What is especially important about the intellectual work accomplished in the excerpt above is that participants regarded the teacher herself as one of the agents who had the right, and indeed the obligation, to make certain aspects of teaching problematic. An image of the teacher as an active agent poses a sharp contrast to the image of the teacher as a pawn pushed around by the fingers of habit, standard procedure, and expert outsider knowledge.

Posing Problems of Practice

Charles A. Beard School, part of the large city school system, provided two educational alternatives to parents—"the open classroom track" and "the traditional track." The hallmark of the culture of teaching in the open classrooms was an ongoing effort to learn from children's language and work, to draw from observations of single cases teaching strategies that could be used in other cases, and to construct curriculum that strengthened children's abilities by building on their own resources. The existence of two distinct traditions of teaching provided ongoing grist for comparison and an informal culture of critique. As one teacher talked to the student teachers about her teaching history, she described the culture of reform of which she and others in the group had been part for many years:

It was the beginning for me of seeing how much what we do affects what the children produce and how much we limit them with unspoken messages when we give them worksheets and when we give them dittos and fill-ins . . . it was very, very hard to be in a place where you knew that you could do something for children that would be meaningful and relevant for them, but the powers-that-be had other ideas about what school was all about. And it really became an ongoing theme in my life, and I think in many people's lives, that whatever culture the kids are from, the school culture becomes yet another piece that is overlaid on them. And when it doesn't have any fit with their own culture, with what they've brought, it really becomes very hard for them to see school as relevant and to be able to feel themselves as valuable people. And I finally had to leave that place because I just felt I was so stymied in what I wanted to do. . . . I realized that we had to take hard looks at the kids and do the kind of work that they were already showing us was important to them.

Charles A. Beard was a small desegregated school with a strong history of parent-teacher cooperation and a commitment to community involvement. Although as a school it did not have a commitment to open education, the teachers who were members of the teacher research group were heavily involved in a teacher-initiated, long-term, and primarily outside-of-school culture of activism, reflection, and progressive education. They were founding members of a 12-year-old teachers' cooperative group that met weekly in members' homes to reflect on their work, and they were participants in many local and national forums on teaching, learning, and evaluation.

Within a culture of commitment to public education and to the social and democratic construction of knowledge for teaching, the Charles A. Beard teacher research group frequently used guidelines from "Descriptive Review of a Child" and other Prospect School documentary processes (Carini, 1986). These begin with a teacher's focusing question about a specific child or issue to be explored through systematic observation and oral inquiry. In site meetings over the course of a year, a frequent focus of the group's intellectual work was the development of questions, or what Schön (1983a) describes as "problem setting." Schön reminds us that problems of professional practice do not present themselves ready-made, but rather that practice "is complex and uncertain, and there is a problem in finding the problem" (p. 129).

In one teacher research group conversation, for example, student teachers were struggling to choose individual children whom they would observe over time in the classroom and then present to the school-site group as a case study or descriptive review. Their cooperating teachers emphasized posing problems from which they could learn how to teach the individual child, as well as other children. Their emphasis was consistently on understanding the generalities of teaching by exploring its particulars.

Sharon Bates, Cooperating Teacher, Grade 4: The key thing is to pick a child you have a question about and that you honestly want to describe and get feedback on. . . . You have to think of a question for the child. This is the hardest part. It has to be with you and the child. It can't just be centered on you.

Karen Johnston, Cooperating Teacher, Grade 3: There might be a third grader [about] whom you feel, "Am I going to know that child any better when I leave here?" or, "How am I going to work with this child when I feel some of these barriers?" That would be one kind of question. It's not just, "How am I going to work with this child?"

Rita Greenberger, Cooperating Teacher, Grade 1: Another kind of question might be, "How am I going to get this child to know I mean business?" or "How can I get this child to be a functioning part of the group—to improve his reading or improve the way he relates to other children?"

Sharon Bates: It also could be a question about reading and writing, like "How can I help someone to read?" Those questions seem to be the ones that you seem to be more comfortable with through what you have already learned in the [university] classroom. And some of these questions about social relationships and management are the harder ones.

Jenny Gold, Student Teacher, Grades 3/4: Does it have to be a question, or can it be an analysis of somebody?

Rita Greenberger: It can be an issue.

Karen Johnston: What is *your* question? [addressing Sharon Bates, who had mentioned earlier that she would be making a presentation about a child at a teacher research conference the following week.]

Sharon Bates: It's about how to help [a particular child]. He's a person who with reading checks things out a lot with adults when it doesn't make sense . . . I think you [addressing Jenny Gold] experience him as very disruptive a lot of the time. He's always up and down.

Jenny Gold: With activities on the rug I do.

Sharon Bates: My question is how to support him in his reading to keep the questioning that he does, because it is really very valuable to him, but to help him become more independent, so that he won't be frustrated when he gets into a classroom situation in which he might not get his questions answered . . . He's captured into reading now, but you have to hold him still . . . so my question is how to support him in this path.

In this and other conversations, members of the group explored together the process of finding questions or setting problems about individual children.

The teachers described and demonstrated the ways they constructed questions out of close observations of children, from multiple perspectives. The questions the cooperating teachers posed were not simply versions of how to teach something or how to apply theory to practice. Sharon Bates, for example, posed a problem about how to understand one child as reader, learner, and asker of questions. She asked about how over time to connect with his resources in order to strengthen them, and then used this question to explore with the inquiry group how to teach other children.

The cooperating teachers at Charles A. Beard helped student teachers frame and reframe questions, repeatedly directing them to return to observations from the classroom, uncover the prior questions that were embedded in present ones, and develop generative structures of inquiry. Their process of mentoring was not unlike Schön's (1983a, 1983b, 1987) description of the ways supervisors in architecture and psychotherapy work with students—by reframing their ways of looking at the problems of design and counseling and by both implicitly criticizing the students' own ways of framing the problems and also suggesting new ways to think about solutions.

One of the most striking aspects of problem setting is the image it conveys to student teachers about the teacher's relationship to knowledge. The teacher implicit in the conversations at Charles A. Beard was not separated from the knowledge of teaching, nor was the teacher simply the practitioner or applier of others' theoretical principles. Rather, she was a builder of knowledge and theory. In their discussions, teacher researchers collaboratively built theory and knowledge frameworks out of the experience of specific cases that also cut across classrooms, age levels of children, and cultural backgrounds. In this way, they were intimately involved in a process of transforming the social life of the school.

Constructing Curriculum

Edgeview Elementary School served a diverse working-class community of mostly White families, a small number of Black families, some recent immigrants from Korea and Greece, and many families from other cultures who had lived in the community for a number of years. There was a strong culture in the school of positive community involvement, friendly relations among children, teachers, principal, and parents, and an ecumenical tolerance for various teaching "styles." Although there was a comfortable sense of congeniality at Edgeview Elementary School, teachers worked largely by themselves, and as is the case in many schools, there was a culture of isolation. The three experienced teachers who were part of the teacher research group were united by their belief in alternative reading/language arts programs that utilized literature and children's writing.

The curriculum and assessment policies of the school district were traditional, and a few years earlier, the district had begun to place increased emphasis on standard procedures and curriculum uniformity. The culture of reform of Edgeview Elementary School's teacher-researcher group was bound up with the construction of an alternative reading/language arts curriculum and with demonstrating that children could learn to read from real literature rather than from texts constructed specifically for the purpose of instruction. During the year prior to the school-site meetings mentioned here, the teachers had struggled with administrators over whether or not literature could be used at the second grade level. One of the teachers described the struggle to her student teacher:

> They fought us about novels last year [because some people think] our children's backgrounds are lacking and they haven't got support from home and experience in reading . . . [They think] they need things simpler. They need the, "See Dick run. See Jane run," and the novel isn't written in that form. It's not simplified. And [they think] they're not ready except for the smart kids . . . So our principal finally said to us, "You can use novels, but you have to test the children in the tests for the reading series, and you have to teach the same skills that are in the reading series." . . . So I do it. And we showed him. I mean, I have folders full of stuff . . . where the kids are learning short *"a"* and long—all the things that he thinks they need to learn . . . This year I never even went and discussed it with him. I'm just assuming that I am going to do it . . . If we hadn't won that battle, I probably wouldn't have come back.

As part of a group effort aimed at curriculum reform working within a larger school-system culture of standardized teaching and assessment, the teacher-researcher group at Edgeview Elementary School raised many questions that can be thought of as *constructing curriculum*. This was more than deciding how to teach the material predetermined in a teacher's guide or a pupil's text. It required that teachers consider the long-range consequences of what and why they teach, as well as the daily decisions about how they teach it. In the conversation below, they critiqued a school district in-service session designed to get them to think of literature as a supplement to, but not an alternative to, the "real" curriculum of basal reading materials.

Charlie Dougherty, Cooperating Teacher, Grade 5: One of the points that was being made to us was the possibility to use novels as a supplement. Now that is what I think is ludicrous to do.
Leslie Franks, Cooperating Teacher, Grade 5: For us.

Charlie Dougherty: You can't do it. *Either* you are going to use the basals *or* the novels.

Leslie Franks: You can't go back and forth . . . because it squashes the enthusiasm. And what happens is the kids tend to moan and groan through the whole basal unit that you are doing, and you're ruining their growth. And when you go back to the novels, they know it is for a one-night stand. A one-night stand! And then they are back again to basals, which is like suicide.

Charlie Dougherty: It's a silly idea . . .

Leslie Franks: And also as they progress in years, when you talk about standardized testing, that is one of the big things that you find . . . It's the little paragraph that you have to read now [on the tests]—What is the main idea? Now what do you want to do first? What were the supporting details? And if you can do that with the novel, you are so much more in tune to detect these [on the test]. Case in point—our kids have done beautifully on [standardized comprehension] testing.

Charlie Dougherty: They blew the top off!

Phyllis Kim, Student Teacher, Grade 5: I don't think I understand basals well enough, but I really don't understand why you can't go back and forth using basals and novels if you were using the same approach—an inferential [approach]?

Mary Thailing, Cooperating Teacher, Grade 2: Yes, if you were just giving a child a book [and not using the teacher's manuals and workbook exercises], you could do whatever you wanted with it.

Phyllis Kim: I was thinking that if I were in a school district next year where I have basals and I could only use novels when I could afford to buy them, could I do something like that?

Mary Thailing: [You could do with] a basal story everything that you do with a novel . . .

Charlie Dougherty: I don't know if you can.

Mary Thailing: Yes you can. If it's a story that is a *real* story. I mean that's in there [in the basal] . . .

In this conversation the group struggled with the problem of combining two kinds of materials for reading instruction that are grounded in basically incompatible perspectives on language learning. Zumwalt (1989) argues that a "curricular vision of teaching" is essential for all beginning teachers if they are going to be prepared to function as professional decisionmakers in their field. Without it, she cautions, the beginning teacher tends to settle for "what works" in the classroom rather than what could be. Also underlying this discussion was the conflict among teachers and administrators (and among teachers themselves) about their roles as curriculum implementers and tinkerers, on the one hand, versus critics and creators on the other.

Confronting the Dilemmas of Teaching

At Stephen R. Morris Elementary School, the slender threads of the open classroom tradition were knotted and entangled with the broader strands of the history of segregation and desegregation in the city. Morris offered a small "open" track, a "traditional" track, and a "midway" track from which parents could choose options for their children. The culture of teaching in the open track was built on a commitment to closely observing children, providing a rich environment out of which children's own curiosities could drive the curriculum, and continuously reflecting on practice in the company of other committed professionals. Morris served more than 1,200 children who, for complex historical reasons, were from poor Black homes, while the middle-class Black and White parents in the immediate and immediately adjacent neighborhoods had chosen to have their children bussed to other desegregated city schools or sent to private schools. Conditions at Morris were difficult, special programs were limited, and the culture of teaching in the school at large was traditional. Teachers in the Morris teacher-researcher group had a transformative vision of education, but they worked within a context of poverty, increasing school district testing and curriculum strictures, and few opportunities for collaboration. One teacher noted to the student teachers:

> At the end of the year, I look over the year and I always feel there's more I could have done. And there are parts of the year I really feel good about and parts of the year I don't feel good about. But you're still only one human being. You can't do everything. I feel that what I offer children is very rich, and if children just get a little bit of that or if they get the idea that not everything has to be the same all the time [then it's worth it]. And there's this thing called thinking, I felt that what I did was important for those children. It gave them a little experience that maybe will stick with them. . . .
>
> One of the thoughts I have is that I'm 63. Technically, you can teach until you're 70. At this point I would like to teach forever. I can't imagine doing anything other than teach. But it's not as enjoyable as it used to be. I mean . . . just being in an environment where I feel I'm unappreciated makes it very, very hard. It's okay once the door is closed, and I'm in here, but it's very hard to walk out of the door.

As a school community, Morris did not have a commitment to the principles of progressive education or teacher empowerment. But the Morris teachers who were members of the school-site group were actively involved in a long-standing culture of teacher inquiry and British primary school traditions and, like the Charles A. Beard teachers, were founding members of a teacher collaborative that met weekly. In teacher research group meetings at Morris, teachers struggled with many questions that had no answers, and many problems that had no solutions. Borrowing language from Berlak and Berlak (1981) and Lampert (1985), I refer to this form of intellectual work as *confronting the dilemmas of teaching*, a process of identifying and wrestling with educational issues that are characterized by equally strong but incompatible and competing claims to justice.

In one teacher-researcher meeting at Morris, for example, the group had talked about recent court decisions that affected girls' and boys' schools in the area. They also discussed the negative consequences and the possible advantages for minority children of *segregated* schooling situations. The fact that one of the student teachers in the group was a Black woman who had attended mostly White schools throughout her educational history, and that all three experienced teachers in the group were White women who had made long-term personal and professional commitments to teaching in mostly Black public schools, were critical factors in the discussion.

Ellen Freeman, Cooperating Teacher, Grade 3: One question I have is about middle-class teachers who don't have the experiences of the children they teach . . . I have noticed something about . . . a few of the Black boys that I've taught, and I came to some conclusions about them and what would be the place for them—what kinds of teachers would be best for them to have. And I don't know, I mean, I don't know if this is racist or not. There were some very bright Black children in that class. They were in a desegregated class. They were learning to read and write and spell and all that, but there was also a group of extremely bright White boys in the class, . . . and the White boys were well-behaved . . . They always did the "right thing." And the Black kids often misbehaved, and they often baited me in some ways.

Later in fourth grade . . . [one of them] was [taken out of the desegregated class] and put into the class of a Black teacher with all Black kids . . . At the end of the year, he won a behavior award in the school. What it made me think was that . . . we need to have all boys' high schools *de*segregated because it's important for boys to be in school with girls. But we [also] need girls' high schools for girls to excel without men, without boys—I wonder, sometimes, if . . . some

Black children need to be in schools that are not desegregated where they see themselves as leaders within their community—I don't know—I mean it really is a question, and I've thought a lot about it ... It's just a question because I think we need girls' high schools *and* I think we need all boys' schools to be *de*segregated. ...

Teresa Green, Student Teacher, Kindergarten: I think that the point Ellen brought up is important ... I know from previous experience that an integrated situation versus a segregated situation can do positive or negative things for you ... I've been a minority in predominantly all-White situations from the time that I was six or seven. And it does make a difference. And some of the differences are negative. And it's important to find out that sometimes people can be stronger when they are with people that they need to be with—when they are in supportive environments. ...

Polly Spellman, Cooperating Teacher, Kindergarten: But I don't think you learn how to be strong in the abstract. Just as I don't think you learn how to use freedom unless you have freedom. Freedom isn't something you read about and then follow directions. It's something you have to experience. Well, I feel it's the same thing about kids in schools. Though I could see some positive things to girls' schools ... I just don't think that we get any closer to learning how to operate by having exclusions. ...

Teresa Green: But you're talking the ideal! The reality is of the world. The reality of the situation is that Black kids cannot go into predominantly White situations and come out with the same kind of security, the same kind of support that they would get in a different environment. ...

Polly Spellman: So, let's go back to segregated schools?

Ellen Freeman: It's not really a segregated school, Polly. That's not what I'm talking about either. I am talking about choices ... But I guess I'm *not* talking about choices for everybody. I have to say that. I don't agree with Karen about boys' high schools. I do *not* think that the people who have traditionally been in power should be allowed—*allowed*—to have choices ...

Teresa Green: But that's contradictory—

Ellen Freeman: I know it is—

Karen Garfield, Cooperating Teacher, Grade 5: What Ellen is saying is that the heavy power [that] has always been a certain way needs to skew the other way ...

In this discussion, teachers worked together to confront the dilemmas created by race, class, and gender segregation of educational opportunities.

They wrestled to reconcile the irreconcilable issues of the possible advantages for minority children of going to school with children of their own race or gender groups versus the clear disadvantages of being segregated from the culture of power. It is significant that there was no consensus in this conversation, especially in the comments of Ellen Freeman, who knew full well that what she was saying was, in a certain sense, both contradictory and critical.

A key aspect of this conversation is that members of the group named one of the dilemmas of teaching and wrestled with the fact that there was no answer to it within the current structures of schooling and society. Their conversation makes it clear that there is a distinction between a dilemma of teaching and a problem of teaching. A problem is a question posed for solution or at least action, a situation that may be perplexing and difficult, but *not* one that is ultimately unapproachable. A dilemma, on the other hand, is a situation of teaching that presents two or more logical alternatives, the loss of *either* of which is equally unfavorable and disagreeable. A dilemma poses two or more competing claims to justice, fairness, and morality. The dilemma confronted above probed the means-ends relationships of schooling and raised critical questions about the interests served by the current structures of schooling. Fenstermacher (1990) points out that in current controversies over the professionalization of schooling, the moral dimensions of teaching, although primary, are often either ignored or forgotten. At Stephen R. Morris School, the group identified and confronted one of the moral dilemmas of teaching. Their intellectual work did not "solve" the problem nor adjudicate which side of the scale should be more heavily weighted in matters of race, gender, and educational opportunity. But their work clearly announced that there *was* a moral base to teaching, not just a knowledge base, and that prospective teachers had to confront that moral base in order to reclaim their responsibility in the classroom.

STUDENT TEACHERS AS REFORMERS

It is clear in the conversations above that student teachers did not dominate, and in many instances did not take equal part in, teacher research group meetings. In most instances, cooperating teachers rather than university-based supervisors or student teachers themselves took the lead. However, the student teachers' emerging theories of practice were influenced by their observations and conversations with experienced mentors who worked against the grain, as well as by their readings of and writings about a rich and diverse collection of theoretical and pedagogical literature. This was indicated in the lessons and units they designed, the questions they raised, and their efforts to understand their own efforts as urban teachers, as is illustrated in some detail in Chapters 3 and 4 of this book.

Though a deep intellectual discourse among student teachers and their school and university mentors is essential in light of the larger reform agenda for U.S. education, it is uncommon and difficult to sustain during the student-teaching period. And yet, as the excerpts in this chapter demonstrate, it *is* essential and possible. Indeed, the conversations that occurred in school-site meetings over the course of a year provide a "proof of possibility" of rich and complex discourse among experienced teachers and student teachers. This discourse is more provocative than the exchanges common in clinical supervision and wider ranging than the feedback usually given in response to particular lessons or teaching techniques. It is clear, however, that conventional supervisory structures are unlikely to generate this kind of discourse (Zeichner, 1986; Zeichner & Liston, 1985).

A combination of several program structures made this kind of discourse possible. Most importantly, the foundation for all the structures was a deep commitment to the development of "collaborative resonance," or intensification of opportunities to learn from and about teaching through the joint work of learning communities. These communities were composed of school-based cooperating teachers, university-based program directors and course instructors, and student teachers and supervisors who straddled the ground between them. Underlying the work of the community was respect for the knowledge and expertise of those who had invested their professional lives in work inside schools, as well as those who had developed their knowledge of teaching through work about, but primarily outside of, schools. Student teachers were invited, and indeed expected, to raise questions and pose problems in the language of both school and university. They were expected to weave their emerging critiques with the threads of both insider and outsider knowledge.

The commitment to building collaborative resonance was instantiated in several key social and organizational structures: university-site monthly seminars where teacher-researcher teams from all school sites met together over the course of a year to consider teaching and learning across grades, schools, and school systems; three publications, distributed locally, featuring news, opinion, and essays by past and present project participants; dissemination and discussion of common readings in the various sites; co-planning by teacher educators and school-based teachers of seminar topics, student teachers' assignments, and program strategies; and participation by project members (including students) in local, regional, and national networks of teacher researchers.

Second, as part of a community of co-learners, the roles of all project participants were redefined. Student teachers were expected to construct their own emerging theories of teaching and learning, call into question conventional practices, write about their work, and participate with their experienced mentors as inquiring professionals. It was understood that the primary role of students was *not* to imitate the instructional styles of their mentors. Concurrently it became clear that the role of cooperating teachers was much more extensive than the demonstration and evaluation of teaching strategies. Some cooperating teachers had been active for many years in teacher organizations that promoted collaborative inquiry, social responsibility, progressive education, and curriculum reconstruction. They brought an inquiry-centered perspective to their roles and worked to articulate their perspectives to student teachers and support students' initial forays into inquiry. In addition, the role of the university supervisor was redefined to include research on practice and co-inquiry. Supervision-as-inquiry meant that in addition to their regular meetings with students and cooperating teachers, supervisors also met regularly with project leaders to reflect on their work as teacher educators and compare the nature of their interactions with students and teachers to the goals and intentions of the program. This provided a connection between supervisor and preservice curriculum that is sometimes missing in student-teaching programs.

Finally, the very existence of weekly school-site meetings helped to make possible an intellectually based student teacher/experienced teacher discourse on teaching and learning. Site meetings of at least 45 minutes per week were built into the requirements of the program, allowing enough time for the beginnings of substantive discussion. Students' teaching placements for a full year permitted continuity of discussions and supported the development of each teacher-researcher group as a community, across grade levels and experiences. This was possible in part because group members came to know one another's contexts of reference and to see one another's growth from the long view. Finally, and perhaps most importantly, school-site meetings were *not* set up according to the conventional model of clinical supervision, which more or less necessitates that the topic of discussion is feedback and evaluation of individual lessons. To the contrary, in the site-meeting context, individual lessons could not be the topic of conversation since the seven to nine participants in each group worked in different classrooms. Together these critical features of the program—the larger collaborative community, the redefinition of roles, and the weekly, year-long inquiry sessions—created participation structures (Erickson, 1981) for school-site conversations that had built into them the expectation of serious talk about teaching and reforming teaching, and made it possible for these kinds of conversations to occur.

One of the most important things that happened at school-site meetings was that student teachers were exposed to certain visions of teaching that are not necessarily in keeping with the norms of the profession. Braided into the social and intellectual relationships of student teachers and experienced reforming teachers is exploration of alternative ways to think about and talk about teaching, ways perhaps not normally seen by teachers and administrators who work *with* the grain but also not normally seen by university-based teachers and researchers who work *outside of* schools. Working with experienced school-based reformers exposes student teachers to alternative visions of teaching that enrich but also alter the perspectives they learn in their university courses, as well as the perspectives they learn form the larger culture of teaching.

Reformers' visions of teaching include alternative ways of interpreting classroom events, thinking through conflicts with parents or administrators, and interpreting children's strengths and vulnerabilities. They include alternative ways of documenting and measuring learning, transforming and constructing curriculum, and thinking through issues of race, class, and culture. Struggling along with experienced teachers who are working to reform teaching within complicated and highly specific situations inside of schools is the only context within which student teachers can have theory- and practice-based conversations that deal with the extraordinary complexity of teaching and reforming teaching. There is a paradox, then, in learning to teach against the grain—it is only in the apparent "narrowness" of work in particular classrooms and in the "boundedness" of discussions of highly contextualized instances of practice that student teachers actually have opportunities to confront the broadest themes of reform. Essentially this means that the only way for beginners to learn to be both educators and activists is to struggle over time in the company of experienced teachers who are themselves committed to collaboration and reform in their own classrooms, schools, and communities.

There are many people who are involved in the struggle for educational reform—teachers, administrators, parents, teacher educators, researchers, consultants, and supervisors. In some instances, reformers are located in small pockets within much larger institutions; in other instances, whole faculties or large subgroups of faculties are working together to reinvent school and institutional structures, alter roles and responsibilities, and recreate curricula. One significant way to expand and build on reform efforts is to link student teachers with experienced and new educational reformers. As communities of school- and university-based teachers develop, they become known outside of their own groups, and others come to join them in their work. Experienced reformers share their strategies as well as their questions with colleagues who are newer to the enterprise of teaching against the grain. In a community based on colabor, each individual's opportunity to learn from teaching is intensified and enriched by the questions, struggles, and triumphs of every other individual.

CHAPTER 3

Color Blindness and
Basket Making

Our present educational system is dysfunctional for disproportionately large numbers of children who are not part of the racial and language mainstream (Delpit, 1988; Heath, 1983). Although there are important general principles, there are no universal specific techniques for teaching about cultural diversity or for teaching children who are culturally and linguistically different from one another, from their teachers, or from "majority" students. Indeed, it is contradictory to the concept of cultural diversity itself to expect that educational experts can enumerate specific practices that all teachers should learn and then apply uncritically across schools and communities with different histories and different needs. But it is also not advisable for teachers or children to mistake color blindness for educational equity or to learn "the characteristics" of people of various races and cultures. These practices decontextualize teaching and learning and often result in bolstering the very stereotypes they are intended to dispel (Cazden & Mehan, 1989).

To alter a dysfunctional system, we need teachers who regard teaching as a political activity and embrace social change as part of the job, teachers who enter the profession not expecting to carry on business as usual but prepared to join other educators and parents in major reforms. In this chapter, I argue that teacher educators cannot carry on business as usual. The ways we have traditionally initiated students into the discourses and practices of teaching—especially through widespread versions of "the lesson plan" based on linear analysis of objectives and methods for teaching and management—are not likely to result in an activist's stance on teaching nor meet the needs of an increasingly diverse population of schoolchildren. I argue, then, that what we need in teacher education are not better generic strategies for "teaching multicultural education" or "teaching for diversity" nor more lessons about basket making and other customs in non-Anglo cultures (Sleeter & Grant, 1987). Instead I propose that what we need are generative ways for prospective teachers, experienced teachers, and teacher educators alike to work together in communities of learners—to explore and reconsider their own assumptions, understand the values and practices of families

46

and cultures that are different from their own, and construct pedagogy that takes these into account in locally appropriate and culturally sensitive ways.

LEARNING THE DISCOURSE OF TEACHING: CONTRASTING APPROACHES

A nearly universal tradition in preservice education is to introduce student teachers to teaching by having them write and carry out "the lesson plan." Most models of lesson planning have a series of steps: explicitly stating objectives and goals, choosing appropriate learning activities, organizing and sequencing those activities, and specifying evaluation procedures. A growing body of research on teacher planning and teacher thinking (Clark & Peterson, 1986) suggests that experienced teachers do not proceed in a linear fashion when planning for teaching, but instead plan in ways that are significantly more recursive and cyclical, more learner-centered, and structured around larger chunks of content and time than those of the single lesson. In fact, although experienced teachers use a wide range of planning strategies over the course of a school year, *lesson* planning appears to play a modest or even insignificant role. Nevertheless, the lesson endures as the major unit for planning and improving teaching in preservice education, and lesson plans endure as the single form of planning taught explicitly in programs across the United States. Hence they continue to represent what is arguably the most visible way teacher education institutions initiate student teachers into the discourses and practices of teaching.

Taken as artifacts of the cultures of teaching and teacher education, typical lesson plan assignments imply that both planning for teaching and teaching itself are linear activities that proceed from a preplanned opening move to a known and predetermined endpoint. They suggest that knowledge, curriculum, and instruction are static and unchanging, transmitted through a one-way conduit from teacher to students, rather than socially constructed through the transactions of teachers, children, and texts. This perspective assumes that we can accurately predict how children make sense of ideas, texts, and information and that all children understand and connect these to their own prior knowledge and experience in the same ways. Most importantly, writing and conducting lessons of the sort described here endorse and perpetuate a view of teaching and learning that hinges on mastery, method, and scripted communication.

Implicit in the lesson plan and similar assignments for student teachers is the notion that uniform mastery of "bits" of information and knowledge is the goal of every lesson. In elementary school teaching, both the bits to be mastered and the sequence of steps for getting there are spelled out in detail in the teacher's manuals that increasingly accompany textbooks in every curricular area from spelling and language to math, health, and science. The dominance of the teacher's manual is most apparent, however, in basal reading programs, which provide carefully scripted plans for every single lesson and which are pervasive throughout elementary teaching, accounting for some 90% of reading instruction nationwide and the lion's share of total instructional time at the elementary level (Goodman, 1988; Shannon, 1988). Basal scripts not only tell the teacher exactly when and what to say but also control the children's part in the script by stipulating precisely which responses are to be elicited and accepted. Notwithstanding occasional directives to the teacher to "accept any reasonable answer," it is clear that both teacher and children are expected to stick to the script, which leaves little room for improvisation, originality of perspective, or diversity. Variations in the cultural and linguistic resources that children bring to school with them, in the verbal and nonverbal interaction patterns to which they are accustomed, and in the kinds of knowledge and prior experiences they may have had are not figured in. Because both the content and the sequence of events are preestablished in the lesson plan, the major task for the prospective teacher is not to learn how to understand the diversity of ways children construct meanings, but to get through lessons with a reasonable amount of decorum—establishing order, keeping children on the task at hand, pacing questions and activities, occupying those who finish quickly, and maintaining control.

The image of teaching underlying an inquiry or teacher research-centered approach to teaching directly challenges the dominance of mastery, scripted discourse, and method. Although there are variations in approaches, when teacher research plays a central role in teacher education (Clift et al., 1990; Cochran-Smith & Lytle, 1993; Gore & Zeichner, 1991; Tabachnik & Zeichner, 1991; Teitelbaum & Britzman, 1991), student teachers are generally invited to treat their classrooms and schools as research sites embedded in the contexts of culture and community, to understand their work by raising questions and collecting data, and to discover meanings in the variations in children's behaviors and interpretations of classroom events and interactions. Teacher research is based on the notion that teachers and children together construct knowledge and curriculum through their ongoing classroom interactions by drawing on and mingling their varied language and cultural resources and experiences. Teacher research is not intended as a strategy to help student teachers implement or translate theory into plans for practice. Rather it is intended to help student teachers uncover and develop "theories of practice" or "theories in practice"—that is, neither theories divorced from practice nor practice unaware of its own underlying theories (Edelsky, Altwerger, & Flories, 1991; Sanders & McCutcheon, 1986; Schön, 1983b). Implicit in teacher research is the image of teachers as among those who construct knowledge about teaching, learning, and schooling and who regard knowledge from the academy as potential frameworks for thinking about and altering practice rather than as scripts for reproducing practice and hence ultimately reproducing the inequities embedded in schooling.

CONSTRUCTING AND CONFRONTING DILEMMAS

Five perspectives on race, culture, and language diversity are essential to preparing teachers who see themselves as both educators and activists, who work with others against the grain of schooling that is inequitable for students of color, and who know how to gain and use cultural and other knowledge to meet the needs of students within particular local contexts. When they are initiated into teaching through systematic and self-critical inquiry, student teachers have opportunities to develop these perspectives: (1) *reconsidering personal knowledge and experience*, (2) *locating teaching within the culture of the school and the community*, (3) *analyzing children's learning opportunities*, (4) *understanding children's understanding*, and (5) *constructing reconstructionist pedagogy*. In the pages that follow, I analyze these perspectives and show how they were developed through teacher inquiry during the preservice period.

Reconsidering Personal Knowledge and Experience

In order to learn to teach in a society that is increasingly culturally and linguistically diverse, prospective teachers as well as experienced teachers and teacher educators need opportunities to examine much of what is usually unexamined in the tightly braided relationships of language, culture, and power in schools and schooling. This kind of examination inevitably begins with our own histories as human beings and as educators—our own cultural, racial, and linguistic backgrounds and our own experiences as raced, classed, and gendered children, parents, and teachers in the world. It also includes a close look at the tacit assumptions we make about the motivations and behaviors of other children, other parents, and other teachers and about the pedagogies we deem most appropriate for learners who are like us or not like us. In Project START, student teachers were invited to examine these assumptions by drawing on their own experiences and ideas as well as on the work of other university- and school-based teachers and researchers.

Along with all members of the START learning community (cooperating teachers, university-based supervisors, project directors, and course instructors), student teachers wrote personal narrative essays about their lives and the experiences that have shaped their views of race, culture, and diversity. The intent in narrative essays was for all members of the community to explore for themselves but also to provide for other members a sense of who they were as teachers, as learners, and as human beings. Student teachers also wrote critical essays designed to promote thoughtful responses to program readings in which they posed their own questions about the topics they found central. The intent in these essays, in which students were invited to address the generic question, "What do you think you think about _____?" was to use other people's research to uncover their own interpretive frameworks and to explore the implications of these connections in ways that were tentative and evolutionary. Both kinds of essays—those that were narrative and personal and those that linked the student teacher's emerging understandings to empirical and conceptual research in education and related fields—were essential to a stance that enabled prospective teachers to learn how to construct and confront the dilemmas of cultural diversity and to teach effectively both their own and others' children.

In the excerpt that follows, a student teacher who had entered teaching after several years as a homemaker and mother confronted the realization that the current arrangements of schools and society provided unearned privileges for members of the majority including herself and her own children. She also realized, however, that that same system handicapped the children she was teaching in her student teaching classroom, children who were not part of the majority in either language or race.

Excerpt 1

"Hegemony" is a large and complex concept. It is also a lofty way to say prejudice. Except this concept is covert, insidious, and oftentimes unconscious, which makes it much more difficult to battle. Many times it is even hard to recognize. However, it is a useful concept that has helped to clarify so much of what I am witnessing in my [student teaching] school and in my life.

McIntosh's article [(McIntosh, 1989)] spoke about me when it said, 'I think Whites are carefully taught not to recognize White privilege.' I know I was. I was taught everyone was equal. It never occurred to me that I got what I did because I could fit into the system . . . I recognize I am a classic by-product of this system. How, as I teacher, can I impart another set of values? Hunter [an urban public school with a large Hispanic population in a poor area with serious drug and crime problems] is a perfect example of hegemony, but more importantly so is Merion [a public school in an affluent White suburb where nearly all children go to college]. I student teach at Hunter; I am the proud parent of a second grader at Merion. Neither school is trying to change the system and therefore Merion will always succeed in reproducing the "future executives" and Hunter will always be struggling to have its children merely come to class daily. Merion will be able to win all the awards because standardized tests seem to be stacked in its favor while Hunter [won't] measure up.

I feel the unfairness is the consequence of hegemony. I am wrestling with its implications. But how do I fight against a system that gives my own children the life I want them to have? I moved from the city to give them the same advantages I had. My husband and I chose Lower Merion Township because it offered the lifestyle and schools we wanted. I will have a tough time bucking a system that works for myself and my children. Does that mean I am part of the problem and not the solution?

This excerpt provides insights into the ways a student teacher constructed and confronted the dilemmas of race, culture, and language in teaching by reconsidering and reconnecting personal experiences and knowledge. Part of what is important in this sort of inquiry is that students struggle with the idea that racism includes not simply what McIntosh (1989) calls "individual acts of kindness or meanness" (p. 10), but also and in much larger measure the privileges and disadvantages that both shape and are embedded in the institutions we live by, especially our educational institutions. For some students, the process was literally a reseeing of their lives not as morally neutral and average but filled with the privileges conferred by race. The toughest part of this kind of self-critical reflection was for student teachers to locate themselves as active agents within those institutions—not by accepting blame or guilt because they had been part of a system based on hegemony rather than meritocracy. Rather they did so by reconsidering the ways they, as educators, would from now on understand and act on the successes and failures of individual students and groups of students, the actions and apparent inactions of parents and community members, and the educational categories and labels assigned by experts and other educators.

Locating Teaching in the Culture of the School and Community

Cazden and Mehan (1989) argue that one of the most important things teacher education needs to do is provide opportunities for student teachers to learn "experientially about students and their families" and "how to gain information from the local community and transform it for pedagogical use" (p. 55). A central aspect of this is for student teachers to understand that the teaching and learning they observe and participate in is located within the culture of teaching in individual classrooms as well as within the culture of a particular school and community.

One way to do this is to begin the student teaching experience with group research projects about the schools and communities where student teachers are placed. Inquiry helps student teachers raise questions by closely observing inside and outside school, interviewing teachers, students, parents, and other school personnel and community members, visiting community centers and action groups, and examining school documents as well as children's work and other artifacts of teaching and learning. What is most important in an inquiry project of this kind is that prospective teachers try to understand what is going on in their schools from the meaning perspectives of the participants—teachers, parents, and children—and in relation to the history and values of the community.

For example, a group of student teachers placed at Howell School, a public elementary school in northeast Philadelphia, worked together to explore the culture of their school and its surrounding community. They gathered statistics about programs, test scores, graduation, households, income, rental costs, race, language, occupation, and enrollments and also took photos of the school, classrooms, surrounding areas, and neighborhoods. They interviewed school personnel, families, and community members. And they asked children to draw pictures that represented the school for them and also asked about favorite things, typical days, and language usage. The group also consulted school documents such as site-management plans, grant applications, and histories as well as literature from community and cultural centers in the surrounding neighborhoods, newspaper articles, and promotional information. They attended teacher orientations, back-to-school nights, parent-teacher meetings and conferences, and faculty in-service programs, and they visited community centers and community action groups. The student teachers also observed extensively in their own student teaching classrooms, interviewed their cooperating teachers, and analyzed curriculum guides and textbooks.

Pooling their data, student teachers in each school-site group presented an overview of the culture of their school and community to others in the program. Individually, each student teacher also wrote about the culture of the school and community as the context within which she or he located all other inquiry projects. The excerpts below, each from a different student teacher's description of the culture of the school and community, provide a sense of the ways they began to understand the school and the community during their first few months.

EXCERPT 2

The neighborhood is trying to change itself, to become more organized in order to fight drugs, clean up the streets, and provide a better lifestyle. The effort is being spearheaded by the Neighborhood Project ... Since I have been at the school, I have read three different newspaper articles about their work here ... The school administration as well as the majority of teachers are White and female. Some speak Spanish, [but] there is only one Hispanic teacher. Most live outside the community and return home without ever venturing out of the school. There is little commerce in the area, which limits interaction ... (But) the school is also trying to serve the community better. It employs a local community representative whose job it is to go into the homes to find out why a child is truant.

In this excerpt, the student teacher worked to understand what was going on in the school from the points of view of participants rather than simply making judgments about teachers' or parents' actions based on her own frames of reference. She also tried to locate issues within the history and politics of the community rather than treat them as ahistorical or value-free. By considering multiple perspectives, student teachers began to realize the complexity of issues, as the following excerpts suggest.

EXCERPT 3

[The school] must demonstrate a steady improvement in students' test scores in language arts and math in order to qualify for federal funding ... This pressure to maintain funding guidelines has a definite impact on curricular decisions, both schoolwide and by individual teachers in their classrooms. With this in mind, I find it interesting that [the school] has taken a position schoolwide favoring an approach which does not square smoothly with standardized testing models of language proficiency. While it is not a unified philosophical shift, the school principal voiced her support of whole language at the beginning of the year and appears concerned that teachers work to find what they perceive to be the most beneficial approaches for their children.

EXCERPT 4

Almost all of the students speak Spanish. For many of them, Spanish is the only language spoken at home and the parents have little or no

knowledge of or use of English . . . [yet] the use of Spanish is dis-
couraged in school . . . In classes Spanish is not spoken during formal
lessons, but some children use it in talking with each other . . .
Although most of the teachers do not speak Spanish, all but two of
the teaching assistants are Spanish-speaking. They often interpret for
teachers who need to communicate with parents or students who do
not speak English. [But] the students are not permitted to speak or
write in Spanish for the purpose of academic work.

The excerpts above touch on some of the tensions inherent when a school
with a White European American faculty serves a Latino population or when
a principal and some teachers attempt to incorporate whole language perspectives while still having to answer at the central office level to achievement criteria based on skills-based standardized tests. What is most important
about this kind of inquiry is that student teachers began to understand that
"the learner," "the teacher," "the school," and "the community" do not exist
in teaching—rather, the condition within which teachers construct curriculum and make educational decisions is the local and messy context of "these
learners," "this teacher," "this school," and "this community." The examples
that appear in the following sections make it clear how this kind of knowledge informs pedagogy and curriculum decisions.

Analyzing Children's Learning Opportunities

When student teachers conduct small-scale studies about their own
schools and classrooms, they engage in active classroom teaching, curriculum construction, and analysis of classroom data, including children's written work, group discussions and other verbal interactions, group and
individual child observations, and textbooks and other materials, in order
to learn from teaching. This allows them to analyze the learning opportunities that are or are not available to children within various academic tasks
and social participation structures (Erickson, 1981), particularly those of
scripted and unscripted programs of instruction.

For example, student teachers taught one lesson from a set of elementary
level basal reading materials, following as closely as possible the script in the
teacher's manual. Based on data from this experience and on language and
learning theory, they then constructed a modified lesson using similar materials. Student teachers formulated research questions in order to compare, for
example: children's responses to original literature and to abridged or vocabu-
lary-controlled stories, interaction patterns that resulted from open-ended
questions and from single right-answer questions, or quality of comprehension when children read complete connected text and when they read parcelled-

out smaller segments of texts punctuated frequently with interruptions in the form of teachers' questions. In essence, through their own research, prospective teachers considered the impact on children's learning opportunities when control of understanding was shifted from text and teacher to children themselves and to the transactions of children, teachers, and texts.

To illustrate, I use an excerpt from a student teacher who worked over the course of a year with a sixth grade class at a Quaker school in center-city Philadelphia. The student teacher described the first lesson in which she followed the teacher's guide as closely as possible.

EXCERPT 5

Stage two [of the scripted lesson] was silent reading. I asked the students to read the story and then we would discuss it. This was an agonizing twenty minutes, or more, for me. The children all read at varying speeds; the faster readers quickly turning page after page while the slower readers took constant breaks by glancing at the others, seeing where the others were in comparison to where they were, counting how many pages remained, looking around the room, laughing at hallway noise and looking at their watches . . . I never before had considered what makes a slower reader, slower. Is it lack of interest in the material to be read? Lack of proficiency in reading? The personality of the reader—easily distracted, competitiveness with others, feeling pressure to read under time constraints? . . . Maybe the reason many basal programs require reading aloud is to keep everyone at the same place at the same time. . . .

This experience prompted me to make my first conscious alteration for the modified basal lesson—I [decided to] have my next group of students read the story at their own pace at home the night before the lesson.

By doing research on contrasting lessons, student teachers often discovered that management issues were, at least in part, artifacts of the structure of lessons wherein everyone was supposed to proceed in unison, know the same things, and interpret texts in the same ways. Further, they discovered not only that there were far fewer opportunities to read connected literary discourse for children who were assigned to low and remedial reading groups than there were for those in higher groups. On the other hand, student teachers also recognized the safety net of the teacher's manual and the power of workbook pages, exercises, and other unison social structures and academic tasks to avoid many behavioral problems in the first place. Close observations of students' and teachers' actions and interactions led student teachers to construct the dilemmas inherent in moving away from scripted prepackaged programs and to see the interrelationships of interactional patterns, management strategies, grouping procedures, and reading material.

As a result of teaching her first by-the-script lesson, the student teacher above constructed teacher research questions about what would happen to discussion, comprehension, and student engagement when different kinds of questions were asked and when different group structures were developed. Her conclusions are reflected in the excerpt that follows.

EXCERPT 6

When I think back to these basal lessons, the difference in amount of student engagement is staggering. Moving from literal, one-correct-answer questions, to open-ended questions generated and pursued by the students transformed a flat, boring lesson to one that was stimulating . . . I could not help but be painfully aware of the effect the first basal lesson was having on my students. The lines of authority were clearly demarcated. The teacher was the asker of questions and acknowledger of correct answers. The students were expected to be suppliers of these correct answers with little or no opportunities to ask questions of their own . . . Basal reading systems that dominate reading instruction in many elementary classrooms are so comprehensive (including graded books for students to read, teachers' manuals telling teachers what and how to teach, workbooks and dittos for the students to complete, sets of tests to assess reading skills, etc.), very little room or time is left for the inclusion of other kinds of reading activities. I believe this approach to reading discourages students from developing and exercising the critical literacy and thinking skills needed to participate fully in a . . . democratic society.

Basal reading programs are controversial in the field of reading/language education: although they have been soundly criticized by some members of the scholarly community, they are regarded by many of those who control educational policy as a complete technology for reading instruction, and they continue to dominate instruction. What is most important about inquiry projects such as those described here, however, is that student teachers learn to critique materials and practices not simply by eschewing convention or imitating the critiques of their professors. Rather, prospective teachers have the opportunity to treat reading groups and other social arrangements for instruction as sites for research. They learn to look closely at how particular materials, instructional practices, and participation structures limit or support children's language learning opportunities.

Understanding Children's Understanding

A fourth perspective that is central to learning to teach in a culturally and linguistically diverse society is learning to understand children's understanding, or learning to do what Duckworth (1987) calls "giving reason" to the ways children themselves construct meanings and interpretations, drawing on experiences and knowledge developed both inside and outside the classroom. A major opportunity for this kind of learning during the preservice period is observation and study of an individual child over time. Here, in consultation with more experienced school-based mentors, the student teacher develops a research question about ways to support a particular aspect of one child's development in the classroom and then gathers multiple data sources in order to come to know that child from various perspectives and formulate concrete recommendations. The image of the teacher implicit in this kind of research is not one who simply accepts the knowledge of outside experts about the appropriate placements, groupings, labels, expectations, and limits for a particular child. Rather, the teacher is taken to be a builder of knowledge and theory as well as an advocate on the child's behalf. Similarly, the child is not regarded as simply the object of other people's actions, but as a knower and agent actively involved in making sense of what is going on around him or her.

Through inquiries about individual children, prospective teachers often recognize that their efforts to respond to cultural, linguistic, and social diversity in their classrooms are located not only in the nested contexts of families, communities, and institutions but also and in large measure, in their own preconceptions, experiences, and assumptions about learning and teaching.

Teacher research can provide student teachers with opportunities to understand individual children by analyzing classroom data in light of learning and sociocultural theory as well as categories for describing and understanding children, such as Carini's (1986) categories for "Descriptive Review of a Child" and conceptual frameworks for describing the uses of language and literacy in communities and schools.

The following excerpts are drawn from the child observation inquiry project of a student teacher who focused on one third grade student at a public elementary school in northeast Philadelphia where the population was about one third Asian, including children from Vietnam, Korea, Cambodia, Laos, and Thailand, one third African American, and one third White European American. The focus child was born in Vietnam and had arrived in the United States from China 2 years earlier speaking no English. The student teacher's question emerged soon after she began observing and was formulated in keeping with the pattern of Carini's (1986) documentary processes: How can we, as teachers in this classroom, help to engage [this child] more fully in classroom activities and help him become more motivated to learn in this setting? The following excerpt from the student teacher's description emphasizes her careful use of rich observational data and her attempts to come to know from the child's perspective:

EXCERPT 7

[The child] is a good reader, but always insists on pictures . . . He once wrote in his reading response journal that he didn't like a particular book because there was no color in the pictures. Questioning reveals that he does understand a story when it is read to him without pictures. He just seems to have a real need to know what [things] look like . . . While most classroom reading is done in pairs (each child has a reading partner), he prefers to read alone. During one reading partner activity, he let his partner read the entire book. He told me this was because he prefers to read by himself. I asked if he would like to borrow the book and read it at home on his own. He did, and came back the following day excited about the story. When reading, he occasionally flips back a page or two and studies the pictures. I'm not sure why he does this, but wonder if he likes to read alone because it gives him the opportunity to take his time and squeeze every bit of meaning out of the book—pictures and text.

The student teacher attempted to understand this child's understanding through the lenses of three patterns in his life at school that she identified by looking across all the observational and documentary data she collected and in light of the language and learning theory she was reading. Then, as the Descriptive Review process calls for, she made a number of concrete recommendations about how to alter the curriculum and classroom routines to support his learning. It is especially important to note her first recommendation.

EXCERPT 8

Cazden and Mehan (1989) discuss the importance . . . of trying to understand a child's many embedded contexts, including family, community, and other sociocultural institutions, and looking at how those contexts might determine meaning for the child. I feel at a significant disadvantage in this respect, in that [the child] is of a culture very different from my own, and that culture must have a significant impact on how he makes sense of what happens in the classroom. I know very little of his culture. I don't know for in-

stance, how books are used at home, which according to Heath
(1983) might determine how he uses books in the classroom.

My first recommendation, then, is to learn more about his
culture in order to better understand how [he] makes sense of his
world in general, and more specifically, in the classroom.

As the semester progressed, this student teacher and her cooperating teacher
developed a number of ways to learn more about this child's family, community, and culture, including locating fiction and nonfiction about Vietnam and China, visiting with his older sibling, talking to members of his
family and community, and giving him opportunities to share information
with the other children in the class. Often teachers can most readily understand, make accurate predictions about, and provide strategic support for
those students who are like them in culture, race, and ethnicity. It takes much
more effort and time to understand and support those who are not like them.
For student teachers, the struggle to understand children's understanding
emphasized teachers' responsibility for knowing all the children in their care
and for educating themselves about language and cultural resources unlike
their own.

Constructing Reconstructionist Pedagogy

When student teachers are initiated into teaching within a learning community that promotes self-critical and systematic inquiries about teaching
and learning, they also learn to construct reconstructionist pedagogy; that
is, pedagogy intended to help children understand and then prepare to take
action against the social and institutional inequities that are embedded in
our society (Sleeter & Grant, 1987). One of the sites for learning about pedagogy of this kind is the social studies, math, or literature study group. Like
the basal reader inquiries described above, study group inquiries also require
student teachers to engage in active teaching with children and to use classroom data in order to learn from and about learning and teaching. In planning for study groups, however, student teachers do not set out simply to
modify scripted lessons or tinker with instructional practices but are instead
invited to construct curriculum by locating and drawing on alternative texts
and materials and altering both the social participation and the academic
task structures of conventional instruction.

What follows are excerpts from the literature study inquiry project of
a student teacher who worked with a group of fifth graders at a Philadelphia public school with a population that was 100% African American.
The student teacher, who was African American, began her report by re-
membering her own childhood reading experiences when she was encour-

aged by teachers to read stories with White characters and, as she later realized, White values and language. The student teacher wanted to expose the children to powerfully written literature with positive African-American characters in contrast to books like Laura Ingalls Wilder's *Little House on the Prairie*, which they had been reading. She used several of the works of Mildred Taylor, an award-winning African-American author of children's historical novels that chronicle the experiences of an African-American family during the depression. Drawing on tape recordings of the group's discussions as well as the children's writing and her own notes, she described the group's work as follows.

EXCERPT 10

Several times during the reading we came across the word, "nigger." [I] anticipated a response from the students. Nothing came from them with the use of that all too familiar word . . . However, [when] I read several lines from the [dialogue] of the elderly Black man's character, I noticed the . . . most displeasure. The first response of the students was laughter, then one of the students said:

[*Child 1*]: That ain't funny. Why y'all laughin'? He talkin' all stupid. He can't even talk!!

[*Child 2*]: I know, why he talkin' like that?

[*Student Teacher (ST)*]: Well, have you ever listened to the way that you talk sometimes? Do you think that you sound like Mr. Bee does when he talks in the book? Sometimes the way we talk now is the way people talked back in Cassie's day.

There really was nothing wrong with the way he talked because he was speaking the way others around him spoke. Can you find other characters who spoke differently?

[*Child 3*]: Yes, the White people do. They talk all proper, but in this book they were talking like the Black people do.

[*ST*]: What do you mean, "like the Black people do"?

[*Child 4*]: Like talk's countrified, like "How y'all doin'" (laughter) and stuff like that. White people don't really talk like that. It's really only Black people from down south that talk like that.

[*Child 1*]: But sometimes the White people down south talk like that too 'cause they never finished school, so they don't know no better.

[*ST*]: So what you're saying is that how long a person spends in school makes them use language better?

[*Group*]: Yes!

[*ST*]: Well, would you say that you talk like the White people in the
    book or the Black people in the book? We all go to school, right?
    Sometimes don't we still talk like Mr. Bee does, and does that
    mean that we don't know better?
[*Child 1*]: No, that just means that we talk like Black people talk.
[*ST*]: Do Black people always sound the same in different [situa-
    tions]? Do White people always talk "proper"?

The discussions the student teacher led were tricky. She missed some opportunities that a more experienced teacher might have exploited and pursued
some lines of discussion that were misleading or ineffective. But the student
teacher herself was in the process of learning to understand the interrelationships of race, culture, and language and also in the process of learning to
work with children. From the beginning, she banked on the power of Taylor's
characters, on the rich language she crafted, and on the compelling story to
help open up new ideas to the children. From the beginning she also believed
in the children's ability to understand, to explore, and to raise significant
questions. In the final group session, many of the children concluded that if
they had a choice between being Laura Ingalls (of *Little House on the Prairie*) or Cassie Logan (of *Roll of Thunder*), they would choose Cassie "because she was strong" or "because she was Black" and there "weren't any
Black people in Laura's story anyway."

What is most significant about the student teacher's inquiry project is
not that she got it all right in her teaching, but that she set out to alter the
curriculum by offering a quite complex and powerful text with rich vocabu-
lary and language that featured strong African-American characters and thus
to construct culturally responsive and challenging curriculum. She also set
out to alter her children's perceptions of themselves as African Americans
by making issues of language, culture, dialect, and power an examined part
of the curriculum and of their lives.

Not all of the literature study inquiries that student teachers did were aimed
so directly at altering both the curriculum and the system. But all of them, like
the one above, were based on a belief in the efficacy (rather than the efficiency)
of teachers, individually and collectively, to change their own teaching lives
and to influence the world of schooling. And every one of them was based on
the premise that children are active knowers, capable of dealing with rich and
complicated content, with the ability to think critically, to pose and solve real
problems, to construct interpretations of texts, and ultimately to participate
in a democratic society. Hence, each had the potential to function as reconstructionist or transformative pedagogy by challenging the dominance of tracking, abridged texts, and teacher control of knowledge transmission.

BEYOND COLOR BLINDNESS AND BASKET MAKING

What I have been suggesting in this chapter is that if we are going to prepare teachers to work intelligently and responsibly in a society that is increasingly diverse in race, language, and culture, then we need more teachers who are actively willing to challenge the taken-for-granted texts, practices, and arrangements of schooling through participation in systematic and critical inquiry. Teachers who are inquirers do not have to be color blind in order to be fair to all students, teach basket making in order to "do" multicultural education, or wait for the experts of universities or research institutes to tell them "*the* teaching strategies" that are most effective for "*the* culturally diverse learner." Rather, these teachers are involved [in] daily pursuits to pose and try to answer some of the toughest questions there are about how to work effectively in local contexts with learners who are like them and not like them.

Teachers who are struggling to move beyond color blindness and basket making need to work in the company of experienced teachers and teacher educators who are also struggling to do so. Clearly this approach to the issues of diversity in teaching and teacher education is fraught with obstacles and challenges. It goes against the grain of much of current school practice and risks constructing new roles for teachers as knowledge generators and curriculum creators as well as new relationships among teachers, supervisors, and administrators.

Despite teacher educators' efforts to establish closer connections between school and university, student teachers sometimes find themselves caught in the middle between what the university is encouraging them to think and do and what the school-based teachers they work with advocate. Sometimes new teachers who have been prepared in an inquiry and reform-centered program "fail" at certain aspects of their early teaching experiences because they do not fit smoothly into the system or because they view teaching as a process of questioning assumptions and challenging traditions rather than adopting the practices modeled by much more experienced educators. Sometimes teacher educators are also caught between helping their students learn the practices that will signify to many school administrators and supervisors that they are good beginning teachers (e.g., how to write and carry out lesson plans), on the one hand, and practices that aim to reinvent classroom knowledge and discourse so that it builds on and is attentive to the resources of all children (e.g., how to construct curricula with materials from both the canon and alternative bodies of literature, history, and culture and how to make issues of diversity explicit parts of the curriculum), on the other.

Teacher educators can perhaps best handle the tension between the lesson plan stance and a transformative, inquiry stance on teaching by arming their student teachers with thorough knowledge of current practice as well as the ability to construct and act on a trenchant critique of that practice. Students cannot teach effectively against the grain if they do not have a thoughtful understanding of what "the grain" is and what its strengths as well as weaknesses are. Teacher education programs that aim to be transformative have a dual agenda, then, much like the dual agenda facing new teachers who are attempting to meet the needs of an increasingly diverse student population. For student teachers the dilemma is how to educate children who know about not only the canon of literature, language, and history, but also their own history, language, and literature; not only how to negotiate their way through the system's gatekeepers but also how to work to dismantle the inequities of the system. For teacher educators the dilemma is how to educate student teachers who know not only about "best practice" in schools but also about alternative practice, not only how to display in traditional ways their competence as beginning teachers but also how to strategically justify and demonstrate a different kind of competence. How to do both is a yearlong theme for many of the student teachers I have worked with and, I would venture, a lifelong theme for many of us as teachers and teacher educators.

Student teachers also need to learn about the power of collaboration in learning communities where other teachers are struggling to understand and ultimately to improve the social relations of schools and classrooms. The days of the isolated though exemplary teacher who closes her classroom door and works miracles with her children are over. The odds against the efficacy of the lone teacher are overpowering, given the problems of urban poverty, family disintegration, and widespread social failure. The collaborative experiences student teachers have in learning communities with one another and with their experienced teacher mentors are among the most powerful influences during the critical preservice period. But an explicit part of the preservice curriculum also needs to be preparing student teachers to find and work in existing networks of reform-minded teachers in their own schools or across schools and school systems as they begin their careers as teachers. If such networks do not exist, student teachers need to know how to begin to build networks of their own and find colleagues with whom to collaborate.

CHAPTER 4

Teaching for Social Justice

For the past 20 years, I have asserted that among the most important goals of teaching and teacher education are social responsibility, social change, and social justice. As the previous chapters indicate, I have argued that there are no recipes, no best practices, no models of teaching that work across differences in schools, communities, cultures, subject matters, purposes, and home-school relationships. Instead I have emphasized that the teacher is an intellectual and a knowledge-generator, that teaching is a process of coconstructing knowledge and curriculum with students, and that the most promising ways of improving teaching across the professional life span are based on learning within inquiry communities rather than training for individuals.

Over the years, my students have more or less accepted the idea of teaching for social justice. With their school-based and university-based mentors, they have struggled to interrogate their implicit assumptions about teaching and learning. They have written thousands of pages of inquiry about teaching and learning and about the arrangements of schooling and its role in maintaining or disrupting the inequitable distribution of resources within our society. Inevitably the question my students ask is this one, "But what does teaching for social justice really mean—in a concrete way?" and its many variants: "What does it look like in the classroom?" "What do you actually do with the students?" "You can't really teach for social justice with five year olds, can you? Don't they have to be older?" and "When do we get to the part in the program where we actually learn how to do it?"

In this chapter I attempt to offer an answer to this question by analyzing examples of student teachers' work for social justice within urban classrooms. Drawing on the words of student teachers themselves, these examples are intended to clarify what it means to learn to teach for social justice—both what it looks like within particular contexts and how the student teachers working in those contexts understand what they are doing. In the pages that follow, I pose six guiding principles accompanied by examples of student teachers' work, each revealing something of what it means to learn to teach for social justice and at the same time, demonstrating how a given principle is played out within a particular school setting. Then, I look more closely at one student teacher's experiences to emphasize the role of an inquiry stance in learning to teach for social justice. All of the examples used in this chapter draw on the work of students who were in Project START, which is described in Chapter 2.

TEACHING FOR SOCIAL JUSTICE: SIX PRINCIPLES OF PEDAGOGY

In the first chapter of this book, I suggested that terms such as "teaching and teacher education for social justice," "social change," and "social responsibility" have generally been used to emphasize that although teachers cannot substitute for social movements aimed at the transformation of society's fundamental inequities, their work has the potential to contribute to those movements in essential ways. Based on the conceptualization of teaching for social justice in Chapter 1, this chapter poses six principles of pedagogy for social justice that are drawn from a synthesis of the literature related to the knowledge, skills, and experiences of teachers who work in the increasingly diverse contexts of urban schools (Cochran-Smith, 1997), and a theoretical framework for teaching and teacher education for social change that links knowledge and interpretive frameworks, political perspectives, teaching practice, and inquiry contexts for professional development (Cochran-Smith, 1998). These two reviews are based on the literature of multicultural education, urban and minority education, culturally responsive curriculum and pedagogy, and related sociological, linguistic, and anthropological research on schools, classrooms, and community cultures. Both reviews also draw on a body of lesser known writing and research on urban education by teachers themselves. The six principles that I identify are informed by and intended to represent the major pedagogical themes that recur in this larger body of conceptual and empirical research by university-based and school-based researchers. In this sense they build on the work of many other people, and none of the ideas that inform the principles in this chapter is, in and of itself, original. In keeping with the goals of this chapter to clarify what learning to teach for social justice actually looks like in student teaching classrooms, I use relatively straightforward terms and a minimum of citations to describe and illustrate each principle. Readers are directed to the two reviews for a more extensive discussion of the literature that informs these six principles as well as a more recent comprehensive review of the literature related to multicultural teacher education (Cochran-Smith, 1997, 1998; Cochran-Smith, Davis, & Fries, 2003).

I use the term "principles of pedagogy," and not terms like "best practice," "models of teaching," or "essential teaching skills" to describe and analyze student teachers' learning to teach for social justice. The language of "principles" is intended to emphasize that teaching practice is tightly linked with knowledge and interpretive frameworks, on the one hand, and with politics and ideological commitments, on the other. Another way to make this point is to emphasize that teaching for social justice is not so much a matter of practice but of "praxis," a term used variously by educational philosophers and social theorists to refer to "the interactive, reciprocal shaping of theory and practice" (Lather, 1986). Although the examples that follow are intended to provide a way to describe and understand practice, then, they are in no way intended to suggest that there are generic methods or specific strategies that are "typical" of student teachers working for social justice and hence generalizable—full-blown—to other contexts. To the contrary, my analysis does not follow from, and is in no way intended to bolster, formal/practical or theory/practice distinctions about teachers' knowledge and/or the activity of teaching (Cochran-Smith & Lytle, 1998). Rather, what I am suggesting is that across contexts, student teaching for social justice is guided by a set of common principles that are instantiated differently depending on the particularities of specific contexts.

Principle 1: Enable Significant Work Within Communities of Learners

I use the phrase "enabling significant work within learning communities" as shorthand for several interrelated features of social justice pedagogy. Specifically, student teachers who enable significant work assume that all students are makers of meaning and all are capable of dealing with complex ideas. They have deep knowledge of subject matter and how to translate and represent that knowledge appropriately. They have high expectations for all of their students and provide opportunities for them to learn academically challenging knowledge and skills. Akin to high expecations for students, teachers for social justice have high expectations for themselves, working from a sense of their own efficacy as decision makers, knowledge generators, and change agents. Finally, enabling significant work means fostering learning communities, an approach that explicitly eschews homogeneous grouping and/or tracking and instead fosters a shared sense of responsibility for learning within collaborative groupings.

In the excerpts that follow, the student teacher provides a striking example of what it actually looks like to enable significant work within a learning community and, just as importantly, what it looks like for a student teacher to struggle to make sense of that work. Over the course of a year, the student teacher taught in a class of 16 first graders in a primarily working-class elementary school in urban Philadelphia. Her class was uncharacteristically small because, as she wrote, the children "were skimmed from the perceived 'bottom' of the first grade population"—that is, they were children who had been designated "at risk" by their teachers, earmarked for remedial instruction, and expected to spend at least 2 years in first grade.

In the excerpts that follow, the student teacher analyzes her experiences with a literature study group designed to explore multiple versions of the three little pigs story. Although she began with high expectations, she also had many doubts.

> We had never attempted anything as open-ended as a literature study in this classroom because the teacher had assumed that the students would be overwhelmed by any activity that lacked strict, teacher-controlled structure. Though I believed that my teacher had woefully underestimated our students' potential throughout the year, I worried that six months in this classroom setting had conditioned the childen to focus only on minutiae, like individual letters and words, rather than on ideas. I had to prepare myself for the possibility that the students would not be able to meet the challenge of a project which asked them to think deeply about books [and] to pose and wrestle with questions that had no clear-cut answers.

Maimon's report on the group's work as well as her title for that report, "Little Pigs and Big Ideas" (Maimon, 1996) make it clear that her high expectations were not disappointed.

Maimon's analysis demonstrates that a small learning community of "at-risk" first graders were able to engage in quite sophisticated intellectual work. In one session, for example, Maimon had the children draw pictures and offer their opinions about story characters. She wrote:

> I found Timmy's sympathy for the wolf so interesting that I wanted to include the entire class in our exchange. After Tim described his picture to everyone, I asked him, "Do you think the wolf deserved to be eaten at the end of the book?" He answered with a definite no. He explained. "You know why? Because the pig was mean. He came at different times and he wasn't waiting for the wolf. It wasn't fair. That's why he shouldn't get eaten." In response, Colleen stated strongly that the pig's deception was a necessary evil. "He had to do that or he would have been eaten."

In the days that followed, Maimon and her students discussed, wrote, drew, and read. In addition to versions of the traditional story that varied in language and illustrations, they read parodies of the tale that played with point of view, narrator reliability, and characters.

In commenting on the literature study project as a whole, Maimon reflected on her children's abilities as learners as well as the damaging effects of a learning culture based on low expectations. In concluding, she wrote:

> As for my question about the childrens' ability to think independently, I have no doubt that my students are as insightful and courageous in their convictions as their counterparts at [any other school] . . . I rejoiced to see them articulate a variety of viewpoints, debate with each other, back up their ideas with examples from texts, change their minds when persuaded by classmates, refuse to accept information presented in a book at face value . . .
>
> In spite of my doubts about the good that can come out of this project while the students remain confined to our classroom, I am ecstatic about (and quite moved by) this experience we shared . . . I have been told so many times, "You can't do this because they can't do this," and "You don't understand the way you have to teach *these* children." . . . In response to these words of suppression, I hold up the powerful, angry, exicted, exciting, deep, enlightening, funny, brave, complex, strong responses that these "at-risk" students produced over the course of our literature study. Our exploration has been their and my vindication.

In one way, it may seem that what Maimon did is just common sense—after all, how can students learn at high levels if their teachers do not expect them to do so? In actuality, however, teachers frequently demonstrate just the opposite to their students—"dumbing-down" the curriculum (Irvine, 1990), especially for "the low group" and "at-risk students." Rather than a pedagogy of social justice, then, what often occurs in urban schools is what Haberman (1991) has described as a "pedagogy of poverty" emphasizing lower-order skills, memorization, and few opportunities to read connected texts while omitting higher order concepts, challenging texts, and alternative points of view, the latter of which are commonplace in higher tracks and middle-class schools (Anyon, 1994).

First and foremost, then, pedagogy for social justice means providing opportunities for all students to engage in significant intellectual work. To do so, as the above example suggests, student teachers strive to work from a sense of efficacy, hold high academic expecations for all students, provide opportunities for learning academically challenging knowledge, and foster communities of learners.

Principle 2: Build on What Students Bring to School with Them—Knowledge and Interests, Cultural and Linguistic Resources

Building on what students bring to school means that student teachers acknowledge, value, and work from the cultural and linguistic resources as well as the interests and knowledge of their students. Especially in urban schools, classrooms increasingly contain widely diverse student populations and/or large numbers of students whose cultural backgrounds are different from the teacher's. In each case, it is important to develop social participation structures and narrative and questioning styles that are culturally and linguistically congruent with those of the students. In addition, it is important to construct curriculum that is multicultural and inclusive so that students can connect meanings in their own lives to traditional content. Social justice pedagogy rejects transmission models of teaching and instead assumes that knowledge is socially constructed and that curriculum is coconstructed by teachers and students.

Marisol Sosa Booth taught for a year in a fourth grade urban classroom in a school that was almost completely Puerto Rican in population. Her writing gives a sense of some of the issues faced by a student teacher attempting to connect to the children's cultural and linguistic backgrounds. Her writing also makes it clear that simply because the teacher and students share certain aspects of culture and language, they do not automatically connect with one another or with multicultural materials, as is sometimes assumed.

> One of the first lessons I taught as a student teacher was about Christopher Columbus. This particular issue was especially sensitive because of the common Puerto Rican background of my students and me. I wrote in my journal, "I want to present a traditional and then a contemporary revisionist story about Columbus because I want the children to begin understanding that sometimes stories change because of new facts and information."
>
> *Encounter* by Jane Yolen is a story documenting the Taino Indians' perspective on Columbus's arrival. I pointed out to my students that the Taino, Arawak, and Carib Indians are part of our heritage, that they were our ancestors. A few of them were disgusted by the thought. I was taken aback. . . . There were remarks like, "They're not *my* ancestors," and "They look funny." I heard these reactions with a certain amount of irony and surprise. My children had internalized Eurocentric perceptions. They were disgusted by the faces of their own people.

Booth talked with the children about two different versions of Columbus's voyages, raising questions about history and "truth." The class explored some of the information in primary documents including Columbus's own journal describing his voyages. Eventually the children seemed to come to a different perspective about the Columbus story, and Booth understood some of the complexities involved in constructing a curriculum that is inclusive of varying perspectives and world views.

> After I read both the traditional telling and Yolen's revisionist version, some of the students called the traditional story "phony" or said that it was "telling lies." To my surprise, they felt that Jane Yolen's *Encounter* was closer to the reality of what "truly" transpired.
>
> bell hooks said, "Our struggle has not been to emerge from silence into speech but to change the nature . . . of our speech." My goal was to place my students at the center of a curriculum that is inclusive of a Latino perspective and embraces their legacy as one that should be heard. This is by no means a simple task, but it's a challenge I'm willing to meet.

Reinventing the curriculum by using more inclusive and multicultural materials is only part of what goes on when teachers try to build on their students' resources and interests. Some of the more taboo topics of school life are also exposed—for young children, this may mean the physical features of racial groups—and a different set of rules emerges about what one can and cannot discuss in school (Fine, 1994).

As this example suggests, then, part of teaching for social justice is building on what students bring to school with them. In order to do so, student teachers coconstruct knowledge with students by building on their interests and questions, construct curriculum so that it includes multicultural and inclusive content and perspectives in addition to traditional content, and develop culturally and linguistically congruent interactional and questioning patterns.

Principle 3: Teach Skills, Bridge Gaps

Learning to teach for social justice with its emphasis on coconstruction of knowledge and on giving all children opportunities to deal with "big ideas" is sometimes taken to imply that there is no attention to skills. To the contrary, an indispensable part of learning how to teach for social justice is learning how and where to help students connect what they know to what they do not know and use prior skills to learn new ones. Obviously this requires that teachers start wherever students are and, as suggested above, build on prior knowledge to scaffold new learning. Some children, particularly those who live in poor urban areas, do not come to school with tacit knowledge of mainstream language and social participation patterns, which are the invisible basis of classroom interaction, and/or do not come with *a priori* knowledge of the literacy and numeracy concepts that are the implicit starting point of much of primary grades instruction. For these children, student teachers have to learn how to teach skills but also bridge gaps between what is often assumed children know and what they actually do know. To do so, first and foremost, student teachers have to learn to pay attention to children and to the sense they are making of whatever it is student teachers think they are teaching.

Ronit Eliav provides an intriguing example of a student teacher's evolution in learning this aspect of teaching for social justice. In an unusually candid essay about her own learning over the course of the preservice period, Eliav looked back on the year, pointing out that when it began, she had assumed that her role was to transmit knowledge and skills. She began her essay with a Vivian Paley quotation about becoming a teacher:

> In September, I thought I understood what Vivian Paley expressed [about gradually shifting attention away from oneself and toward children as learners]. Today, I realize that I did not. Growing up, I thought of teachers as the carriers of knowledge. I defined teaching as the transferring of knowledge. I viewed a good student as someone who studied that knowledge and was able to retrieve it upon demand . . . As the year progressed, the sources from which I sought answers evolved . . . As I started to think more about what it means to look at children, I realized that they were my greatest teachers. I began to see that when I understood how they learned and thought about a concept, I was better able to teach them that concept. This realization marked the turning point in my education and development as a student teacher.

Eliav provides access into the usually implicit and internal process of a student teacher's evolving sense of what it means to teach skills within the larger framework of teaching for social justice.

As the following excerpt reveals, there were specific moments in her experiences as a student teacher that were mileposts in the evolution of her ideas about how to teach skills effectively. In one essay, Eliav reflected on her first "real" lesson—a mini-lesson in mathematics where the children answered questions about number sentences. In the next part of the lesson, she switched to a more open discussion in which the children were to apply their knowledge. She hoped for greater participation and involvement in this part of the lesson.

I did not think to ask how the children were perceiving what I thought I was teaching them. Many children were coming up with the correct answers to my examples, which I saw as an indication that they were understanding the lesson . . . I entered this experience thinking about myself, my teaching, and my lesson plan. At no point in this process did I consider the children's prior knowledge or needs until a little boy raised his hand.

I was so excited that right away a student was participating and could answer my question. When I called on him with the expectation that he would have a response, he said, "Miss Eliav, what does a number sentence mean?" . . . I asked the class if anyone could define a number sentence, and to my surprise, no hands went up. . . . In choosing this lesson, however, I thought it was grade-level appropriate. However, had I looked to the children prior to planning it, I would have seen that their needs and background knowledge had not prepared them for the lesson that I had planned. I did not meet my students where they were. Why did I assume that they were at a level at which they were not? Why did I not think to look at their prior knowledge and understanding before choosing this lesson?

Beginning to teach "where the children are" is certainly one of the most common aphorisms in teacher education. However, learning to teach skills is often located in "the lesson plans" that student teachers, almost universally, are required to complete. In the traditional lesson plan assignment of preservice education, the skills children are supposed to learn are preestablished in what amounts to a script for teaching and learning, as pointed out in Chapter 3, and variations in children's prior knowledge and skills are not accounted for.

A major part of learning to teach for social justice, then, means learning how to discern and take account of children's prior conceptions and understandings at the same time one introduces and reinforces new skills. To do so, as the above example suggests, student teachers start where children are in terms of prior knowledge and skills, teach skills by linking prior knowledge to new information, and pay attention to what sense students are making of what is being taught.

Principle 4: Work with (Not Against) Individuals, Families, and Communities

I use the phrase "working with (not against) individuals, families, and communities" to emphasize that teaching for social justice means drawing on family histories, traditions, and stories as well as demonstrating respect for all students' family and cultural values. But it also means consciously avoiding functioning as a wedge between students and their families by conveying negative messages, even if subtly or unintentionally, such as the idea that to succeed is to escape from one's community and become "an exception" to one's race or cultural group. Particularly important here is that student teachers demonstrate that they are connected to, rather than disengaged from, or (worse) afraid or condescending toward their students and their communities.

Student teachers generally have few opportunities to work directly with parents and/or to become genuinely engaged in the communities in which they work. The relatively short duration of student teachers' time in schools coupled with their inescapable status as "guests" in other people's classrooms make it unlikely that student teachers can link with families and groups in the ways experienced teachers are sometimes able to do—living in the communities in which they work, learning the cultural references and language patterns of parents, visiting homes and taking children to religious or social events, or joining neighborhood efforts to challenge local regulations or fight crime.

What student teachers can do, however, is notice and critique the implicit messages conveyed about students and their families, consciously rethinking their assumptions and avoiding the imposition of their judgments on others. In the excerpts that follow, Susan Moore provides a glimpse of a student teacher attempting to work with (not against) families and communities in a school located in a Puerto Rican neighborhood. Despite "Puerto Rican History Month" and many jointly sponsored parent-teacher celebrations, Moore realized that there were also powerful negative messages being sent by teachers at her school.

> Most egregious for me was the school-wide celebration of Columbus Day in October. My classroom had been on a field trip during Puerto Rican History Month in which we had discussed the fact that the Puerto Rican culture is a mix of Spanish, African, and Taino Indian cultures due to Columbus's importation of African slaves to obtain gold for him because the Tainos were dying off with his introduction of European diseases to the island. This led me to the erroneous conclusion that a school with a majority of Puerto Rican students would not be apt to celebrate Columbus's conquest of the Americas. . . . Columbus Day should never pass uncritically in a school populated by the descendants of those that this "hero" oppressed.

As the year progressed, Moore also recognized subtle contradictions about the children's cultural heritage and their identities as people of color. She noticed that students' spontaneous comments about race or culture were almost always diverted or silenced in the classroom. When teachers talked among themselves, they proudly claimed to see "only children, not color" in the school. Books read aloud or displayed on classroom shelves had few African-American and no Latino characters. Moore wrote:

> It is crucial to explore issues of race and culture with our students and to embed these issues in the curriculum. It is important that we White teachers recognize that aspect of our students' identity and resist denying it due to guilt over our own place in the hegemony. We simply must acknowledge our students' racial minority position in the United States if we are to begin to prepare them to negotiate a system which will be cruel to them.

What is particularly interesting about Moore's experiences as a student teacher is that she did not simply spout liberal ideology about the teacher's role in opening a discourse about racism and oppression. She also struggled with what it really meant to avoid being a wedge between children and their communities. For example, Moore's cooperating teacher had told her that valentines seemed particularly important in Latino culture and that mothers went to great lengths and expense to send gifts for teachers and valentines for children to trade with their classmates. Moore reflected in her journal:

> In my mind [Valentine's Day] is just one big money-making venture ... yet if I teach in a place where the community loves to celebrate Valentine's Day, how will I make room for both their enthusiasm and my cynicism? ... I made sure to hand craft individual Valentines for each of the kids this year—yet I will also not let the holiday pass uncritically. I will raise the issue with the kids of how much money is spent each year on candy, cards, etc. .... I will try to get them to consider who profits from Valentine's Day expenditures. ...

The excerpts above reveal some of what it looks like when a student teacher tries to make sense of the tensions between competing claims to justice. She struggles to respect community traditions, on the one hand, and teach her students to critique marketing campaigns that urge unnecessary expenditures, on the other.

Part of learning to teach for social justice, then, is learning to appreciate the complexities of working with (not against) individuals, families, and communities. To do so, student teachers respect the cultures and cultural traditions of families; ensure that the messages about race and culture conveyed directly are consistent with those conveyed more subtly; understand issues in terms of the tensions between community values and social critique; and support (and join in) activities that strengthen rather than suggest escape from neighborhoods, communities, or cultural/racial groups.

Principle 5: Diversify Forms of Assessment

It is now well documented that most standardized testing practices perpetuate inequities in the educational opportunities available to various groups, particularly that they limit opportunities for poor children and children of color (Beckum, 1992; Darling-Hammond, 1995). Beckum urges educators to "diversify assessment" as a partial response to this situation by using a wide variety of evaluation strategies for formative as well as cumulative assessments (e.g., portfolios, performances) and by not relying on standardized tests as the sole or primary indicator of students' abilities and achievement in schools. Part of the idea here is that over time assessment and instruction can blend into one another, and ongoing assessments can be designed in ways that support students' learning rather than truncating it.

In many school contexts, student teachers have few opportunities to "diversify" assessment if the more experienced teachers and administrators with whom they work are not already doing so. In fact, cumulative assessments of children's achievement are often out of student teachers' control completely, and although they may contribute to more formative assessments of their students, student teachers seldom have the opportunity to do away with certain kinds of assessment systems and introduce new ones. Instead, student teachers who are struggling to teach for social justice focus on understanding the assessment systems that are in place in their own schools, interrogating the connections between assessment and educational opportunity, access, and standards.

Jamie Kim-Ross's experience as a student teacher is instructive along these lines, although clearly not typical. Kim-Ross worked in a large and quite diverse public elementary school with many children for whom English was a second language. Unlike most of their colleagues, her two cooperating teachers, who worked as a team, had rejected the use of test scores and other numerical grading systems in their own classroom. At the beginning of the year, Kim-Ross was unfamiliar with assessments that were not numerically based, although she quickly saw their benefit. Partly because she herself had painful memories of her high school experiences as an "ESL student" who had come to the United States from Korea during high school, however, Kim-Ross was also concerned about the implications of diversified assessments for non-native speakers.

When I started student teaching, I volunteered to build a database to
help my cooperating teachers keep track of their students' test scores.
My cooperating teachers responded that they would have nothing to
put into the database, because they did not make use of test scores or
grades. Instead, the children are evaluated based on the progress they
make over their three years in the program; progress is monitored by
keeping a portfolio of each child's work . . . I initially found this
method bizarre. How could a child's ability be measured objectively
under such a system? How could the performance of different
children be compared? Could not teachers' preferences be prejudicial
to the fair evaluation of some children?

It was not long, however, when I realized that the system
worked precisely because it was not designed to measure how much
the children had learned versus a common standard; rather, it was
designed to monitor the progress of each child in a context that made
sense given the particular facts and circumstances that related to that
child. This aspect of the system was especially useful given the large
numbers of ESL [English as a Second Language] students for whom
most standardized tests would be grossly inappropriate. Many of
these students understood the underlying concepts being taught quite
well but lacked the language skills to explain their understanding
on paper. In assessing such students' knowledge, my cooperating
teachers recognize that the language barrier should not prevent
students from having their hard work praised.

I quickly saw how the individualized nature of the assessment
system helped build self-confidence . . . However, I am still not sure
. . . Can we really be sure students are progressing? If so, what about
the ESL students? Can we really be sure that these children are
keeping pace with their peers in traditional classrooms? Is there no
chance that individual progress is being overemphasized to the
detriment of high academic standards?

Kim-Ross's experiences touch on some of the issues involved in diversifying
assessment. Like other aspects of teaching for social justice, there are tensions and competing agendas to try to reconcile. Many student teachers,
however, have experiences that are quite different from hers, obligated to
utilize assessments that they judge to be biased or struggling to introduce
portfolios or other diversified means of assessment into even the smallest parts
of curriculum and instruction. Although it is sometimes not possible, then,
given the narrow realm of influence that most student teachers have, those
who are working for social justice critique standardized assessments, use a

range of alternative assessments that focus on students' abilities and achievements, and connect assessment and instruction.

Principle 6: Make Inequity, Power, and Activism Explicit Parts of the Curriculum

Student teachers whose work is animated by a sense of social justice encourage their students to think critically about the information to which they are exposed and make explicit in the curriculum issues that are often kept underground. Part of what this means is helping students name and deal with individual instances of prejudice as well as structural and institutional inequities by making these issues "discussable" in school. This also means challenging some of the practices and assumptions that are taken for granted. Finally, making inequity explicit means modeling activism and/or helping students explore how they themselves can question the status quo.

The excerpts that follow reveal how one student teacher attempted to make power and inequity an explicit part of the curriculum and, perhaps even more importantly, how he posed questions about the work and struggled to understand the complexities. Mark Paikoff was a student teacher over the course of 1 year at a large urban elementary school with an African-American population. Prompted by his cooperating teacher to choose a story with an African-American theme for Black History Month, Paikoff chose Mildred Taylor's *The Friendship* for use with his reading group.

> Black History Month is much more than George Washington Carver, Jesse Jackson, and Jackie Robinson. I wanted to ensure these students knew . . . of the biases that have been created against them. In this way, they will best be able to tear down the walls constructed to keep them from climbing society's ladder.
>
> I had many questions . . . How will the students react to a story that does not have a "happy ending"? How will they deal with blatant racism present in the story? What will they say or do after reading the word "Nigger" in a story? . . . How can I most effectively guide them to a grand conversation about a topic I feel anxious about? . . . What will my reaction be to theirs? How do I as a White person teach five African Americans about racism?

As his experiences with the group reveal, this last question proved to be especially important. In vivid detail that stays close to the children's own words and to their unfolding understandings of the story, Paikoff described the group's responses after they had read the first section of the book.

I closed the lesson with a return to the journals, and the students wrote for a while. Ryanne was the first to share, "I don't like the story because I am Black, and anyone Black who reads this story, *The Friendship*, will not like it either. It is a really sad story because Black people should be treated right and the Black people in the story aren't treated right." She told me she did not want to read the story anymore.

Ultimately Ryanne decided to stay in the group, partly in reponse to Paikoff's explanation of how important it was to know about "what really happened." Throughout their reading of the novel, however, student teacher and students wrestled with the visceral emotional response the story evoked. Paikoff wrote:

> I saw the word "Nigger" approaching on the next page and warned the students, "Something that will probably bother you is coming up on the next page." . . . I posed one simple question, "How does that word make you feel?" Ryanne said, "It doesn't make me feel good because they called it to a Black person only because he's Black." Regina said, "I feel if the White people want respect, they got to earn respect." Nicole said, although the word bothered her a lot, she understood the usage: "It adds to the story because we can tell it was the deep south and feel like we're there."
>
> [But] the students were visibly upset—eyes drooped and they looked angry. Tarell said, "Why we reading this anyway?" Nicole, who only moments earlier had said she understood the word usage in the story, said, "What does this have to do with friendship? Why is the name *The Friendship*?"

Public discussions of inequities and injustices are difficult. Some student teachers worry that such discussions are depressing, making young children feel worse than they already do, while others are concerned that they may be inflammatory and divisive for older students. Paikoff's report reveals the complexities involved in prompting children to think critically about topics that are difficult even for adults, and it also suggests that the race of the teacher vis-à-vis that of the students plays a complicated part in the ways each responds.

As these examples suggest, however, part of learning to teach for social justice is struggling to make visible and explicit—at whatever level is developmentally appropriate for students—the inequities of society and the institutional structures in which they are embedded. To do so, students teachers encourage critical thinking and activism about information, texts, and events;

openly discuss race and racism, equity and inequity, oppression and advantage; and work against the social, organizational, and structural arrangements of schooling and society that perpetuate inequity.

ONE STUDENT TEACHER'S EXPERIENCE:
INQUIRING INTO SOCIAL JUSTICE

The six examples above make it clear that learning to teach for social justice is as much a matter of learning how to make sense of one's experiences over time as it is learning how to act in particular ways in the classroom. "Making sense" includes the kinds of questions student teachers ask about their work, the problems and dilemmas they pose, the interpretive frameworks they construct, the assumptions they are prompted to rethink, as well as the ways they connect emerging ideas to the theories, research, and experiences of other teachers and researchers. Each of these is part of what Susan Lytle and I have called an "inquiry stance" on teaching and learning to teach (Cochran-Smith, 1994, 1997; Cochran-Smith & Lytle, 1993, 1999). Inquiry is a central part of both the context within which learning to teach for social justice occurs and the vehicle through which much of that learning is worked through and expressed.

An inquiry stance is reflected, either implicitly or explicitly, in all of the examples I have already offered. Inquiry allowed Gill Maimon to raise questions about whether her "at-risk" first graders could reason independently and debate the multiple perspectives of a story; it also fueled her belief that they had the right to try. Inquiry supported Marisol Sosa Booth's tentative explanations about her students' initial disgust at pictures of their own Taino ancestors as well as her determination to give them voice and place in the curriculum. Ronit Eliav's inquiry about her first "real" lesson prompted her to rethink the assumptions she had been making about her students' prior knowledge and also allowed her to shift her focus away from herself as teacher and toward the meaning the students were making of what was going on in the classroom. Susan Moore's inquiries allowed her to interrogate the overt as well as hidden messages in the curriculum and also to struggle with what she saw as conflicting claims to justice—respecting families' values, on the one hand, but also fostering critical perspectives about mass market practices, on the other. Likewise, through inquiry, Jamie Kim-Ross posed a problem with multiple and competing perspectives—she considered both the importance of assessing ESL students' learning in ways that tapped into their cognitive understandings rather than simply their (lack of) language skills and, at the same time, the need of parents and educators to have comparative assessments of progress. And finally, an inquiry stance legitimated Mark

Paikoff's uncertainty about how young African-American children would respond to a novel that focused on racism just as it legitimated his commiment to make that topic part of the curriculum.

To elaborate on the role of inquiry in learning to teach for social justice, I draw in this final section on the work of Mary Kate Cipriani who student-taught for a year in a public elementary school in a working-class neighborhood in Philadelphia. In the portfolio that represented Cipriani's work for the year, there are many examples that illustrate the six principles of teaching for social justice that I have outlined above. I have selected the excerpts that follow, however, to focus more on the underlying intellectual stance that Cipriani developed as she struggled to work for social justice.

In the critical essay that introduced her porfolio, Cipriani described not only what she learned about teaching over the course of a year but also how she learned it—that is, the internal processes that prompted her to think and rethink her experiences as well as the social and organizational structures that supported her learning.

> I am a twenty-seven-year-old white female. I am a student. I am a teacher. I am a teacher researcher. I am comfortable with myself and happy with my choice to return to school to become a teacher. I am coming to the end of a positive, fulfilling, difficult, rewarding, confusing, and satisfying time of my life. I am, however, continuing upon an ongoing journey to teach, research, learn, and be an agent for change. I am someone who in this past year has worked harder than I have ever worked in my entire life. I am certain that I will always work this hard as I continue on my journey. I am someone who has learned a lot but still has a lot to learn. . . .

With these words, Cipriani makes it clear that she sees social change as part of the job of the teacher (and student teacher). But, just as importantly, she makes it clear that she sees learning to teach as an ongoing process—filled with questions—that will continue over the course of her lifetime as a teacher rather than one that will have closure when she graduates from her preservice program.

Cipriani's use of the journey metaphor, which was a central image in many discussions of the program, emphasizes the continuous and distinctly nonlinear character of the process of learning to teach. It is worth noting also that Cipriani explicitly designates herself as learner as well as teacher. Part of being a learner (rather than an expert, a transmitter, or some sort of repository of knowledge) is acknowledging that one does not know everything and that, indeed, knowledge is not a "thing" that is accumulated like garbage or money in the bank (Eisner, 1985). As Cipriani's essay continues, she articulates her philosophy about learning how to teach, emphasizing that "not knowing" comes with the territory.

> Teachers are expected to know. We are expected to transmit what we know to the next generation. But teacher researchers believe that is OK not to know . . . NOT TO KNOW? Could that be? Yes, because there is a difference between knowing and knowing how. We learn how to teach not by looking for answers, but by continuously searching for meaning in our classrooms. Our search for meaning is ongoing. We begin with uncertainty. Through observation and reflection we attempt to make meaning of this uncertainty. Based on our interpretations, we implement new strategies in our classrooms. In the end we are left with a new uncertainty which causes us to begin this process all over again. . . . We have learned to look to our students to guide us. By understanding who they are and what they bring to our classrooms, we allow the children to teach us how to teach them.

Learning to teach for social justice is supported by inquiry that acknowledges ongoing uncertainties, confusions, misgivings, and concerns. An inquiry stance contradicts the certainty that many student teachers expect to find during their preservice programs. For some student teachers, this is unsettling, to say the least; others are more comfortable with the ambiguity.

Finally, Cipriani also writes specifically about the importance of being part of a learning or inquiry community as the context within which she learns to teach for social justice—various groupings of schoolchildren, preservice teachers, experienced teachers, and university-based supervisors and instructors, all of whom function as learners and researchers across the professional life span. In a certain sense, this community is both the invisible "audience" for many of the reflections student teachers write and, at the same time, it is the context wihin which they worked.

> My salvation became the teacher communities I [was part of] . . . The term "communities" is used broadly because it encompasses many kinds of support groups and moments. It includes the mornings when [the other student teachers who taught with me at the school] would come by my classroom to ask me questions that ranged from, "Have you ever used pattern blocks," to "How are things going in your life?" . . . It includes the ethnography paper group and Sunday nights we spent beside [our professors's] fireplace wrenching and writhing over our journals and papers, looking for themes. It includes [my cooperating teacher] and me chatting about our students' academic

behavior and who likes who this week. It includes dinners at [my supervisor's] house, classes at Penn and special events like the Ethnography Forum and the AERA annual meeting . . . I am a teacher because we are a teacher community and because we are a teacher community, I am a teacher.

Being part of a learning community with multiple and nested contexts for inquiry was the context within which Cipriani and all of the student teachers quoted in this chapter were learning to teach for social justice. They read a wide variety of challenging literature from many perspectives—both university-based and school-based—about topics related to diversity, literacy and learning, culture and language, race and racism, privilege and oppression, and teacher inquiry itself. They looked closely at individual children, examined the language and substance of classroom practice and school policy, and interrogated their own and others' assumptions about difference, culture, and the purposes of schooling. They wrote frequently about all of these. Their work was deliberately structured so that multiple viewpoints and experiences were represented. Their schedule included long periods of time for groups to work together to hash out issues and think through disagreements. They shared the data of their classrooms with one another, shaping and reshaping both questions and interpretations.

CONCLUSION: LEARNING TO TEACH FOR SOCIAL JUSTICE

Perhaps more than anything else, the excerpts quoted in this chapter emphasize that teaching for social justice is difficult and uncertain work. It is work that is profoundly practical in that it is located in the dailiness of classroom decisions and actions—in teachers' interactions with their students and families, in their choices of materials and texts, in their utilization of formal and informal assessments, and so on. At the same time, however, it is work that is deeply intellectual in that it involves a continuous and recursive process of constructing understandings, interpretations, and questions. To describe learning to teach for social justice, then, we must describe not simply "what it looks like"—the question my own student teachers so often asked, but also "how teachers make sense of it"—how they struggle to think about and understand what they are doing. In this sense, learning to teach for social justice is as much a matter of developing a particular kind of pedagogy as it is learning to theorize pedagogy and participate in a community of professionals also engaged in this work.

CHAPTER 5

Blind Vision

In this chapter, I have attempted to explore and write about *un*learning racism in teaching and teacher education. I do not begin in the scholarly tradition of crisply framing an educational problem by connecting it to current policy and practice and/or to the relevant research literature. Instead I begin with a lengthy narrative based on my experiences as a teacher educator at a moment in time when issues of race and racism were brought into unexpectedly sharp relief. I do so with the assumption that narrative is not only locally illuminating, as Barbara Hardy's (1978) theoretical work on narrrative suggests, but also that it has the capacity to contain and entertain within it contradictions, nuances, tensions, and complexities that traditional academic discourse with its expository stance and more distanced impersonal voice cannot (Fine, 1994; Gitlin, 1994; Metzger, 1986).

The idea that racism is something that all of us who are involved with teaching and teacher education must constantly struggle to *un*learn is profoundly provocative (Britzman, 1991; Cochran-Smith, 1995a; King, Hollins, & Hayman, 1997; Sleeter, 1992; Tatum, 1992). For many of us, it challenges not only our most precious democratic ideals about equitable access to opportunity but also our most persistent beliefs in the possibilities of school and social change through enlightened human agency (Apple, 1996; Giroux, 1988; Leistyna, Woodrum, & Sherblo, 1996; Noffke, 1997). Attempting to make the unending process of unlearning racism explicit and public is even more provocative. I go public with the stories in this chapter not because they offer explicit directions for unlearning racism but because they pointedly suggest some of the most complex questions we need to wrestle with in teacher education: In our everyday lives as teachers and teacher educators, how are we complicit—intentionally or otherwise—in maintaining the cycles of oppression (Lawrence & Tatum, 1997) that operate in our courses, our universities, our schools, and our society? Under what conditions is it possible to examine, expand, and alter long-standing (and often implicit) assumptions, attitudes, beliefs, and practices about schools, teaching, students, and communities? As teacher educators, what should we say about race and racism, what should we have our students read and write?

BLIND VISION: A STORY FROM A TEACHER EDUCATOR

A White European American woman, I taught for many years at the University of Pennsylvania, a large research university in urban Philadelphia whose population was predominantly White, but whose next-door neighbors in West Philadelphia were African American and Asian schools and communities and, in parts of north and northeast Philadelphia, Latino as well as racially mixed schools. Seventy-five to 80% of the students I taught were White European American, but they worked as student teachers primarily in the public schools of Philadelphia where the population was often mostly African American or mostly Latino. In schools that appeared on the surface to be more ideally integrated, the racial tension was sometimes intense with individual groups insulated from or even hostile toward one another.

The teacher education program I directed had for years included in the curriculum examination of race, class, and culture and the ways these structure both the American educational system and the experiences of individuals in that system. For years, my students read the work of James Comer, Lisa Delpit, Henry Giroux, Shirley Brice Heath, and John Ogbu, as well as Molefi Asante, Carl Grant, Peggy McIntosh, Luis Moll, Mike Rose, Christine Sleeter, and Beverly Tatum. I thought that the commitment of my program to urban student teaching placements and to devoting a significant portion of the curriculum to issues of race and racism gave me a certain right to speak as a teacher educator. I thought so with some degree of confidence until an event that was to change forever the way I thought about racism and teacher education. This event was to influence the work I did with colleagues in the Penn program over the next 6 years as well as the work in which I am presently engaged.

At the end of a powerful presentation to my student teachers about his own experiences of racism as both student and teacher, the guest speaker—a Native American who worked in a teacher education program at another university—began to ask my student teachers about their program at Penn. I had no qualms. Our program was well known and well received. Students often raved about it to visitors from outside. Knowing and sharing the commitment of my program to exploring issues of race, my guest asked in the last few minutes of our 2-hour seminar, "And what does this program do to help you examine questions about race and racism in teaching and schooling?" Without hesitation, one student teacher, a Puerto Rican woman, raised her hand and said with passion and an anger that bordered on rage, "Nothing! This program does nothing to address issues of race!" After a few seconds of silence that felt to me like hours, two other students—one African American and one

Black South African—agreed with her, adding their frustration and criticism to the first comment and indicating that we read nothing and said nothing that addressed these questions. I was stunned and frankly grateful that my face did not betray my feelings as class time ran out. With another class waiting to enter the room, students—and I—quickly exited the room.

In the days that followed, I counted up the ongoing efforts I had made to increase the diversity in our supervisory staff and in our pool of cooperating teachers. I had insisted that we send student teachers to schools where the population was nearly 100% African American and Latino, schools that some colleagues cautioned me were too tough for student teachers and some student teachers complained were too dangerous. I talked about issues of race openly and, I thought, authentically in my classes—all of them, no matter what the course title or the topic. I thought about the individual and personal efforts I had made on behalf of almost all of those students—helping them get scholarships, intervening with cooperating teachers or supervisors, working for hours with them on papers, loaning books and articles. I constructed a long and convincing mental argument that I was one of the people on the right side of this issue. Nobody can do everything, and I was sure that I already paid more attention to questions of racism and teaching than many teacher educators. How could she say that? I was stunned by what had happened and deeply hurt—surprised as much as angry.

During the first few days after that seminar session, many students— most of them White—stopped by my office to tell me that they thought we were indeed doing a great deal to address issues of race and racism in the program but they wanted to learn more, to figure out what we should do differently. Some students—both White students and students of color, stopped by or wrote notes saying that they thought we were currently doing exactly what we should be doing to address issues of race in the program. And a few students—all White—stopped by to say that all we ever talked about in the program and in my classes was race and racism and what they really wanted to know was when we were going to learn how to teach reading.

I knew that the next meeting of the seminar group would be a turning point for me and for the program. I struggled with what to say. It was clear to me that I was about to teach my student teachers one of the most important lessons I would ever teach them. I was about to teach them how a White teacher, who fancied herself pretty liberal and enlightened, responded when confronted directly and angrily about some of the issues of race that were right in front of her in her own teaching and her own work as a teacher educator. The very different responses of my students and my own shock and hurt at some of those responses pointed out to me on a visceral level the truth that many of the articles we were reading in class argued on a more intellectual level: How we are positioned in terms of race and power vis-à-vis others has a great deal to do with how we see, what we see or want to see, and what we are able not to see.

In the end, I commented briefly, then opened up the two hours for students to say whatever they wished. I tried to sort out and say back as clearly as I could both what I had heard people say at the seminar and the quite disparate responses I had heard in the ensuing week. It was clear from these, I said, that nobody speaks for anybody or everybody else. As I spoke, I tried not to gloss over the scathing critique or make the discrepancies appear to be less discrepant than they were. Especially for many of the students of color in the program, I said that I had clearly heard that there was a feeling of isolation, of being silenced, a feeling that we had not dealt with issues of race and racism in a "real" way . . . Notwithstanding the view expressed by some students that all we ever talked about was race, I reported a strong consensus that an important conversation had been opened up and needed to continue.

I concluded by saying that despite my deep commitments to an antiracist curriculum for all students, whether children or adults, and despite my intentions to promote constructive discourse about the issues in teacher education, I realized I didn't "get it" some (or much) of the time. This seemed to be one of those times.

What I remember most vividly about that seminar were the tension and the long silence that followed my comments and my open invitation to others to speak . . . All of the women of color in the program spoke, most of them many times. A small portion of the White students participated actively. Students critiqued their inner-city school placements . . . They said we needed more cooperating teachers and more student teachers of color . . . They spoke passionately about the disparities they had observed between their home schools and the schools they had cross-visited—disparities in resources and facilities but even more in the fundamental ways teachers treated children in poor urban schools, on the one hand, and in middle-class urban or suburban schools, on the other. They complained that our faculty and administrators were all White, naming and counting up each of us and assuming I had the power and authority, but not the will, to change things. . . . Many students of color were angry, bitter. They spoke with a certain sense of unity as if their scattered, restrained voices had been conjoined, unleashed.

Many White students were silent, some almost ashen. Some seemed afraid to speak. One said people were at different levels with issues of race and racism, implying that others in the room might not understand but she herself was beyond that. Another commented that she too had experienced racism especially because her boyfriend was African American. One said that when she looked around her student teaching classroom, she saw only children, not color. Another complained that she didn't see why somebody couldn't just tell her what she didn't get so she could just get it and get on with teaching. I cringed inside at some of these comments, but several of the women of color rolled their eyes, whispered among themselves . . . The only man of color in the program, who sat apart from the other students, said all he wanted to do was to be an effective teacher. He did not want to be seen as a Black male teacher and a role model for Black children, but as a good teacher. The women of color immediately challenged him on the impossibility and irresponsibility of that stance.

For nearly 2 hours, the tension in the room was palpable, raw. As leaders, we said little, partly because we had little idea what to say, partly because we had agreed to open up the time to the students. We nodded, listened, took notes . . . We asked for recommendations. There were many suggestions but only a few that we could actually do something about in the 6 weeks or so that remained before the students graduated.

It would be an understatement to say that these events were galvanizing as well as destabilizing for me, for the people I worked closely with, and for the students who graduated just a few months later. Everything was called into question—what we thought we were about as a program, who we were as a community, what learning opportunities were available in our curriculum, whose interests were served, whose needs were met, and whose were not. But it would be inaccurate to say that these events *caused* changes in the program over the next 6 years or that we proceeded from this point in a linear way, learning from our "mistakes" and then correcting them.

It is also important to say that the above account of what happened is a "fiction" of sorts—not reality or truth, but my interpretation of my own and other people's experience in a way that makes sense to me and speaks for me. Although part of my intention in telling this story is to uncover my failure and unravel my complicity in maintaining the existing system of privilege and oppression, it is impossible for me to do so without sympathy for my own predicament. My experience as a first-generation-to-college, working-class girl who pushed into a middle-class, highly educated, male profession has helped to give me vision about the personal and institutional impact of class and gender differences on work, status, and ways of knowing. But my life long membership in the privileged racial group has helped keep me blind about much of the impact of race. In fact, I have come to think of the story related above as a story of "blind vision"—a White female teacher educator with a vision about the importance of making issues of race and diversity explicit parts of the preservice curriculum and in the process, grappling (sometimes blindly) with the tension, contradiction, difficulty, pain, and failure inherent in unlearning racism.

Of course, it is what we do after we tell stories like this one that matters most or, more correctly, it is what we do afterward that makes these stories matter at all. In the remainder of this chapter, I examine what we tried to do in our teacher education community after this story was told. We wanted to do nothing short of total transformation, nothing short of inventing a curriculum that was once and for all free of racism. What we *did* do—over time—was much more modest. Over time we struggled to unlearn racism by learning to read teacher education as a racial text (Castenell & Pinar, 1993), a process that involved analyzing and altering the learning opportunities available in our program along the lines of their implicit and explicit messages about race, racism, and teaching as well as—and as importantly—acknowledging to each other and to our students that this process would never be finished, would never be "once and for all." In the pages that follow, I analyze and illustrate this process, examining the evolution of three courses I consistently taught during the years that followed these events; the changes we made over time in the program; and the persistent doubts, questions, and failures (as well as successes) we experienced as recorded in notes, reflections, conversations, and other correspondence.

READING TEACHER EDUCATION AS RACIAL TEXT

Reading teacher education as racial text is a conception that draws from three interrelated and somewhat overlapping ideas—that teaching and teacher education can be regarded and read as "text," that preservice teacher education has both an explicit text and a subtext, and that any curriculum can and—given the racialized society in which we live—ought to be, read not simply as text but as racial text.

A number of recent writers have forwarded the idea that the work of teaching can be regarded as "text," which can—like any other text—be read, reread, analyzed, critiqued, revised, and made public by the teacher and her or his local community. This assumes that teaching, like all human experience, is constructed primarily out of the social and language interactions of participants. To make teaching into readable "text," it is necessary to establish space between teachers and their everyday work in order to find what McDonald (1992) calls "apartness" or "step[ping] outside the room, figuratively speaking, and search[ing] for perspective on the events inside" (p. 11). Along related but somewhat different lines, we have suggested that oral and written inquiry that is systematic and intentional, "transforms what is ordinarily regarded as 'just teaching' . . . into multi-layered portraits of school life" (Cochran-Smith & Lytle, 1992). These portraits and the ways teachers shape and interpret them draw on, but also make problematic, the knowledge about teaching and learning that has been generated by others at the same time that they help to build bodies of evidence, provide analytic frameworks, and suggest cross-references for comparison. "Rereading teaching as text" means representing teaching through oral and written language as well as other means of documentation that can be revisited, "RE-searched"—to use Ann Berthoff's (1987) language, connected to other "texts" of teaching, and made accessible and public beyond the immediate local context.

As text, teacher education is dynamic and complex—much more than a sequence of courses, a set of fieldwork experiences, or the readings and written assignments that are required for certification or credentialing purposes. Although these are part of what it means to take teacher education as text, they are not all of it. This also means examining its subtexts, hidden texts, and intertexts—reading between the lines as well as reading under, behind, through, and beyond them. This includes scrutinizing what is absent from the main texts and what themes are central to them, what happens to the formal texts, how differently positioned people read and write these texts differently, what they do and do not do with them, and what happens that is not planned or public. Ginsburg and Clift's (1990) concept of the hidden curriculum in teacher education is illuminating here. It calls attention to the missing, obscured, or subverted "texts" of teacher education—what is left out, implied, veiled, or subtly signalled as the norm by virtue of being unmarked or marked with modifying language.

It is necessary to read teacher education not just as complicated and dynamic text but as *racial* text. Castenell and Pinar (1993) locate current curriculum issues within the context of public debates about the canon and about the racial issues that are embedded within curriculum controversies. In forwarding this view of curriculum, they imply that it is critical to analyze any curriculum to see what kind of message or story about race and racism is being told, what assumptions are being made, what identity perspectives and points of view are implicit, and what is valued or devalued. This conception of curriculum links knowledge and identity, focusing particularly on issues of representation and difference.

Getting Personal: Using Stories About Race and Racism in the Curriculum

For the teacher education community referred to in the opening narrative of this chapter, reading teacher education as racial text came to mean making issues of diversity (particularly of race and racism) central, not marginal, to what we read, wrote, and talked about. Consciously deciding to privilege these issues meant rewriting course syllabi and program materials, reinventing the ways we evaluated student teachers, changing the composition of faculty and staff, drawing on the expertise and experience of people beyond ourselves, and altering the content of teacher research groups, student seminars, and whole community sessions. For example, in response to the events described above, we worked the following year with a group of outside consultants in a series of "cultural diversity workshops" jointly attended by students, cooperating teachers, supervisors, and program directors. During the next year, we focused monthly seminars on race and culture in sessions led by Charlotte Blake Alston, a nationally known African-American storyteller and staff development leader. In the years to follow, we participated in sessions on Afrocentric curriculum led by Molefi Asante, on Black family socialization patterns and school culture led by Michele Foster, on multicultural teaching in urban schools led by Deborah Wei, by Sonia Nieto on Hispanic children's literature, and on racial identity led by Beverly Tatum. In addition, we had sessions on using children's cultural and linguistic resources in the classroom and constructing antiracist pedagogy led by the program's cooperating teachers.

Telling Stories

A central part of these activities was "getting personal" about race and racism, or putting more emphasis on reading, writing, and sharing personal experiences of racism and digging at the roots of our own attitudes at the same time that we also continued to read the more intellectualized, and thus somewhat safer, discourse of the academy. This meant making individual insider accounts (even though not as well-known as the writing of the academy) a larger part of the required reading. Along with the usual reading of Comer, Delpit, Ogbu, Heath, and Tatum, then, we began to do more reading of pieces by Daryl Foreman, David Creighton, and other student teachers, cooperating teachers, and supervisors in our program.

All of us in the community wrote and read personal accounts about race and class that were published in-house and used as the starting point for many discussions. For example, Daryl Foreman, an experienced cooperating teacher, wrote about her experiences as a child whose mother took her north to Pennsylvania for a summer visit. She wrote about the sights and scenes of 1960s Harrisburg and then turned to one unforgettable experience:

> It had been four days since my mother left Harrisburg. . . . She left us in the warm and capable hands of my aunt. We'd been behaving as

tourists. But now, my younger sister and I had to accompany my aunt to work. For years, she'd been employed by a well-to-do White family whom I'd never met . . . At four o'clock, I was starving and my aunt informed me that it was "normal" for us to eat in the kitchen while [the family] dined elsewhere . . . Before dinner, the woman of the house entered the kitchen offering to set the tables— one in the kitchen and the other in the dining room. She grabbed two sets of dishes from the cupboard. She delivered a pretty set of yellow plastic plates to the kitchen dining area and a set of blue china to the dining room. After dinner she came back and thanked my aunt for the delicious meal, then prepared to feed the dog. She walked toward the cupboard and opened it. Her eyes and hands traveled past the pretty set of plastic dishes and landed on the blue china plates. After she pulled a blue china plate from the cupboard, she filled it with moist dog food and placed it on the floor. He ran for the plate. I shrieked! . . .

To this day, I'm not sure if I shrieked at the shock of [people] sharing dinnerware with a dog or because the dog got a piece of blue china while I ate from yellow plastic.

David Creighton, a student teacher, wrote about working in an Italian restaurant in South Philadelphia in the 1990s:

"Yo, Dave, what *are* you anyway?" said Tony Meoli, a waiter in LaTrattoria.

"Whaddaya mean?" I, the new busboy, said.

"Like, uh, what's your nationality. You know, where are you from? I mean, you're obviously not Italian."

"Oh. Well, I'm Russian with some German mixed in," I said.

"Well, just as long as you're not Jewish," said Tony. "We don't like Jews around here."

"Actually, I am Jewish," I said.

"Oh, sorry, I was just kiddin' you know."

"Don't worry about it," I said. . . .

Reading and writing first-person accounts like these as starting points for interrogating unexamined assumptions and practices can evoke a shared vulnerability that helps a group of loosely connected individuals gel into a community committed to dealing with issues of race more openly. Accounts like these can move a preservice curriculum beyond the level of celebrating diversity. They also have the capacity to contain many of the contradictions, nuances, and complexities that are necessary for understanding the roots and twists of racism and the many ways these interact with the social life of schools and classrooms. But the considerable power of accounts that "get personal" about race is also their pitfall. They can use some people's pain in the service of others' understanding, as I suggest below, and they can also imply that we all share similar experiences with racism, experiences that, beneath the surface of their details and contexts, are the same. Over the years, I have come to realize that this lesson in unlearning racism, which is an especially difficult one to hold onto, helps to explain some of the depth of anger expressed by the student teachers in the story with which this chapter began.

Stories about Whom? Stories for Whom?

Several of the students of color in the blind vision story related above claimed we had done nothing in the program to help students understand issues of race, that we did not talk about it in "real" ways. Factually, this was not the case. We had read a large number of articles by both White scholars and scholars of color, and we had shared some personal incidents in class as well as had more intellectualized discussions. It is clear to me now, though, that these discussions were framed primarily for the benefit of White students who were invited to learn more about racism through stories of other people's oppression. The stories were not sufficiently linked to larger issues or framed in ways that pushed everybody to learn not regardless of, but with full regard for, differences in race, culture, and ethnicity.

This is a lesson that seems to need to be learned over and over again. Although I thought I had learned it years ago, I learned it again recently from Tuesday Vanstory, an African-American woman who was a supervisor but had also been a student in the program years before. We had had a difficult discussion about race in our supervisors' inquiry group where we had considered ways to respond to a particularly troubling journal entry written by a White student teacher. In it she had complained about the students of color in the program sometimes separating themselves from the others, sitting together on the perimeter of the classroom and/or not participating in certain discussions. The journal writer used the phrase "reverse discrimination" and questioned how we could ever move forward if everybody would not even talk to each other. Several White members of the supervisors' group voiced somewhat similar concerns. They were genuinely distressed, wanting open conversations and resentful of the figurative as well as literal separation along racial lines of some members from the larger group when certain topics arose.

Vanstory had sat silent for a long time during this discussion, then finally burst out and demanded, "But *who* are those discussions *for*? *Who* do they really serve?" There was silence for a while and then confusion. She wrote to me that same day about the discussion:

> I must say that I was very upset after today's supervisors' meeting. There's nothing like a discussion on race, class, and culture to get my blood boiling, especially when I am one of a few who is in the "minority." . . . I wanted to remain silent, tranquil. Instead I spouted off in what felt like a very emotional and, at times, a nonsensical response . . .

> And to come to school and have to play "educator" to the others who want to discuss race or understand, or release some guilt, or even in a very few cases, people who want to see a real change . . . It gets tired . . .
> Marilyn, I think that you are very brave and genuine to ask the tough questions that you ask yourself and your White students. But the truth is, your perspective, your reality does not necessarily reflect ours.

In *Teaching to Transgress* (1994), bell hooks makes a point that is remarkably similar to Vanstory's. Although hooks discusses White feminist writers rather than teachers or teacher educators as Vanstory was, her comments highlight the perpetuation of the status quo in old paradigms of scholarship and education.

I am convinced that reading and writing accounts about race and racism that get personal as well as reading more intellectualized arguments about these issues are vital to preservice teacher education. As I have tried to suggest, however, reading teacher education as racial text reveals that this is also an activity that is complex and fraught with problems. The more compelling the better, personal stories often evoke a strong sense of empathy for others (Rosenberg, 1996), a false sense that all of us have experienced hurt and frustration varying in degree but not in kind, that all of us—underneath—have the same issues. In addition to using some people's experience in the service of others' education, then, personal narratives can also obscure more direct confrontation of the ways that individual instances of prejudice are *not* all the same—that some are deeply embedded in and entangled with institutional and historical systems of racism based on power and privilege, and some are not. Reading teacher education as racial text means helping all of the readers and writers of such stories understand that schools and other organizational contexts are always sites for institutional and collective struggles of power and oppression (Villegas, 1991), not neutral backdrops for individual achievement and failure (McCarthy, 1993).

The foregoing discussion is not meant to suggest that racism was or should be the only topic in the teacher education curriculum or that everything else is secondary. I am not suggesting here that student teachers and their more experienced mentors should talk only about racism or that if we learn to talk about race and racism constructively, we do not need to learn anything else in the teacher education curriculum. But issues of language, race, and cultural diversity are implicated in and by all of these topics, as I illustrate in the next section of this chapter, and it is a fallacy to assume that there is a forced and mutually exclusive choice in preservice education—either emphasizing pedagogical and subject matter knowledge *or* emphasizing knowledge about culture, racism, and schools as sites for power struggle.

Reading Between the Lines:
Perspectives, Identity, and Difference

Understanding curriculum as racial text requires thorough scrutiny of implicit perspectives about race and careful attention to issues of identity and difference. Following the events recounted in the blind vision story above, our teacher education community attempted not only to make issues of race "up close and personal," but also to "read between the lines" of the curriculum. As director of the program and instructor of core courses on language, learning, and literacy, I had earlier examined how my students constructed issues related to race and racism and how they linked these to their roles as prospective teachers. But at this point, as part of our group's larger, more intensive efforts, I wanted to get at the implicit, more subtle perspectives by scrutinizing what was included and omitted from readings and discussions in my courses, how issues were sequenced and juxtaposed with one another, which messages were consistent and fundamental, and—inevitably—which were not.

What I found was in one sense exactly what I expected to find. Over the years we had increased the amount of time and attention we gave to questions of culture, race, and racism. In fact, these issues had become a central theme of my courses and of the program in general. But what I found when I read between and under the lines of the curriculum as racial text was a contradiction. On the one hand, the first part of my courses presented heavy critique of the inequities embedded in the status quo and how these were perpetuated by the current arrangements of schooling. On the other hand, the latter part of the course privileged pedagogical perspectives drawn from theories and practices developed primarily by White teachers and scholars of child development, language learning, and progressive education. There was as well an underlying White European American construction of self-identity and other, of "we" and "they."

White Theory, White Practice

My courses were intended to help students think through the relationships of theory and practice, learn how to learn from children, and construct
principled perspectives about teaching and assessing language and literacy
learning. Two themes that were not about literacy and literature per se but
were intended to be fundamental to these courses and the entire program
were: (1) understanding teaching as an intellectual and political activity and
the teacher as constructor of knowledge and curriculum; and (2) developing
critical perspectives about race, class, culture, and schooling.

A between-the-lines analysis revealed a sharp contrast in the subtle
messages my courses projected about these two themes. The notion of teacher
as constructor of meaning and active decision maker was consistent in readings and discussions. Research and writing by experienced teachers from the
local and larger inquiry communities were part of the required reading for
every topic on the syllabi. In addition, the knowledge and interpretive frameworks generated by teachers were regarded as part of the knowledge base
for language and literacy teaching. They were *not* mentioned only when the
topic was teacher research itself or when the point was to provide examples
of classroom practice or of the application of others' ideas. Teachers' ways
of analyzing and interpreting data, creating theories, assessing children's
progress, and constructing and critiquing practice were foregrounded and
valued as much as those generated by researchers based outside classrooms
and schools. Reading between and under the lines exposed little discrepancy—
with regard to teachers' roles as knowledge generators and change agents—
between the texts and subtexts of the curriculum.

By contrast, the same kind of close reading with regard to critical perspectives on race and racism led to different and more troubling insights. In
my two-semester language and literacy course, a major segment early in the
syllabus had to do with race, class, and culture. For this segment students
read selections by the well-known scholars mentioned earlier. This part of
the course gave students the opportunity to "rewrite their autobiographies,"
or reinterpret some of their own life stories and experiences based on new
insights about power, privilege, and oppression and "construct uncertainty,"
or pose and investigate questions of curriculum and instructional strategies
informed by their experiences as raced, classed, and gendered beings and
contingent upon the varying school contexts and student populations with
whom they worked. The remainder of the course was organized around
major topics in elementary school language and literacy: controversies about
learning to read and write; teaching reading and writing in elementary classrooms; and interpretation and use of assessments in language and literacy.
For each topic, underlying assumptions about the nature of language, children

as learners, teaching and learning as constructive processes, and classrooms/ schools as social and cultural contexts were identified and critiqued. The pedagogy that was advocated was more or less "progressive," "whole language," "developmental," and "meaning-centered," with emphasis on children as readers and writers of authentic texts and the classroom as a social context within which children and teachers together construct knowledge. There was a distinct bias against skills-centered approaches that taught reading and writing in isolated bits using texts constructed specifically for that purpose. Instead it was emphasized that language skills emerged from authentic language use.

Reading between the lines forced other realizations. The pedagogy I advocated was drawn from theories and practices developed primarily by White teachers and scholars. The prominent names on this part of the syllabus were revealing—John Dewey, James Britton, Ann Berthoff, Donald Graves, Lucy Calkins, Carol Edelsky, Anne Haas Dyson, Vivian Paley, Louise Rosenblatt, and Kenneth Goodman, as well as teachers and teacher groups at the North Dakota Study Group, the Prospect School, the National Writing Project, the Breadloaf School of English, the Philadelphia Teachers Learning Cooperative, and other local teachers and practitioner groups. What was absent from these segments of the syllabus and from our discussions were contrasting cultural perspectives on child language learning and socialization. Also absent were rich accounts of successful pedagogies, particularly with poor children and children of color, that were not necessarily "progressive" or "whole." Notwithstanding the fact that students read Lisa Delpit, Shirley Heath, Kathryn Au, and others earlier in the course, it became clear to me by reading between the lines that the subtle message was that pedagogy developed primarily from research and writing by and about White mainstream persons was the pedagogy that was best for everybody. This subtle message implied that "progressive" language pedagogy was culture-neutral, although just weeks earlier the course had emphasized that all aspects of schooling were socially and culturally constructed. Because "progressive language pedagogy" was unmarked as cultural theory or culturally embedded practice, however, the subtle message was that it was an acultural position about how best to teach language and literacy that applied across contexts, historical moments, and school populations.

Part of what this meant was that my courses offered student teachers no theoretical framework for understanding the successful teachers they observed in their fieldwork schools who used traditional, skills-based reading and writing pedagogies with their students, particularly in urban schools where there were large numbers of poor children and children of color. Although my courses explicitly emphasized the importance of teachers' knowledge, there was a contradictory and perhaps more powerful implicit message: the knowledge of some teachers was more valuable than others, and the knowledge of teachers who worked (successfully) from a more or less skills-based, direct instruction perspective was perhaps not so important, and the pedagogy of these teachers was misguided and out of date. Reading between the lines of my students' discussions and writings revealed that they were confused about what to make of the successes they observed in urban classrooms when the pedagogy we read about and valued in class was not apparent. On the other hand, my students had a powerful framework for critique and could easily conclude that many urban teachers were unsuccessful because they were too traditional, too focused on skills, not progressive enough.

What was missing were theories of practice developed by and about persons of color as well as rich and detailed analyses of successful teachers of children of color, particularly poor children of color, who used a variety of pedagogies including those that would not be called "progressive." Ladson-Billings's work (1994, 1995b) had just been published at the time I was struggling to read deeply between the lines of my courses and our larger curriculum. Hers and related analyses of culturally appropriate, culturally relevant, and/or culturally sensitive pedagogies (Au & Kawakami, 1994; Ballenger, 1992; Foster, 1994; Hollins, King, & Hayman, 1994; Irvine, 1990; Irvine & York, 1995; King, 1994) were extremely useful in my efforts to rethink the ways I taught my courses and structured the program. In fact, Ladson-Billings's book *The Dreamkeepers: Successful Teachers of African American Children* (1994) speaks directly to the issue of skills and whole approaches to language instruction by contrasting very different but highly successful teachers of African- American children. Ladson-Billings's commentary lifts the debates about literacy instruction out of the realm of language theory and practice *only* and into the realm of ideology and politics as well—that is, into the realm of teachers' commitments to communities, to parents, and to activism. Her analysis of successful and culturally relevant pedagogy for African-American children repeatedly emphasizes teachers' ties to the school community, teachers' beliefs in the learning ability of all children (not just an exceptional few who, through education, can make their way "out" of the lives common to their parents and community members), and teachers' strategies for establishing personal connections with students and helping them connect new knowledge to previous experiences and ideas. When I revised my language and reading courses, Ladson-Billings's *The Dreamkeepers* was one of the central texts, and I included in discussions about reading/writing pedagogy many other readings about culturally relevant language pedagogy. In addition to readings about language and literacy theory, debates about pedagogy, and so on, new additions were intended in part to alter the curriculum read as racial text. Particularly they were intended to provide frameworks for understanding successful and unsuccessful teaching of poor and privileged White children and children of color—frameworks that were not dichotomous and that included, but were more complex than, whole language versus basals.

Identity and Difference: We and They

Understanding the racial narrative that underlies a curriculum is a process that requires intense self-critical reflection and analysis, as Castenell and Pinar (1993) have made clear:

> Debates over what we teach the young are also—in addition to being debates over what knowledge is of most worth—debates over who we perceive ourselves to be, and how we will represent that identity, including what remains as "left over," as "difference." (p. 2)

Reading between the lines of my own courses and of the larger teacher education curriculum revealed a White European American construction of self-identity and "other." "We," I came to realize, often referred not to "we who are committed to teaching elementary school differently and improving the life chances of all children," but to "we White people (especially we White women) who are trying to learn how to teach people who are different from us." In a certain sense, one could make a persuasive case that a White European American and female construction of self and other is just what the preservice teacher education curriculum ought to have given the demographics of the teaching and student populations. On the other hand, the program I directed had 20–25% students of color and 15–20% male students. A curriculum for "White girls" was surely not the answer. Rather we were committed to constructing a curriculum that helped all student teachers—with full acknowledgement of differences in race, culture, and gender—prepare to teach in an increasingly multiracial and multicultural society. To do so, we had to revise the story the curriculum told about identity and rewrite the characters who were central in that story, particularly who "we and they," "self and other," "regular and left over" were.

One example from my required course in literature for children illustrates the ways I tried consciously to alter the assumed definition of self and other or "we and they" in my courses. What I wanted to do was to construct discussions where "we and they" shifted *away from* "we White people who are trying to learn to teach those other people—those people of color" *and toward* "we educators who are trying to be sensitive to, and learn to teach, all students—both those who are different from us and those who are like us in race, class, and culture." I began to use Lynne Reid Banks's *The Indian in the Cupboard* as one of the novels my students read in common for the literature course. My course had for years included many children's books that were highly regarded for their portrayals of the perspectives of African-American, Asian, and Hispanic family and childhood experiences (Harris, 1986), and the course had for years focused on the politics of children's literature (Taxel, 1993). The point of adding *The Indian in the Cupboard* was *not* to add "the Native American experience" to the list of cultures represented in the course. Rather the point was to prompt an altered conception of self and other, an altered sense of who "we" were as teachers.

Published in 1980 when the *New York Times* called it "the best novel of the year," *The Indian in the Cupboard* continues to be highly acclaimed and widely used as a whole-class text in upper elementary and middle schools. A fantasy about Omri, a British boy who receives as a present a collector's cupboard, the book revolves around a plastic Indian figure who comes to life (but remains 3 inches high) when the boy casually places him inside the cupboard and closes the door. A toy cowboy and soldier eventually come to life too and interact with the Indian and the boy. The book is charming in many ways, well written and pivoting on premises that are extremely appealing to children—being bigger than adults, having toys come to life, and keeping a powerful secret. But in addition to positive reviews about the popularity of the book and the high quality of its writing, the book has also been criticized as racist, perpetuating stereotypes about Native Americans at the same time that it charms and appeals.

The first year I used the book, all of my students were prospective teachers, many of whom were just completing a year of student teaching in urban schools where the population was primarily African American, Asian, and/or Puerto Rican. I asked the class to read the novel and jot down their responses and then read the critical commentary I had assigned. In an excoriating critique of images of Native Americans in children's books, MacCann (1993) argues that the vast majority of children's books with Native American characters or themes are written from a non-Native perspective, portraying Native American cultures as futile and obsolete. In *Through Indian Eyes* (Slapin & Seale, 1992), a collection of articles written primarily by Native Americans, the review of *The Indian in the Cupboard* and its sequel is also wholly negative. My students read these critiques after they had read and responded to the novel and came to class prepared to discuss both.

Most of my students reported that they were completely engrossed in the unfolding story, and some were shocked by the negative critiques and even embarrassed that they hadn't noticed the racist overtones (and undertones) until after they finished the book. Many were uncertain about what to think. The discussion was intense and animated, with students divided about what they thought of the book. Many saw it as more or less harmless, assuming that those who considered the book racist were self-interested extremists, interested only in what was "politically correct," or manufacturing problems where there were none. Others strongly disagreed, assessing the book as promoting shallow stereotypes with little redeeming social value. At some point in this very intense discussion, I inserted, "What if it were *The Jew in the Cupboard* or *The Black in the Cupboard*? Would that be all right?" For a few minutes there was dead silence. The looks on the faces of my students, many of whom were Jewish, African American, or Hispanic, indicated that it would decidedly *not* be all right to have a children's book with those titles or those story lines. Why then, I asked, was it all right for elementary and middle school teachers each year to teach to the whole class a children's book that had an Indian in the cupboard?

This was a turning point in the course, one that prompted some of the best discussion of the semester. Several students, African American and Hispanic, talked about how this opened their eyes to racism in a different way. Everybody seemed to have new questions, and nobody seemed as sure as they had been about the answers. I believe this was so in part because in this discussion there was a different underlying construction of identity and difference, an altered perspective on what was assumed to be the standard from which we defined "regular and different," "self and other." When "other" was Native American and "self" everyone else in the room, there were new opportunities for students to interrogate their assumptions, new opportunities to struggle with the issue of what it means to teach those who are different from and the same as our multiple selves.

Telling the story of what happened when I added *The Indian in the Cupboard* to my course is in no way intended to suggest that all we have to do in teacher education is figure out who is "not in the room" and then construct that person as the "other." The point is that it is critically important to scrutinize the often very subtle messages about identity and difference that float between and under the lines of the curriculum and consciously work to construct opportunities where all the members of the community have opportunities to interrogate their constructions of "self" and "other."

CONCLUSION: LESSONS LEARNED AND UNLEARNED

What are the lessons here—the lessons learned about unlearning racism? One has to do with the power of narrative *in* teacher education and, as importantly, the power of teacher education *as* narrative. As I have tried to show throughout this chapter, the personal as well as fictional stories about race and racism we invite participants to read and write can break down the barriers of distanced, academic discourse and make possible potent revelations about positionality, identity, and standpoint. Stories can help a group gel into a community, can serve as touchstones for shared experience and commitment. As a primary way we understand and construct our professional lives and our multiple identities, stories can help us scrutinize our own work and theorize our own experience. But stories can also be extremely negative, particularly when the stories of some groups are used—unintentionally or not—in the service of others' desire to learn and/or when powerful emotions are unleashed and then participants are left to fend for themselves in their aftermath. Stories can be negative if they prompt a false sense of sameness and personal empathy that is unconnected to historical and institutional racism, to schools as sites for power struggles, or to ownership of the roles privilege and oppression play in everyday life. It may also be the case that there are some stories that individuals should not be coaxed to share in mixed racial groups and some that group leaders should not attempt to solicit. Finally, it must be understood that the narratives we use as tools and texts in the teacher education curriculum confound and are confounded by larger and more deeply embedded messages, messages that are revealed only when the curriculum is interrogated, or consciously read as racial text.

The second lesson is connected to the title of this chapter, which implies two contradictions: blind vision, a phrase that suggests simultaneous seeing and not seeing; and *un*learning, a word that signifies both growth and the undoing or reversing of that growth. These contradictions are intentional, chosen not only to signal the enormous complexities inherent in the ways race and culture are implicated in teaching and teacher education but also to caution that blindness may be an aspect of seeing, that failing is an inherent aspect of unlearning racism. I am completely convinced that "reading the curriculum as racial text," in the sense that I have described it in this chapter, is critical to a vision for preservice education. But I am also convinced that this is a slow and stumbling journey and that along the way difficulty, pain, self-exposure, and disappointment are inevitable. To teach lessons about race and racism in teacher education is to struggle to unlearn racism itself—to interrogate the assumptions that are deeply embedded in the curriculum, to own our own complicity in maintaining existing systems of privilege and oppression, and to grapple with our own failure.

CHAPTER 6

The Outcomes Question in Teacher Education

In Chapters 2 through 5, I have conceptualized teacher education for so-cial justice as a learning problem by exploring the learning of prospective teachers, their school- and university-based mentors, and their K–12 pupils. Chapters 6 through 8 are quite different. They take up the idea of teacher education for social justice as a political problem by examining from a poli-tical lens several of the major policy debates and issues that affect teacher education. This chapter focuses on teacher education outcomes, assess-ments, accountability, and bottom lines—issues that have been sharply debated since the mid-1990s and have driven reform in teacher education. As I pointed out in Chapter 1, from the early 1980s until the middle of the 1990s, prospective teachers were assessed primarily according to their knowledge and skills, and their teacher education programs were assessed according to the coherence of their curriculum and its alignment with the burgeoning knowledge base for teaching and teacher education. Toward the end of the century, however, the emphasis shifted from knowledge-based to performance-based accountability. Sharp and highly politicized debates about how to reform teacher education revolved around the issue of out-comes, especially the question of whether or not collegiate teacher prepa-ration adds value to the performance of classroom teachers as measured by their pupil's scores on high-stakes tests and what kind of outcomes pro-grams ought to be able to demonstrate. These debates about the outcomes of teacher education have had and continue to have an enormous influ-ence on teacher education programs, professional organizations, licensing and accreditation agencies, and governmental regulations. In this chapter, I analyze the outcomes debate in teacher education from a political per-spective. I argue that the education community must reject narrow views of teaching and learning and, at the same time, insist that social justice issues remain on the agenda.

SORTING OUT THE OUTCOMES QUESTION

The outcomes question is a particularly complicated one in teacher education in that its various iterations usually rest on differing sets of assumptions about what teachers and teacher candidates should know and be able to do, what K–12 students should know and be able to do, and what the ultimate purposes of schooling should be. These assumptions shape the ways terms are defined, the ways data are selected and analyzed, and the interpretive frameworks within which conclusions are formulated.

Generally, the outcomes question has to do with the connection the public has a right to expect among teacher education, teaching practice, and student learning. In a certain sense, every discussion related to the outcomes question assumes that the ultimate goal of teacher education is student learning and also assumes that there are certain measures which, depending on the unit of analysis, can be used to indicate the degree to which this outcome is or is not being achieved for teacher candidates, K–12 students, teacher education programs and institutions, and the education profession itself. At a general level, then, the outcomes questions that are being debated and constructed in teacher education are: (1) What should be the outcomes of teacher education for teacher learning, professional practice, and pupil learning? and (2) How, by whom, and for what purposes should these outcomes be documented, demonstrated, and/or measured?

It is important to note that unanimity about the outcomes question begins and ends here, at this rather surface level of understanding. If we move one level deeper in terms of specificity or elaboration, we uncover disagreement. If we attempt to describe the relationship between teacher learning and professional practice, attempt to explain what we mean by teacher learning and student learning, attempt to elaborate the theoretical bases and consequences of the kind of student learning we are trying to account for, or even attempt to define what we mean by "students" (Which students? How many? All of them, or some statistically significant portion of them?), we uncover differences, some of which represent deep philosophical and political divides. Notwithstanding the growing—and many say unprecedented—consensus about standards for teaching and teacher education within the profession itself (Darling-Hammond, 1996, 2000e; Hawley & Valli, 1999), it is important to acknowledge that there is considerable variation both within and outside the profession in terms of how the outcomes question is being constructed and upon what grounds it will be decided.

The outcomes question is being taken up in differing ways depending on the policy, research, and practice contexts in which it is posed as well as on the political and professional purposes of the posers. One way to sort out versions of the outcomes question, then, is to consider how "teacher learn-ing," "professional practice," and "student learning" are constructed and assumed to be related to one another; what is assumed to be central and extraneous to teacher learning and student learning and what counts as evi-dence of these; what criteria are used to assess the evidence; and who de-cides all of these matters. It is also important to consider aspects of the context in which the outcomes question is being debated: Who is constructing the question and what unit of analysis is used? What political and professional agendas lie behind the question and the question-asker? And, What larger purposes of schooling are assumed?

Three constructions of the outcomes questions are receiving major atten-tion nationally, at the state level, and within teacher education institutions: the long term or general impacts of teacher education as a profession; the aggregated scores on teacher tests of teacher candidates, teacher preparation programs, and/or institutions; and the professional performances expected of teacher candidates. In many contexts, these questions are used in various combinations to guide decisions about resources, licensing and accreditation, and rankings of programs, institutions, and individuals. Each of these ques-tions limits the range of possible answers and to a great extent determines the outlines of the discourse.

LONG-TERM IMPACT AS OUTCOME

This first construction of the outcomes question in teacher education—long-term impact—is related to larger issues about the general impact of teacher education on teacher knowledge, preparedness, attrition, and rat-ings as well as student achievement. These issues are located within much larger debates about teaching quality and teacher qualifications, teacher licensing and certification, professional standards for teaching and curricu-lum, and the use of student achievement as a valid evaluation measure for teachers and schools.

The long-term impact question that is most visible and most highly con-tested has to do with the impact of teacher education on K–12 students' learn-ing. This question is explored primarily through syntheses and meta-analyses of previous and current work in order to make recommendations about teacher preparation as an educational policy that is either value-added or not, either a good investment or not. In these high-stakes debates, teacher preparation at the preservice level is not considered by itself but as one of several factors related to the quality and qualifications of teachers. The unit of analysis is not teacher candidates—individually or collectively—or even teacher preparation programs and institutions. Rather, in a certain sense, the unit of analysis is the profession itself—teacher preparation as one aspect of a broad category referred to as "teacher qualifications," which includes scores on licensure examinations, graduate level degrees, years of experience, preparation in subject matter and pedagogy, certification in the teaching area, and money spent by school districts on professional development. Student learning is defined as student gains on achievement tests. The relationship between teacher education and student learning (i.e., the *outcome* of teacher education) is taken to be the percentage of variance in student gains accounted for by teacher qualifications when other variables are held constant or adjusted.

The initial report of National Commission on Teaching and America's Future (NCTAF) definitively posed the long-term impact question by linking teacher qualifications—including extent of teacher education—with student learning. Speaking for the commission, Linda Darling-Hammond (1998) argued that "a growing body of research appears to confirm" that teacher knowledge and teacher expertise are significant influences on student learning, as are to a lesser extent class size and school size. Drawing on data from the commission's 50–state survey of policies, case studies at the state level, the 1993–94 Schools and Staffing Surveys, and the National Assessment of Education Progress, Darling-Hammond's synthesis (2000d) examines how teacher qualifications are related to students' achievement. She concludes:

> The findings of both the qualitative and quantitative analyses suggest that policy investments in the quality of teachers may be related to improvements in student performance. Quantitative analyses indicate that measures of teacher preparation and certification are by far the strongest correlates of student achievement in reading and mathematics, both before and after controlling for student poverty and language status . . . This analysis suggests that policies adopted by states regarding teacher education, licensing, hiring, and professional development may make an important difference in the qualifications and capacities that teachers bring to their work. (p. 1)

Framing the outcomes questions in teacher education in terms of general and long-term impact on K–12 students' achievement is part of NCTAF's larger campaign to provide qualified and competent teachers for all students by emphasizing and aligning professional standards across initial teacher preparation, teacher licensure, and teacher certification at the state and regional levels.

There is, however, another take on this first outcomes question that is—at least on the surface—quite similar in construction but diametrically different in conclusions to the one I have just been describing. In fact, economists such as Dale Ballou, Michael Podgursky, and others offer analyses of teacher preparation, licensing, and certification that support the deregulation of teacher education rather than its professionalization and seek to limit rather

than enhance the power of the educational community to control the profession. For example, in what they refer to as a "layman's guide" to teacher
training and licensure, which appears in the Fordham Foundation's policy
statement (Kanstoroom & Finn, 1999) on how to produce better teachers
and better schools, Ballou and Podgursky (1999) conclude:

> [T]eacher ability appears to be much more a function of innate talents than the
> quality of education courses. Teachers themselves tell us that this is so. We come
> to similar conclusions when we examine the determinants of scores on teacher
> licensing examinations. Finally, teachers who enter through alternative certifi-
> cation programs seem to be at least as effective as those who completed tradi-
> tional training, suggesting that training does not contribute very much to teaching
> performance, at least by comparison with other factors." (p. 57)

Furthermore, in a widely-circulated issue of *Teachers College Record*, Ballou
and Podgursky (2000) directly attacked the commission's findings, and Darling-
Hammond (2000b) emphatically refuted their use of evidence and their conclusions. These debates are described in further detail in Chapter 7.

There are a number of efforts in the United States to get to the bottom
of these debates. For example, there are initiatives underway sponsored by
the federal government's Office of Educational Research Initiatives, the
American Educational Research Association, and the Education Commission of the States. However, it is important to note here, as I suggested earlier in this chapter, that no matter what conclusions are ultimately drawn
about the evidence, they will depend to a great extent on complex and prior
decisions about what counts and how it counts as evidence, decisions that
are based on values, goals, and priorities. In this sense, the debate will never
be settled solely through empirical means. Along these lines, it is worth noting that part of what accounts for differences in the conclusions of Darling-
Hammond, on the one hand, and Ballou and Podgursky, on the other, is
information that is buried in the details of how terms such as "alternate
routes," "college majors," and "fully licensed teachers" are defined and the
ways data about these are used in the two analyses.

The differences are also partly explained by differences in the way "the
problem" of teacher education is framed in the first place and how different
framings shape definitions of terms, procedures for data selection, interpretations of results, and formulation of conclusions. Supported by the Carnegie
Foundation and the Ford Foundation, NCTAF (in collaboration with the
National Board for Professional Teaching Standards [NBPTS], the Interstate
New Teacher Assessment and Support Consortium [INTASC], and the National Council for the Accreditation of Teacher Education [NCATE] frames
"the problem" of American education in terms of democratic values (Earley,
2000; Labaree, 1997) and thus begins—and ends—with calls for stepped-

up, standards-driven improvements in teacher education and professional development in order to guarantee a well-qualified teacher for every American schoolchild.

The Fordham Foundation (Kanstoroom & Finn, 1999) and other conservative organizations and politicians, on the other hand, frame "the problem" in terms of a market approach to educational policy making. They criticize the profession's "preoccupation with teacher preparation" (Ballou & Podgursky, 1997), seek to limit the power of the profession to control the market by controlling licensing and approved programs, and push instead for an open-market agenda. Deregulationists in the United States and other places around the world (Apple, 2000) advocate subject matter background rather than professional standards. They thus begin—and end—with calls for alternate routes to certification and pulling down the "needless barriers" that hamper the profession.

TEACHER TEST SCORES AS OUTCOME

The teacher tests required for initial licensing in the majority of states suggest another highly visible way that outcomes are being constructed in teacher education. The construction of test scores as outcomes is really a subset of the first construction of the outcomes question in that it explores one facet of the long-term impact of teacher education. However, because teacher tests have been given so much attention and weight, it is worth considering them separately. Test scores as outcomes are connected to larger debates about quality, licensing, standards, and assessment. They are also embedded in the long history of criticisms of teachers as mediocre students, "semi-skilled" workers, "less than literate" individuals, and members of a minor or "not quite" profession.

With initial licensing tests, the proxy for teacher learning is usually some combination of general knowledge, including communication and literacy skills, with knowledge of specific subject matter and pedagogy, both of which are demonstrated on a paper and pencil exam. There is no clear evidence that teacher testing—as policy—has a positive impact on the performance of classroom teachers (Flippo, 1986; Ladson-Billings, 1998), although there is some evidence that testing has an impact on the "quality" of those entering and remaining in teaching where "quality" is defined as other test scores, grade point averages, and similar measures (Gitomer & Latham, 2000).

Earlier teacher test scores were assumed primarily to measure individual fitness for teaching in a way not unlike the way SATs and GREs are assumed to measure individuals' potential for college and graduate-level academic work. Relatively little attention was paid to the aggregated scores of individuals from the same state or the same teacher education institution. Times changed, however, fueled in part by the dismal performance of Massachusetts teacher candidates on that state's first ever teacher test in spring of 1998—when 59% of candidates failed. The Massachusetts scores fanned the debate about teacher quality and teacher preparation that was already going on in Congress about professional preparation and proposed stipulations for the reauthorization of the Higher Education Act (Earley, 2000; Melnick & Pullin, 2000).

Of particular importance in the Higher Education Act are the mandatory accountability requirements that all states and colleges/universities that receive federal dollars must provide annual information on the performance of all teacher candidates recommended by an institution on each measure required for licensure. As has been widely broadcast, these data will be compiled into institutional and state "report cards" intended to serve as indicators of the fitness of the teacher education enterprise and will provide public, and no doubt highly politicized, rankings of teacher education institutions (U.S. Department of Education, 2000). By switching the unit of analysis from individuals to institutions, recent testing arrangements locate the responsibility for teacher education outcomes squarely at the feet of colleges and universities, some of which may be threatened with closure when the new regulations go into effect (Wise, 1988).

Constructing the outcomes question in teacher education as scores on teacher tests creates a number of problems and has important consequences for the pool of candidates entering the profession. Some statewide teacher tests, for example, are anathematic to the concepts and knowledge taught in teacher education programs (Melnick & Pullin, 2000), particularly in terms of conceptions of literacy, views of student learning, and notions of growth and progress (Luna, Solsken, & Kutz, 2000). Unfortunately, at the same time that there are many efforts to recruit a more diverse pool of teacher candidates, the teacher test is working as gatekeeper to keep some potential teachers out. Fear of poor performance on teachers tests is leading some schools of education to change admissions standards with the consequence that fewer students are applying, and there is increasing evidence that the implementation of teacher tests—like other tests historically that are biased against minorities—may be playing a role in the decline of minority participation in the teaching profession (Garcia, 1986; Gitomer & Latham, 2000; Smith, 1984; Wise, 1988). Further, although some studies have also indicated that teacher candidates prepared in teacher education programs, particularly NCATE-accredited programs, score higher on teacher tests than other candidates (Wise, 1999), there is little evidence that teacher test scores are related to actual teaching performance in classrooms or to students' learning.

PROFESSIONAL PERFORMANCE AS OUTCOME

The third major take on the outcomes question is professional performance as outcome. This construction of the outcomes question focuses on the professional performances that teacher candidates are expected to demonstrate and how these performances are documented, analyzed, and evaluated. The idea of performance as an outcome of teacher education is connected to larger debates about authentic assessments of teaching, the shift from "inputs" to "outputs" as the basis of teacher education accreditation, and rapid revisions in teacher education programs across the country in keeping with new state requirements.

Performance assessments are intended to evaluate teacher candidates' abilities to produce "products" and complete "authentic tasks" that closely resemble the real work of teaching (Madaus & O'Dwyer, 1999). There are a number of differing ideas, however, about what the real work of teaching is.

In the section that follows, I sketch four initiatives that illuminate some of the range and variation in how performance is being constructed as an outcome of preservice education as well as some sense of the consequences of constructing outcomes in various ways. Each of these examples has been highly visible as a result of multiple publications and presentations. Each has been supported by or connected to larger professional foundations, agencies, or organizations, and/or each has been used as a public exemplar of teacher education practice in keeping with a particular agenda.

Ability-Based Performance Assessment

Alverno College's approach to performance assessment for preservice teachers is part of the larger ability-based curriculum of the college. The work at Alverno has been widely cited as an exemplar of preservice teacher education in line with the standards-based professionalization efforts of NCTAF, INTASC, and NBPTS. It is also included in the U.S. Department of Education profiles of "promising practices," for improving teacher quality (U.S. Department of Education, 1998) and as the preservice example in the *Studies of Excellence in Teacher Education* series copublished by AACTE and NCTAF (Darling-Hammond, 2000c).

As Diez and Hass (1997) have pointed out, the Alverno program is based on the idea that performance assessment is not an add-on, but a basic approach that transforms the curriculum. They write: "Teacher candidates' abilities are assumed to be developmental and, because the evidence they require is complex, assumed to demand multiple opportunities for demonstration of abilities and a wide variety of assessment modes" (p. 21). Thus students are engaged in literally hundreds of performances during their preservice preparation. Through portfolios, analyses of lessons and units, essays, letters, case study analyses, observations of teachers, simulations with parents, and development of curriculum materials, teacher candidates are required not simply to demonstrate that their teaching has an impact of students' learning, although they must do that, but also how and why their teaching practices impact student learning within particular contexts that closely resemble the actual contexts of teachers' work.

Performance Understanding

Researchers and teacher educators at Michigan State University, the University of Michigan, and elsewhere have been engaged in professional education for prospective and experienced teachers—particularly in mathematics and social studies—designed to generate teaching strategies "for understanding" (Ball & Cohen, 1999; Cohen & Ball, 1990; Cohen, McLaughlin, & Talbert, 1993). Here teacher education outcomes are framed as the alignment over time of teachers' pedagogy with current curriculum standards (Lampert & Ball, 1998, 1999) and with discipline-based goals for students' learning of complex forms of reasoning, problem solving, and communication (Ball, 1996, 2000). This work has received considerable attention as part of what Hawley and Valli (1999) call the "new professional development," which is closely aligned with national standards for professional development and K–12 curricular reform.

Writing specifically about performance and knowledge, Lampert and Ball (1999) suggest that knowing teaching means understanding in such a way that one is prepared to perform (or practice) in a given situation for which one cannot fully prepare in advance. They emphasize *how* teacher candidates should know what they need to know rather than focusing on simply *what* they need to know (Lampert & Ball, 1998). In their programs, teacher candidates learn by working with artifacts and records of practice to facilitate multiple perspectives, triangulation of interpretations, and retrieval and sorting of ideas in multiple ways.

Teacher Work Samples

Western Oregon University's Teacher Work Sample method has been in place since 1986 when the state of Oregon began to require teacher certification programs to provide evidence that teacher candidates could produce appreciable progress in the learning of all K–12 students (Schalock & Myton, 1988; Schalock, Schalock, & Myton, 1998). Workshops and institutes are now led by Western Oregon faculty to aid teacher educators who are trying to develop systematic means of connecting teaching and learning (Schalock & Imig, 2000).

Schalock, Schalock, and Girod (1997) point out that the teacher work sample method is a "complex, 'authentic' applied performance approach" to the evaluation of teacher candidates that is outcomes-based and grounded in a "context-dependent" (pp. 17–18) theory of teacher effectiveness. The teacher work sample method proceeds as follows:

> Starting with preinstructional data on pupil learning, a student teacher calculates a "percentage correct" score for each pupil in his or her classroom. Using these scores, the teacher then (a) tabulates, from highest- to lowest-scoring pupil, the range of preinstructional scores; (b) sorts these scores into high-, low-, and middle-scoring groups; and (c) calculates the means scores for each of the groups formed and for the class as a whole. These preinstructional groupings provide the structure for both the analysis of postinstructional measures of outcome attainment and the calculation of gain scores. (Schalock et al., 1998)

According to its architects, the work sample approach sharply contrasts with assessments that feature portfolios and teachers' analyses of lessons planned and taught because of its explicit focus on demonstrable teacher effectiveness as measured by student learning gains.

Inquiry as Stance

For a number of years, a group of university- and school-based researchers and practitioners (myself included) at the University of Pennsylvania and the Philadelphia area schools (and more recently at Boston College) have promoted teacher research as a vehicle for generating local knowledge and challenging the status quo by linking inquiry, knowledge, and professional practice across the professional life span (Cochran-Smith & Lytle, 1993, 1999). In these programs, a major outcome of teacher education has been teacher learning and professional practice that promotes rich and rigorous learning opportunities with the goal of equity and social justice for all K–12 students.

With inquiry as stance (Cochran-Smith & Lytle, 1999), the focus is on how teacher candidates work within professional communities to construct local knowledge, open their decision-making strategies to critique, wrestle with multiple perspectives, and use the research of others as generative of new questions and strategies. Professional performances expected of teacher candidates include description and analysis of the cultures of the school and community, analysis of students' learning opportunities based on comparative classroom studies, analyses of individual children as learners and constructors of meaning, and construction of curriculum intended to provide all students with opportunities to engage in significant intellectual work and interrogate issues equity (Cochran-Smith, 1995a, 1995b). Portfolios of teacher candidates' inquiries, samples of teachers' and students' work, and critical narrative essays analyzing teacher learning over time represent a major final performance (Cochran-Smith, 1999).

The examples above provide some sense of the range and variation in how professional performance is being constructued as an outcome of preservice education. In the most general sense, of course, all four construct performance as the intersection of teacher learning, professional practice, and student learning demonstrated in authentic school and classroom tasks.

However, there are important differences as well. In some approaches, the overriding focus is on demonstrable teacher effectiveness as measured by the learning gains of students. In others, the focus is on how teachers' learning and understanding are linked to students' learning. Some evaluate performance against standards aligned with curriculum standards, some with standards of professional practice validated in the field, and some with combinations of these. Along other lines, in some performance assessments, teacher candidates are evaluated in part in terms of their ability to critique, rather than simply comply with, curriculum standards and traditions of practice. These differences in viewpoint about what constitutes competent teaching performance are more than semantic. At the heart are fundamentally different definitions of teaching and learning, how teaching can best be documented and interpreted, where learning is located, and how close to actual schools and classrooms it is assumed one must be in order to learn how to teach (and evaluate teaching).

THE OUTCOMES QUESTION: GROUNDS AND GROUNDWORK

Throughout this chapter, I have suggested that how we construct the outcomes question in teacher education—including how we argue that some outcomes matter more than others—legitimizes particular points of view about the purposes of schooling, the nature of teaching and learning, and the role of the teacher in educational reform, but also undermines other points of view. I turn now to several cautions and concerns about the points of view that are being legitimized but also undermined as grounds and groundwork for the outcomes question.

The Tension Between Consensus and Critique

Many of the discussions that pertain to the outcomes question depend on the claim that there is an unprecedented professional consensus about how to reform education by developing closer and closer alignment of standards for teaching and learning, assessments of students and teachers, and new models of teacher education, licensing, and certification. There is, however, a fair amount of evidence that just below the surface of common language and agreement at the abstract level are deep differences.

The whole movement for the the privatization of schooling (and with it the deregulation of teacher education), driven by a market approach to education reform (Earley, 2000), is an obvious—an enormous—example of the lack of consensus about teacher education in the United States. The deregulation movement (described in some detail in Chapter 7) helps to explain some otherwise puzzling discrepancies within and among state policies concering the preparation and licensing of teachers. For example, many states now have official relationships with NCATE, and/or they are working with INTASC to develop professional standards for the licensing of beginning teachers. However, some of these very same states are at the same time implementing state policies that are fundamentally out of sync with the standards of the professional organizations. Colorado, for example, has removed the word "diversity" from its regulations regarding teacher preparation, Massachusetts Department of Education officials have excised the word "constructivism" from discussions about curriculum, and states such as New Jersey and Texas now advocate alternate routes with a few weeks of teacher training prior to full classroom responsibility as a preferred entry into teaching.

Even if we put the professionalization-deregulation debate aside, however, it may be that what Hawley and Valli (1999) have called "an almost unprecedented consensus . . . among researchers, professional development specialists, and key policymakers on ways to increase the knowledge and skills of educators substantially" is at least partly an illusion—or a wish. For example, only 500 of the 1200 plus institutions in the country that recommend teachers for certification are nationally accredited, and there was considerable disagreement about a provision in the Federal Higher Education Act to encourage accreditation as a means of increasing accountability for teacher education institutions (Darling-Hammond, 2000e).

Some of the differences among teacher education policy makers, researchers, and practitioners may be accounted for as turf battles, some as what Smith, Heinecke, and Noble (1999) call "political symbolism and contention" (p. 158), and some as genuine and rational debate about the meaning and purposes of teaching and learning. But in the face of these disagreements, what accounts for the strong claims that consensus already exists and what propels such strong advocacy of closer and closer alignment of educational outcomes? Yinger and colleagues (Yinger, 1999; Yinger & Hendricks-Lee, 2000) suggest that standards are a powerful professional tool and that consensus is critical to the professionalization process, signaling to the public and to policy makers that a profession has established cognitive jurisdiction. Yinger (1999) argues:

> As consensus develops around national standards for teaching and teacher preparation, it fulfills the needs of both policy makers and the public for simplification of the image of teaching and issues of quality. There was no way teaching could have met these social needs for a unified, scientifically based perception of professional practice as long as academics were arguing publicly about conceptions of teaching and 50 state legislatures were deciding the matters for themselves. (p. 106)

Yinger's analysis points to the fact that we need consensus—whether we have it or not. The danger here—and the caution for teacher education as we construct the outcomes question—is that we will sacrifice or gloss over the healthy and vital contribution of critique for what is arguably the greater professional good of consensus.

In one way, working from consensus and alignment of standards is a rational and much-needed improvement in teacher education that helps to establish professional jurisdiction. In another way, however, the greater the supposed consensus and the tighter the alignment of all the pieces, the less room there is for critique and questioning within the profession and in the preparation of prospective teachers. As we construct the outcomes question in teacher education, a central challenge is how to prepare teacher candidates who can demonstrate what some consider "best" instructional practices, but also know how to challenge those practices when they exclude certain children or fail to serve some students. How will we prepare teachers who know how to "fit" into tightly aligned standards-driven schools and school systems, but also know how to raise questions about whose interests are being served, whose needs are being met, and whose are not being met by those systems?

Problems with Inputs-Outcomes Metaphors

As mentioned above, some people are describing changes in teacher education accreditation standards as a "paradigm shift" from inputs to outputs or from inputs to outcomes in teacher education (Schalock & Imig, 2000; Schalock & Myton, 1988). The dominance of input-output metaphors to describe the outcomes question in teacher education is troubling. In *Metaphors We Live By*, Lakoff and Johnson (1980) suggest that images like these are powerful forces in the social construction of reality:

> Metaphors may create realities for us, especially social realities. A metaphor may thus be a guide for future action. Such actions will, of course, fit the metaphor. This will, in turn, reinforce the power of the metaphor to make experience coherent. In this sense metaphors can be self-fulfilling prophecies. (p. 156)

Input-output metaphors carry with them images of factories and production lines and suggest a linear view of the relationship of teaching and learning for both K–12 students and for teacher candidates.

As the debate continues about what kind of outcomes should be expected from teacher candidates' performances, an important challenge will be to eschew narrow views of teaching, particularly those that begin and end with the assumption that teaching can be defined as instructional practice that leads to increased test scores. If we require teacher candidates to use some kind of calculus that measures and aggregates the learning gains of each K–12 student from pretest to posttest measures for each lesson or unit of lessons, there will be an inevitable narrowing of the curriculum and an inevitable pull toward teaching as transmission and learning as accruing bits of knowledge. There will also be an inevitable emphasis on teaching practice as what teachers do within the boundaries of their classroom walls rather than an expanded view that includes teachers' roles as members of school communities, as activists, school leaders, and theorizers of practice. With Susan Lytle, I have described this broader view of teaching practice as follows (Cochran-Smith & Lytle, 1999):

> We are not suggesting that an expanded view of practice results from *adding* teachers' activity outside the classroom to what they do inside, but rather that what goes on inside the classroom is profoundly *altered* and ultimately transformed when teachers' frameworks for practice foreground the intellectual, social, and cultural contexts of teaching. (p. 276)

In short, I am suggesting that we need outcomes measures that—ironically—make teaching harder and more complicated for teacher candidates (rather than easier and more straightforward) by recognizing its inevitable complexity and uncertainty and by acknowledging the fact that there are often concurrent and competing claims to justice operating in the decisions teacher candidates must make from moment to moment, day to day. Linear models of teaching will not suffice, nor will approaches to the outcomes question that push only for clarity and certainty. Someone once said that "those who have been forced to memorize the world are not likely to change it." It may also be true that those who measure the outcomes of teaching only with pluses and minuses are not likely to see the value of question marks, concentric circles, and arrows that point both ways and sometimes double back.

Teachers (and Teacher Educators) as Saviors and Culprits

In debates about the outcomes question, teachers and teacher educators are being constructed as both the last great hope and the most culpable culprits in what ails American schools. The attention given recently to outcome-based assessment systems that incorporate student achievement data into evaluations of individual teachers and schools reinforce this idea. Sanders and Horn's (1998) Tennessee Value-Added Assessment System, for example, has been widely cited by researchers and policy makers, even those who represent opposing perspectives. Despite their differences, policy makers use Sanders and Horn to make the same point—when other variables are adjusted for or held constant, teacher effectiveness is the primary factor that accounts for differences in student learning, even stronger as a determinant of students' achievement than class size and heterogeneity. This means that teachers are responsible for students' learning despite the mitigation of social and cultural contexts, students' backgrounds, and the match or mismatch of school and community expectations.

My intention here is certainly *not* to argue that teachers—and teacher education—are not important. As we construct the outcomes questions that are driving reform and development in our profession, however, we face the challenge of how to emphasize the centrality of teachers' work without implying that teachers—individually or collectively—are the panacea for the problems of education. Notwithstanding recent research about the impact of individual teachers on students' learning, it may be wise to remember as we construct the outcomes question in teacher education that teachers—and teacher educators—are neither the saviors nor the culprits of all that is wrong with education.

Getting (and Keeping) Social Justice on the Outcomes Agenda

In the standards of NBPTS, INTASC, and NCATE, there is an explicit mandate that teachers and teacher candidates should be able to meet the needs of an increasingly diverse student population by producing demonstrable learning gains for *all* children. Several major proponents of the professionalization agenda have pointed out that the standards of these three organizations provide a remarkably consistent image of the professional teacher as a "knowledgeable and reflective practitioner willing and able to engage in collaborative, contextually grounded learning activities (Yinger, 1999).

It is not clear, however, whether this emerging professional image also includes images of the teacher as activist, as agent for social change, or as ally in antiracist initiatives. As we construct the outcomes question in teacher education, we need to clarify and interrogate what it means to teach "all students" well and/or what it means to adjust teaching practices according to the needs and interests of "all children." In a chapter on preparing teachers for diversity, Ladson-Billings (1999) suggests that

> The changing demographics of the nation's schoolchildren have caught schools, colleges, and departments of teacher education by surprise. Students are still being prepared to teach in idealized schools that serve white, monolingual, middle class children from homes with two parents. (pp. 86–87)

With regard to culturally relevant approaches to teacher assessment, Ladson-Billings (1998) further asserts that these are "dangerous times" for teachers of students of color. She suggests that some aspects of the new presumably more authentic evaluations of teacher competency "may actually serve to reinscribe a narrow set of teaching practices that fail to serve all children well—particularly children of color and children living in poverty" (p. 255). Similarly Irvine has suggested that some aspects of assessments such as those of NBPTS are not in keeping with what we know about the strategies, relationships, and beliefs of teachers who teach children of color most effectively (Irvine, 2000; Irvine & Fraser, 1998).

As we establish the grounds and groundwork for the outcomes question, one of the challenges we face is how to keep social justice—particularly issues of race, class, and language background—on the agenda. Images of the professional teacher—as reflective and knowledgeable, on the one hand, or as transformative and culturally relevant, on the other—are not necessarily inconsistent, and they can and do mutually coexist in various constructions of the outcomes question in teacher education. In fact in some performance assessments where teacher candidates are expected to document student learning but also demonstrate their work as part of communities working for social change, the two images are entirely consistent and mutually reinforcing. But it is also important to note that these two images are by no means *necessarily* coincidental. We could easily imagine performance assessments, for example, that demonstrate that a teacher candidate is reflective, collaborative, and knowledgeable but have little or nothing to do with critiquing the inequities of the educational system or raising questions about the school as a sorting machine that reinforces privilege and disadvantage based on race, culture, language background, and gender. A challenge as we construct the outcomes question is to imagine performance assessments for teacher candidates that require both.

Democracy or Market Forces?

As noted earlier, many of the most contentious debates about the outcomes question in teacher education stem from two fundamentally different approaches to teacher education reform and from two fundamentally different views of the purposes of schooling. The first, which is intended to reform teacher education through professionalization so that all students are guaranteed fully licensed and well-qualified teachers, is based on the belief that public education is vital to a democratic society. The second, which is intended to reform teacher education through deregulation so that larger numbers of college graduates (with no teacher preparation) can enter the profession, is based on a market approach to the problem of teacher shortages, an approach that feeds off erosion of public confidence in education. These two agendas are discussed in detail in Chapter 7.

Constructions of the outcomes question embedded within market approaches to the reform of teacher education legitimize the dominance of "private goods" and undermine the view that public education is an enterprise for the public good in a democratic society. Emphasis on private goods and the privatization of education is a trend that is not limited to the United States. Rather the free-market approach to educational reform is a global phenomenon. Along these lines, Apple (2000); Whitty, Power, and Halpin (1998); and Robertson (1998), among others, have pointed out that the tendency in Australia, New Zealand, the United Kingdom, and in parts of the United States has been to devolve blame for the "failures" of public education to the local level—schools, teachers, and teacher education programs—while at the same time overregulating the content of education and dramatically curtailing the role of universities in teacher education (Thiessen, 2000).

Many of the recent attacks on teacher education are best understood in terms of this larger global debate. There is a striking similarity in many of the attacks on teacher education and in their allegiance to market-driven reforms that make the antidemocracy theme very clear. In many of these attacks, multicultural education is constructed as a villain, and there is the presumption that what would save our schools is the "return" to an earlier and idealized time when American values were uncontested and shared by all, when the "canon" of Western European history and literary works was unchallenged, and when academic standards for all students were rigorous and culturally neutral (Ravitch, 2000). Each of these entirely faulty presumptions and historical inaccuracies has been critiqued and deconstructed in great detail elsewhere (e.g., Apple, 2000; Banks, 2000; Ladson-Billings, 1999).

The similarities among these attacks, however, are not surprising—nor are their explicitly conservative politics and their gestures toward racism—when it is understood that they are part of the larger conservative political agenda for the privatization of American education. Although it claims to be neutral, this agenda begins with the premise that we need to deregulate teacher education and let the market decide which children will have the most qualified teachers. These are anything but neutral premises and neutral assumptions about the purposes of American education, the purposes of teacher education, and the role of public education in a democratic society.

Mary Heaton Vorse once wrote, "In the last analysis, civilization itself will be measured by the way in which children live and by what chance they have in the world" (Maggio, 1997). As we construct the outcomes question in teacher education, we need to keep in mind how we will be measured by our own measures. As researchers, practitioners, and policy makers in teaching and teacher education, we will not measure up unless we preserve a place for critique in the face of consensus and keep at the center of teacher education rich and complex understandings of teaching and learning that are not easily reducible to algorithms. We must also acknowledge that although teachers have a critical role in educational reform, they alone are neither the saviors nor the culprits in what is wrong with American schools and American society. We must remain vigilant in demanding time and space on the outcomes agenda not just for professional discussions about meeting the needs of all students but for deep interrogation of questions related to diversity, equity, access, and racism. At this critical juncture in the reform and development of teacher education, if we do not take control of framing the outcomes question as a social justice question, then the outcomes question will surely frame us and undermine our work as teachers, teacher educators, researchers, and policy makers committed to a democratic vision of society and to the vital role that teachers and teacher educators play in that vision.

Sticks, Stones, and Ideology

Marilyn Cochran-Smith and Kim Fries

Like the previous chapter, Chapter 7 develops the idea of teacher education for social justice as a political problem by examining from a political lens two competing and highly visible agendas for the reform of teacher education—professionalization and deregulation. In this chapter, which is coauthored with Kim Fries, we argue that neither of these agendas is neutral or apolitical. In fact, we argue to the contrary—that both are highly values-driven and ideology-laden. Drawing on policy documents and public debates, we show that although their rhetoric is similar in certain ways, these two agendas are based on sharply contrasting assumptions about the purposes of schooling in a democratic society and the ways teacher education should be held accountable to the public. These contrasting views have dramatically different implications for teaching and teacher education for social justice.

PROFESSIONALIZATION AND DEREGULATION: UNPACKING THE DISCOURSE

Public critiques of teachers and teacher education are not new on the educational scene, nor are scholarly debates within the profession. Arguably, however, there have never before been such blistering media commentaries and such highly politicized battles about teacher education as those that have dominated the public discourse and fueled legislative reforms at the state and federal levels during the last 5 or so years of the 20th century. Many aspects of these debates can be understood as part of two much larger debates about school reform, particularly two larger national agendas, which are overlapping in certain ways but simultaneously competing and even contradictory in many others (Apple, 2000, 2001; Cochran-Smith, 2001a, 2001b; Earley, 2000).

The agenda to *professionalize* teaching and teacher education, which is linked to the K–12 curriculum standards movement, has been spearheaded by Linda Darling-Hammond and the National Commission on Teaching and America's Future (NCTAF) and forwarded through the joint efforts of the National Council for the Accreditation of Teacher Education (NCATE), the National Board for Professional Teaching Standards (NBPTS), and the Interstate New Teacher Assessment and Support Consortium (INTASC) (Gallagher & Bailey, 2000). These projects reflect a broad-based effort to reform teacher education nationwide based on high standards for the preparation, licensing, and certification of teachers. Supported by foundations including the Carnegie Corporation, the Pew Charitable Trusts, the Ford Foundation, and the DeWitt Wallace Reader's Digest Fund, proponents of professionalization advocate standards-based teacher preparation and professional development as well as teacher assessments based on performance across the professional life span. In direct opposition to the professionalization agenda, however, is the well-publicized movement to *deregulate* teacher preparation by dismantling teacher education institutions and breaking up the monopoly that the profession has "too long" enjoyed. Supported by conservative political groups and private foundations including the Fordham Foundation, the Heritage Foundation, the Pioneer Institute, and the Manhattan Institute, the deregulation agenda begins with the premise that the requirements of state licensing agencies and schools of education are unnecessary hurdles that keep bright young people out of teaching and focus on social goals rather than academic achievement. Advocates of deregulation push for alternate routes into teaching and high-stakes teacher tests as the major gatekeeper for the profession.

In this chapter we look closely at how the discourse of these two competing agendas is being publicly constructed, critiqued, and debated. Our intention here is not to determine which agenda is "right" or to reveal the "true" underlying motives of the proponents of either one. Nor is our intention to bolster unnecessary dichotomies between these two agendas. However, since so much of the debate about teacher education is constructed—and interpreted by others—in terms that are oppositional, we believe it is important to unpack the assumptions and values in which the opposition is grounded. Thus we offer here an analysis of the way each constructs its own arguments as well as how each critiques the positions of the other side, using the language of these groups themselves and quoting from published articles and papers as well as other public documents.

We argue that sorting out contradictory assertions will not be accomplished simply through "unbiased" evaluations of "the evidence," although efforts to do so are important and useful. Along these lines, we do not pretend that our own stance about teacher education reform is neutral or apolitical. As teacher education scholars and practitioners, we have long been involved in efforts to prepare new and experienced teachers to educate an increasingly diverse population and respond to the changing economic, social, and political contexts of our time. And we have long been committed to teaching and teacher education for social justice. However, the analysis we offer here is intended to be as evenhanded as possible, unpacking some of the important values and politics underlying the arguments for both professionalization and deregulation.

We suggest that it is also necessary to unpack the values and politics in which these viewpoints are embedded, including their differing notions of evidence, fairness, results, progress, public benefit, the American way, and other key ideas. We suggest that although proponents of each agenda use "ideology" and other value-laden terms as pejoratives to critique the other, both agendas are themselves ideological in the sense that they are driven by ideas, ideals, values, and assumptions about the purposes of schooling, the social and economic future of the nation, and the role of public education in a democratic society. We caution that unless underlying ideologies and values are debated along with and in relation to "the evidence" about teacher quality, we will make little progress in understanding the discourse of reform and the competing agendas that currently dominate the politics of teacher education.

COMMON SENSE ABOUT TEACHER EDUCATION REFORM: THREE WARRANTS FOR ACTION

Discourse analysis is often used to examine how "different versions of the world" are produced through texts and talk (Silverman, 2000). To prepare this analysis, we gathered a group of public policy documents, scholarly articles, and transcriptions of public talk in order to analyze how the discourse of two national agendas for teacher education is being constructed and debated. We concluded that the discourse revolves around three major warrants.

The term "warrant" is derived from the Old German in which it referred to a commission or written document that gave one person or group the authority to do something. We use "warrant" to signify justification, authority, or "reasonable grounds" for some act, course of action, statement, or belief. We suggest that the discourse of both professionalization and deregulation of teacher education revolves around the establishment of three warrants: *the evidentiary warrant, the political warrant,* and *the accountability warrant.* Taken together, these three warrants are used to add up to "common sense" about what should be done to improve the quality of the nation's teachers.

The Evidentiary Warrant: Empirical versus Ideological Positions

The professionalization-deregulation debate has been carried on in scholarly journals as well as in the media and in many policy and professional arenas. In the scholarly literature, the focus has been primarily on the evidentiary warrant, or "what the evidence actually says" about teacher education based on meta-analyses and/or syntheses of previous and current empirical work. The point is to make policy recommendations that, when implemented, will yield value-added investments of state and/or federal resources.

Emblematic of the debate between those who favor professionalization and those who favor deregulation is the ongoing controversy about the impact of teacher quality on K–12 students' learning. Darling-Hammond, the NCTAF, and other proponents of increased professionalism for teachers and teacher educators assert that the evidence shows that teacher education "matters most" in educational reform (Darling-Hammond, 2000a; Darling-Hammond & Sykes, 1999; National Commission on Teaching & America's Future, 1996, 1997). As noted in Chapter 6, Darling-Hammond (2000b) explicitly points out that qualitative and quantitative analyses indicate that student achievement is related to teacher quality and that measures of teacher preparation and certification are the strongest correlates of students' achievement.

On the other hand, Dale Ballou and Michael Podgursky, economists whose analysis appears in the Fordham Foundation's monograph (Kanstoroom & Finn, 1999) on how to produce better teachers and better schools, conclude that teacher education doesn't matter much at all. Again, as noted in Chapter 6, Ballou and Podgursky (1999) assert that evidence from teacher licensing exams as well as studies of alternative certification programs indicate that teacher preparation has little to do with teaching performance. The introduction to the Fordham Foundation's monograph (Kanstoroom & Finn, 1999) reiterates Ballou and Podgursky's conclusion in no uncertain terms:

> We are struck by the paucity of evidence linking inputs [courses taken, requirements met, time spent, and activities engaged in] with actual teacher effectiveness. In a meta-analysis of close to four hundred studies of the effect of various school resources on pupil achievement, very little connection was found between the degrees teachers had earned or the experience they possessed and how much their students learned. (p. 18)

Again it is useful to contrast this conclusion with Linda Darling-Hammond's conclusion in NCTAF's second report, *Doing What Matters Most: Investing in Quality Teaching* (National Commission on Teaching & America's Future, 1997):

> Reviews of more than two hundred studies contradict the long-standing myths that "anyone can teach" and that "teachers are born and not made" . . . teachers who are fully prepared and certified in both their discipline and in education are more highly rated and are more successful with the students than are teachers without preparation, and those with greater training . . . are more effective than those with less. (p. 10)

The battle for the evidentiary warrant is especially clear in the *Teachers College Record* exchange between Ballou and Podgursky and Darling-Hammond, mentioned in the last chapter. In this blunt exchange, both parties go to some lengths to cast their own positions as "strictly" empirical and at the same time question the empirical validity of the other's position. Ballou and Podgursky (2000) directly attack the findings of NCTAF by asserting, "The commission overstates policy implications, ignoring critical limitations of the research. In many instances, the commission flatly misreports and misrepresents what these studies show" (pp. 13–14).

Speaking for NCTAF, Darling-Hammond (2000b) emphatically refutes Ballou and Podgursky's use of evidence as well as their conclusions. She claims:

> In this volume of the *Teachers College Record*, Ballou and Podgursky go further to charge, falsely in each instance, that the Commission has misrepresented research data and findings. In the course of their argument, their critique itself misreports data . . . and variously ignores and misconstrues the research evidence presented in support of the report's key findings. (p. 29)

In this contest to establish the evidentiary warrant, the point is to focus on facts established through standard quantitative research conventions for data collection and analysis. Each side endeavors to undermine the warrant of the other by pointing out methodological errors, incorrect or incomplete data, and faulty logic.

In this way, each side constructs its own case as if it were neutral, apolitical, and value free, based solely on the empirical and certified facts of the matter and not related to a particular agenda that is political or ideological. In fact, it is clear from the discourse that neither side can afford to be cast as ideological. Each therefore implicitly (or explicitly) eschews the notion that there *is* an ideological basis to its position and uses the term as an epithet to undermine the position of the other. James Gee (1996) makes an intriguing argument along these lines with reference to what he calls "Napoleon's move":

> In attacking [the Enlightenment] philosophers, Napoleon used "ideology" as a term of abuse for a social policy which was in part or in whole derived from a social theory in a conscious way. Napoleon disliked the Enlightenment philosophers' social theory and its conclusions because they conflicted with his interests and his pursuit of power. Rather than arguing against this theory by arguing for a rival theory of his own, he castigates it as abstract, impractical, and fanatical. (p. 3)

Gee points out that this move has been used ever since Napoleon to attack and dismiss social theories that conflict with one's own and to suggest that one's opponent is an ideologue, operating within a closed system and unwilling to consider other points of view.

Based on our reading of the documents, we have noted that the deregulationists are more likely to make Napoleon's move in their critiques of the professionalization agenda than vice versa. They are also more likely to be inflammatory in their remarks, casting aspersions not only on the positions they oppose but also on the professional integrity of their opponents. However, debaters on both sides use Napoleon's move in order to cast their opponents' positions as ideological and their own as empirical.

Darling-Hammond (2000b), for example, concludes that Ballou and Podgursky's "one-sided treatment of the Commission's proposals reflects the ideological lens they apply to their work" (p. 29). She also attempts to capture the empirical warrant for her position by reiterating the veracity of her own analyses and dismissing empirical challenges Ballou and Podgursky pose by labeling them as political and ideological in the first place: "Charges of deliberate misrepresentation of data are very serious. Making such charges without ascertainment of sources and accurate rendering of claims may be acceptable in the political realm, but it violates the ethical norms of the research community" (p. 42). On the other hand, in nearly all of their discussions of NCTAF's recommendations, Ballou and Podgursky assert that NCTAF's claims are ideologically rather than empirically driven. They are especially critical of the teaching methods taught in schools of education, which they claim are not based on evidence:

> Poor ideas secure a following in part because the scientific foundation for pedagogical prescriptions is weak. However, ideology also plays a large role in shaping the views of educators, as shown by the influence of the constructivist theory of learning on the teaching practices endorsed by leading schools of education

... [T]eacher educators espouse pedagogical practices for ideological reasons rather than because the evidence indicates they best promote student learning. (Ballou & Podgursky, 1999)

In statements like these intended to persuade the public (Thomas B. Fordham Foundation, 1999a, 1999b), the deregulationists repeatedly use Napoleon's move to dismiss the idea of professionalization.

One of the most provocative applications of Napoleon's move to dismiss a position *because* it was ideological occurred in an evaluation of teacher education programs in Colorado. With tighter regulations for teacher preparation, all teacher education programs in Colorado were required to be recertified by June 2001, or else be shut down. Early that year, Denver newspapers revealed that the National Association of Scholars (NAS) had been commissioned by the Colorado Commission on Higher Education to aid in these evaluations. The NAS report's conclusions about teacher education at the University of Colorado at Boulder—with Napoleon's move front and center—made headlines across the state:

> There are problems here that are so significant that a mere "revision" is unlikely to correct them. Nothing short of a miraculous transformation can reverse the patently overt ideological proselytizing that goes on in the name of teacher education at CU [Boulder]. More than any other reviewed institution, CU's teacher education programs are the most politically correct and stridently committed to the social justice model. (Curtin, 2001)

Authored by David Saxe, the NAS report asserted explicitly that teacher education programs should be based on "objective" standards and "core knowledge" rather than ideology. The critique used "ideology" as a damning pejorative in and of itself in order to discredit the work of certain teacher education institutions and conclude that they should be shut down. The fact that David Saxe and other NAS members were signers of the Fordham's Foundation "manifesto," which explicitly advocates deregulation in the first place, was not mentioned in newspaper accounts.

There is no question in the above examples that the evidentiary warrant is what is being contested. The battle is over which side will capture the right to be termed "empirical," while at the same time avoiding the deprecatory description, "ideological." The major players in the professionalization-deregulation debate jockey to establish the *evidentiary warrant* through three key strategies: providing convincing empirical evidence about the impact of teacher education, discrediting the evidence of the other side through methodological and/or logical critique of procedures for data collection and analysis, and casting the other side as "simply" ideological and therefore readily able to be dismissed and/or ignored.

The Accountability Warrant: Outcomes versus Inputs

Accountability is surely one of the most overused terms in public discussions about schools and schooling. In fact, we argued in Chapter 6 that the outcomes question in teacher education is driving the field and is, to a great extent, influencing policy and practice. In this chapter, we use *the accountability warrant* to refer to the arguments posed on both sides of the professionalization-deregulation debate in order to demonstrate that recommended policies are justifiable and justified by the outcomes and results they produce.

The outcomes emphasis of the deregulation agenda is most clear in "The Teachers We Need and How to Get More of Them," a major statement of the Thomas B. Fordham Foundation (1999a), presided over by Chester Finn and also connected to the Heritage Foundation, the Pioneer Institute, and the Manhattan Institute through interlocking boards of directors and senior associates. These groups are widely known for their government lobbies and their support of the privatization of education, including school reform strategies such as school choice, vouchers, and heavy reliance on high-stakes testing for students and teachers. "The Teachers We Need" is Fordham's "manifesto," signed by William Bennett, E. D. Hirsch, Diane Ravitch, James Peyser, and others. The focus on accountability is crystal clear throughout:

> The good news is that America is beginning to adopt a powerful, commonsensical strategy for school reform. It is the same approach that almost every successful modern enterprise has adopted to boost performance and productivity; set high standards for results to be achieved, identify clear indicators to measure progress towards those results, and be flexible and pluralistic about the means for reaching those results. This strategy in education is sometimes called "standards-and-accountability" . . .
>
> The bad news is that states and policy makers have turned away from this commonsensical approach when trying to increase the pool of well-qualified teachers. Instead of encouraging a results-oriented approach, many states and policy makers are demanding ever more regulation of inputs and processes . . .
>
> A better solution to the teacher quality problem is to simplify the entry and hiring process. Get rid of most hoops and hurdles. Instead of requiring a long list of courses and degrees, test future teachers for their knowledge and skills. Allow principals to hire the teachers they need. Focus *relentlessly on results*, on whether students are learning . . . (pp. 1–2, emphasis added)

In their manifesto, the Fordham Foundation also focuses relentlessly on discrediting professionalization by suggesting that it does *not* focus on results, but instead emphasizes inputs, or what Fordham calls "hoops and hurdles" in the form of courses, degrees, and certification requirements to the exclusion of results and accountability. Positioning deregulation in opposition to professionalization vis-à-vis the outcomes issue is a repeated rhetorical move in Fordham Foundation and related documents, as this excerpt indicates:

> Today, in response to widening concern about teacher quality, most states are tightening the regulatory vise, making it harder to enter teaching by piling on new requirements for certification. On the advice of some highly visible education groups such as the National Commission on Teaching and America's Future, these states are also attempting to "professionalize" teacher preparation by raising admissions criteria for training programs and ensuring that these programs are all accredited. (Thomas B. Fordham Foundation, 1999a, p. 4)

Contrary to the way they are characterized by the deregulationists, however, those who favor professionalization *do* claim to be concerned about accountability and outcomes. They take a very different tack, however, by defining outcomes in terms of quality of teaching, high standards for teacher development, and teachers who are able to teach so all students learn to high standards. For example, Sykes's introduction to *Teaching as the Learning Profession: Handbook of Policy and Practice* (Darling-Hammond & Sykes, 1999) illustrates how proponents of professionalization construct the accountability warrant:

> This book is based on a deceptively simple premise coupled with a hypothesis. The premise is that the improvement of American education relies centrally on the development of a highly qualified teacher workforce imbued with the knowledge, skills, and dispositions to encourage exceptional learning in all the nation's students. The related hypothesis is that the key to producing well-qualified teachers is to greatly enhance their professional learning across the continuum of a career in the classroom. (p. xv)

Along similar lines, Arthur Wise and other NCATE representatives tout their new standards as squarely outcomes-based and claim that they represent a "major shift from curriculum-oriented standards to performance-based standards that focus on what teacher candidates know and are able to do" (Wise, 1999, p. 5).

Wise (1999) points out that NCATE's new system will require schools of education to provide performance evidence of candidate competence:

> The public expects that teachers of their children have sufficient knowledge of content to help all students meet standards for P–12 education . . . Candidates

for all professional education roles are expected to demonstrate positive effects on student learning ... Primary documentation for this standard will be candidates' performance data prepared for national and/or state review ... [including] performance assessment data collected internally by the unit and external data such as results on state licensing tests and other assessments. (NCATE, 1999, pp. 7–9)

The new NCATE standards are in keeping with recent developments in specialized accreditation organizations more generally, where the emphasis has shifted from inputs to outcomes measures (Dill, 1998) and in higher education where there is an "increasing clamor to apply quantitative measures of academic outcomes to guarantee educational quality for consumers" (Graham, Lyman, & Trow, 1998).

It is not surprising that proponents of both deregulation and professionalization are preoccupied with outcomes. This is a seductive idea that has captured public sentiment, and politicians have seized on it in election after election. The power of the outcomes idea, of course, is its "common sense." Who would deny that the public has a right to expect clear connections and links among how teachers are prepared, how teachers teach, and what students learn? Closer examination of the discourse, however, reveals that although parties on both sides of the debate use the language of outcomes and results to establish the accountability warrant, they actually mean quite different things by these words.

Spokespersons for the deregulation agenda mean "outcomes" in a narrow sense—students' scores on mandatory high-stakes standardized tests. The deregulationists' single-minded focus on results is crystal clear in Marci Kanstoroom's (1999) testimony to the U.S. House of Representatives Subcommittee on Postsecondary Education. In this testimony, Kanstoroom, research director at the Fordham Foundation and research fellow at the Manhattan Institute, makes the outcomes point at the same time that she discredits the "inputs" focus of professionalization:

> [F]ocusing on retooling existing teachers through professional development is itself an inadequate strategy for addressing the teacher quality problem. So too is focusing on preservice training of future teachers in colleges of education ...
>
> What principles might guide the Congress in seeking to ensure that every child in America has outstanding teachers? Start by focusing on the one vital result, student achievement. Insist that anything you do for teachers have a payoff in student learning, and insist that states focus their teacher quality policies on this as well, at least insofar as federal dollars are involved ... [Insist] that everything supported with federal funds be judged by evidence that it yields higher pupil achievement. (pp. 1–2)

Likewise, in a critique of the work of the NBPTS, Wilcox and Finn (1999) simultaneously emphasize standardized test scores and discredit teachers' learning as an outcome worthy of attention:

> Board certification focuses on input measures that are inconsistent with [states'] emphases on student and school results . . . teachers whose students show the most improvement on the test should be the ones rewarded, not the National Board certified teachers since there is no evidence that their students do better academically. The Board has made little effort to link its credentialing process to gains in pupil achievement—the holy grail of educational reform. (pp. 181, 188)

Language like "the holy grail" of educational reform and a "relentless focus on results" is intended to signal to the public and to policy makers that the deregulation agenda is a "get tough" approach based on measurable outcomes that are clear and precise while the professionalization agenda is soft and subjective. Although deregulationists are interested in accountability systems that are more complex than just test scores, these are clearly the linchpin in such systems: "The proper incentives are created by results-based accountability systems in which states independently measure student achievement, issue public report cards on schools, reward successful schools, and intervene in or use sanctions against failing schools" (Thomas B. Fordham Foundation, 1999b, p. 8).

As we have mentioned above, however, spokespersons for the professionalization agenda *do* emphasize outcomes. Their notion of outcomes, however, stands in stark opposition to the test score approach of the deregulationists. From the perspective of professionalization, outcomes are defined primarily in terms of teachers' professional performance, including the alignment of teaching practice with curriculum standards, with teachers' ability to have a positive impact on students' learning, and with teachers' skill at reflecting on and learning from their own work. The notion of professional performance as outcome is a central facet of partnerships among accrediting, licensing, and certification agencies across states and the nation (Wise, 1996). Performance as outcome is also behind the move in some states to require teacher education institutions to seek national certification and/or certification by new state-level professional practices boards.

Professional performance as outcome is particularly clear in "NCATE, INTASC, and National Board Standards," an appendix to *Doing What Matters Most* (1997), NCTAF's second report:

> Until recently, teaching has not had a coherent set of standards created by the profession to guide education, entry into the field, and ongoing practice. In the last ten years, such standards have been created by three bodies working

together to improve teaching . . . These standards are aligned with one another and with new standards for student learning in the disciplines, and they are tied to performance-based assessments of teacher knowledge and skill. The assessments look at evidence of teaching ability in the context of real teaching. (p. 63)

All three sets of standards (NCATE, INTASC, and NBPTS) stress the idea that teachers must have knowledge of subject matter and pedagogy and also be able to teach so that all children can achieve in all the subject areas. Although the latter is consistent with the outcomes focus of the deregulationists, advocates of professionalization also stress the importance of teachers' working with diverse learners, meeting the special learning needs of students, providing positive learning environments, collaborating with others, thinking critically about practice, and participating in learning communities. Defining outcomes as professional performance is very different from the bottom-line approach of the deregulationists who see the production of "well-prepared" teachers as an intermediate outcome at best, not important in and of itself, but only—and only if—it produces student performance outcomes. On the other hand, professionalizationists oppose high-stakes tests as the sole measure of students' learning. They focus instead on relationships between student learning and teacher learning with outcomes defined as teaching performance that supports student learning (Darling-Hammond & McLaughlin, 1999).

As we have said, part of the way both deregulationists and advocates of professionalization construct the accountability warrant is to discredit the approach of the other side. In her debate with Chester Finn, for example, Linda Darling-Hammond (Education Commision of the States, 2000) comments explicitly on why the deregulationist approach—with accountability defined only in terms of student test scores and after the fact (i.e., firing ineffective teachers who don't boost test scores)—is simply untenable, while, from her perspective, the approach of the NCTAF is actually more directly focused on accountability:

> [NCTAF] aims at professional accountability—trying to figure out how to hold the system and teachers accountable for getting and using knowledge about what works. . . . The Fordham approach . . . doesn't have a strategy for dealing with the big misassignment problems that occur across the country. . . There is the idea of just leaving it up to school districts who the best-qualified candidates are . . . The other issue is that poor and minority children get the least qualified teachers in virtually every context.

These excerpts suggest that proponents of professionalization construct accountability as quality of teaching, teacher qualifications, and systematic teacher development in line with high standards for curriculum and pedagogy reached through research and professional consensus. Such well-qualified and developed teachers are to be available to *all* students including those [who] attend the poorest and most neglected schools.

The accountability warrant is highly contested. The battle is over which side gets to call itself the most accountable and the most attentive to responsible outcomes. The rhetorical strategies employed in the debate about accountability—on both sides—are similar to those used in debating the evidence: using the language of outcomes, results, responsibility, and accountability (even though defined differently); suggesting that the other side is really *not* about outcomes but is instead *either* about inputs (the deregulationists' characterization of the professionalization agenda) *or* about outcomes defined so narrowly that they are dysfunctional (the profession's characterization of the deregulation agenda); and, casting the other negatively, *either* as favoring rigidity, lock-step procedures, and standardization (the deregulationists' characterization of professionalization) *or* favoring loopholes and leaving good teaching to chance rather than professional knowledge and qualifications (the profession's characterization of deregulation).

The Political Warrant: Public Good versus Private Good

In this chapter, we use the term *the political warrant* to refer to the ways proponents of competing policies in teacher education justify their positions in terms of service to the citizenry and larger conceptions about the purposes of schools and schooling in modern American society. Once again what is most intriguing here is that proponents of both deregulation and professionalization use some of the same language and, at least on the surface, claim some of the same things. They argue, assert, and endeavor to persuade others that they are in favor of an inclusive agenda intended to promote a civil society and serve the good of the public *writ large*. At the same time, they discredit their opponents because they advocate a private agenda for the good of a privileged few. Of course what the two sides mean by "public good" and "private good" is diametrically different.

The "public good" emphasis of the deregulationists is clear in Chester Finn's comments in the Finn/Darling-Hammond debate:

A better way to get good teachers . . . is in fact to open the doors and welcome lots more people into American public schools through lots more pathways . . . I think what this subject [quality teaching] needs today, and some of you may think this uncharacteristic of me, is humility, open-mindedness, pluralism, and experimentalism. . . . This is a plea for freedom, devolution, pluralism, and diversity, all centered on the concept of school accountability. (Education Commission of the States, 2000)

The political warrant—with its highly evocative language of freedom, pluralism, and open-mindedness—is linked rhetorically to the accountability warrant with its emphasis on the bottom line of students' test scores. The Thomas B. Fordham Foundation's manifesto (1999a) is clear on this point:

> The teaching profession should be deregulated. Entry into it should be widened, and personnel decisions should be decentralized to the school level, the teachers' actual workplace. Freeing up those decisions only makes sense, however, when schools are held accountable for their performance.
>
> For principals (or other education leaders) to manage their personnel in such a way as to shoulder accountability for school results, but not only be free to select from a wide range of candidates, they must also have the flexibility to compensate those they hire according to marketplace conditions (and individual performance), and they must be able to remove those who do not produce satisfactory results. (pp. 8–9)

The argument is basically this: In order to improve teaching and quality of life for the public *writ large*, what schools need more than anything else is the freedom and flexibility to open their doors and thus recruit, hire, and keep all teachers who can "up" students' test scores regardless of their credentials (or lack thereof). From this perspective, the "free market" represents the ultimate "freedom" for American society. This rhetoric of the deregulationists is intended to persuade the public that disciplining teacher education (and schooling in general) according to the forces of the free market is the best way to serve the American citizenry and produce the greatest good for a civil society, including the production of better teachers.

The public discourse of the deregulationists also constructs proponents of the professionalization agenda as members of a private club. In Wilcox's critique of the National Board (Wilcox & Finn, 1999), for example, as in other Fordham Foundation documents, the point is repeatedly made that NCTAF was funded by private foundations. Ballou and Podgursky (2000) consistently characterize the commission as a "private body" with representatives from "various educational interest groups" (including the American Federation of Teachers, the National Education Association, the National Council for Accreditation of Teacher Education, and others), all of whom they paint with the same brush: "regulatory authority empowers these organizations to act in ways that serve private rather than public interests, a significant public policy problem that students of regulation have long recognized" (p. 7).

Another strategy of the deregulationists is to portray proponents of professionalization as motivated by private interests out of sync with the views of "the public." A dramatic example is found in the Public Agenda's *Different Drummers: How Teachers of Teachers View Public Education* (Farkas & Johnson, 1997), a survey of some 900 professors of education. Although the Public Agenda is described as a "nonpartisan public opinion research and citizens' education organization" (Public Agenda, 2001), the preparation and publication of *Different Drummers* was in fact funded by the Fordham Foundation. The report concludes that teacher education professors have a liberal education agenda that de-emphasizes teaching as the direct transmission of knowledge, de-emphasizes the "canon" of Western knowledge, and de-emphasizes memorization and right answers. Instead, the report finds that teacher educators believe that enabling all students to be "lifelong learners" is the "absolutely essential" (p. 9) goal of teacher education.

This vision of education, the Public Agenda report concludes, is fundamentally out of touch with the views of "the public" and of "public schoolteachers" whose priorities are discipline and order, punctuality and politeness, and learning basic factual material within a well-managed environment. In short, the report suggests that teacher educators are "idealists" who pay scant attention to the agenda of "real" parents and "real" teachers. What is perhaps even worse, the report suggests, is that teacher educators stand by their commitment to public education even in the face of their own admitted uncertainty about how to remedy the situation.

Sandra Stotsky, a Fordham Foundation standards reviewer as well as an original signatory of its manifesto, is the author of *Losing Our Language: How Multicultural Classroom Instruction Is Undermining Our Children's Ability to Read, Write, and Reason* (1999), a book with themes similar to those mentioned above. In it, Stotsky asserts that elementary school instructional reading materials have been drastically altered over the last 30 years as part of "an approach to curriculum development called multiculturalism," which, she claims, has "a clear race-based political agenda, one that is anti-civic and anti-Western in its orientation" (p. 7). Stotsky concludes that teacher education is a "progressive" force that is harming the interests of the public and ultimately undermining students' achievement.

Like the deregulationists, proponents of the professionalization agenda also construct *the political warrant* in terms of its contribution to the public good and to all members of the citizenry. The surface similarity of their terms, however, is the only similarity along these lines. The position of professionalization is that every child in America ought to have a well-qualified, fully prepared, and committed teacher. This approach is crystal clear in all of NCTAF's major documents, including *What Matters Most* (National Commission on Teaching and America's Future, 1996):

A caring, competent, and qualified teacher for every child is the most important ingredient in education reform and, we believe, the most frequently over-
looked ... (p. 3)

Tens of thousands of people not educated for these demands have been unable
to make a successful transition into the new economy ... Those who succeed
and those who fail are increasingly divided by their opportunities to learn ...
(p. 11)

In this knowledge-based society, the United States urgently needs to reaffirm a
consensus about the role and purposes of public education in a democracy ...
The challenge extends far beyond preparing students for the world of work. It
includes building an American future that is just and humane as well as productive, that is as socially vibrant and civil in its pluralism as it is competitive
... the central concepts that define America, ideas about justice, tolerance, and
opportunity are being battered. We must reclaim the soul of America. (p. 11)

These excerpts from the NCTAF report illustrate how the political warrant—
with, once again, the highly evocative language of justice, freedom, pluralism, civility—is linked rhetorically to the accountability warrant. NCTAF's
executive summary (1996) carries the often-quoted lines that link the two:

We propose an audacious goal for America's future. Within a decade—by the
year 2006—we will provide every student in America with what should be his
or her educational birthright: access to competent, caring, qualified teaching
in schools organized for success. ... Common sense suffices: American students
are entitled to teachers who know their subjects, understand their students and
what they need, and have developed the skills required to make learning come
alive. (p. vi)

The argument of those who advocate professionalization is basically this: in
order to improve the quality of life and economic opportunity for the public
writ large, what schools need more than anything else is teachers who are
fully qualified. From this perspective, equal access to good teachers with rich
opportunities to learn for all students represents the true path to a citizenry
educated for democracy in American society.

It is also part of the rhetoric of professionalization to point out that the
deregulation agenda is far removed from the best interests of the public in a
democratic society. In the debate with Finn, Darling-Hammond pointed out
more than once that the market approach of the Fordham Foundation did
not address the realities of hiring practices in school systems with large populations of poor and minority children.

Poor and minority children get the least qualified teachers in virtually every context across states and across districts . . . in California . . . high-minority schools are nine or ten times more likely to have unqualified teachers than low-minority schools. High-poverty schools are several times more likely to have unqualified teachers. So when the market operates, it does not always operate to provide all children with the best-qualified teachers. (Commission on Multicultural Education, 1978)

This position is stated more fully in Darling-Hammond's (2000e) summing-up piece about NCTAF several years after the initial report:

Advocates for a free-market approach to teacher hiring and teacher education ignore the extensive evidence demonstrating the significant effects of teacher education and certification on student learning . . . Unfortunately, all the evidence that currently exists suggests that the end result of their arguments will be the continuation of the grossly unequal system we currently operate, in which the profession has few means for infusing knowledge into preparation and training; meanwhile the schools that serve the most advantaged students insist on well-trained teachers, whereas those that serve poor and minority students get what is left over . . . (p. 176)

This statement provides a telling overview of how proponents of professionalization interlock the three warrants to make their case for educational reform.

Penelope Earley, vice president of the American Association for Colleges for Teacher Education (AACTE) and David Labaree, professor of teacher education at Michigan State University, each point out that a market approach fundamentally misunderstands the nature of teachers' work, which they characterize as primarily a public enterprise for the common good, in contrast with market approaches to educational reform, which they suggest are about individual competition for what Labaree (1997) calls "private goods." Earley (2000) points to the contradictions between teachers' work and market-driven reforms:

A market policy lens is based on competition, choice, winners and losers, and finding culprits. Yet teachers must assume that all children can learn, so there cannot be winners and losers. Market policies applied to public education are at odds with collaboration and cooperative approaches to teaching and learning . . . However, under the market approach being used in educational policy and reflected in the accountability sections of the same law, teachers and those who design and administer their preparation programs must have as a primary concern competition, being a winner, not a loser, and certainly not being cast as a culprit. The consequence of these pressures is . . . frustrating efforts for teaching to be truly professional work. (pp. 36–37)

Proponents of professionalization suggest that market approaches to education reform legitimize the dominance of "private goods" and undermine the view that public education is an enterprise for the public good in a democratic society.

The *political warrant* is clearly contested. The contest is about which side gets to claim that it is most committed to the public good and to the foundations of American society. Again, the rhetorical strategies are similar to those used to establish the first two warrants: using the language of public interest, civil society, pluralism, and freedom; suggesting that the other side is really not about the public good, but is instead about its own private agenda; and, casting the other side negatively, *either* favoring regulatory strategies that protect private monopolies (the deregulationists' characterization of the professional agenda) *or* favoring status-quo strategies that protect the already advantaged and deny educational opportunities to poor and minority communities (the professionalists' characterization of deregulation).

CONCLUSION: THE HIGH GROUND OF COMMON SENSE

In the conclusion of this chapter, we want to suggest that taken together, the three warrants we have been describing—*the evidentiary warrant, the accountability warrant*, and *the political warrant*—are being used by advocates of opposing agendas to try to capture "the linguistic high ground" (Madaus & O'Dwyer, 1999) of common sense about reforming teacher education and improving teacher quality. In other words, given the way each has constructed "the problem" of teacher education, each side is attempting to persuade others that the "solution" is obvious and logical, based on simple common sense and clearly intended for the common good of the public and of American society.

It is not at all surprising that this rhetorical strategy is used on both sides of the debate, even though the solutions advocated are diametrically opposed. It is only common sense, after all, to want educational policies based on empirical evidence and facts rather than "ideology" in Napoleon's sense of a closed system of ideas put forward by ideologues. Along these same lines, it is only common sense to want state and federal policies regarding teacher quality and teacher education that require educators to be accountable for students' learning rather than permitting them to be romantic about ideas that don't really work or ignorant of the fact that narrow ideas are actually dysfunctional in the real world. And finally, it is only common sense—not to mention patriotic and true to the American spirit—to want reform policies that are devoted to taking care of the people and of the public good *writ large* in our society, rather than dedicated to the private interests of a certain privileged few.

One problem with the "high ground" of common sense, of course, is that it sometimes obscures the lower ground all around it, not to mention what is underneath the visible surfaces or only partially exposed in the high ground itself. This makes it difficult to sort out rhetorical moves from substantive arguments and political maneuvering from innovative policies and practices. When advocates of two very different agendas each stake out the high ground, it is doubly difficult to remember also that the warrants each side uses to make its case are tied to their positions within institutional structures and connected in complicated ways to larger viewpoints on society and social relationships within society, viewpoints that go well beyond schools and schooling.

It is also not surprising that it is the evidentiary warrant that has most captured the interest of academics and other researchers, some of whom have been perplexed and troubled by the publication and announcement of opposing conclusions about the empirical evidence concerning the impact on teacher quality of various strategies for educational reform. Along these lines, there are a number of current initiatives intended to sort out some of the competing claims about teacher education and teacher quality. These initiatives are important, and we ourselves are involved in some of these. We also believe, however, that it is imperative that the participants in these initiatives sort out and expose the various political and accountability warrants implicit in and related to the evidentiary warrants they seek to establish. This means being explicit about the assumptions and motivations that underlie the establishment of different initiatives in the first place as well as the values and political purposes attached to them.

In conclusion, then, we would caution that the most important open questions about how best to reform teacher education and provide quality teachers for America's schools will not be resolved solely by evaluating the evidentiary warrant. Rather we are arguing here that the accountability warrant and the political warrant must also be considered, as well as how these two are intertwined with one another and with the evidentiary warrant. Earley (2000) has commented on the value-laden nature of educational research and its easy use by policy makers to further their own, sometimes quite different agendas. She suggests that "data and evidence used in the policy process will have several levels of bias: that embedded in the data or evidence itself, bias associated with analysis, and the biases of those in the policy world who use the information" (p. 35). We argued in Chapter 6 that the way "the problem of teacher education" is conceptualized in the first place has a great deal to do with the conclusions that are drawn about the empirical evidence and the policy recommendations that are made.

Thus we close this chapter with the same caution with which we began. Unless underlying ideals, ideologies, and values are debated along with and in relation to "the evidence" about teacher quality and unless we examine the discourse of teacher education policy reform, we will make little progress in understanding the politics of teacher education and the nuances and complexities of the various reform agendas that are currently in competition with one another. We will certainly make little progress in understanding the larger project of teaching and teacher education for social justice. We continue this line of argument and analysis in Chapters 8 and 9.

CHAPTER 8

Multiple Meanings of Multicultural Teacher Education

Despite the fact that most teacher education programs report that they have thoroughly incorporated diversity perspectives and multicultural content into the curriculum, external examinations often prove the contrary (Gollnick, 1995). Likewise, as noted in Chapter 1, synthesizers of the research on teacher education have consistently concluded that despite more than 2 decades of multicultural reform, little has really changed in the ways teachers are prepared in college- and university-based programs (Grant & Secada, 1990; Ladson-Billings, 1995a; Zeichner & Hoeft, 1996). Along related but somewhat different lines, institutional and governmental policies purportedly committed to the same goals of providing all children equal access to highly qualified teachers often turn out to be strikingly different from (and sometimes even diametrically opposed to) one another in implementation and ramifications. Discrepancies like these attest to the fact that there are dramatically different takes on "teacher preparation for diversity," "multicultural teacher education," and "teaching for social justice," as well as major disparities (sometimes even among people considered like-minded) in notions of "equity," "teacher learning," "social change," and "highly qualified" teachers for "all students."

Given the importance of these issues and the multiple meanings noted above, this chapter suggests that we need rich conceptual frameworks to help clarify differing underlying assumptions, sort out discrepancies between theory and practice, and analyze the ways they are entangled with competing political agendas. The premise of the framework proposed in this chapter is that within any research study, any particular teacher preparation program or practice (whether collegiate or otherwise), and any governmental or professional policy that is in some way related to multicultural, diversity, or equity issues in teacher preparation, there are implicit or explicit answers to a series of key questions. These answers are mediated by institutional, community, and regulatory forces, all of which are nested within larger social and historical contexts as well as broader agendas for educational reform. To understand the multiple meanings of multicultural teacher education, then, it is necessary to unpack the answers to these questions, analyze the external forces that influence them, and identify the larger contexts and political agendas to which they are attached.

In this chapter, I propose a conceptual framework designed to accomplish these tasks, building its pieces through a series of interlocking figures and also sketching the "answer" to each of the key questions that is suggested by multicultural teacher education theory. The answers suggested by theory, however, are not necessarily (and sometimes not at all) the ones operating in actual teacher preparation policies, practices, and programs. Thus as I describe the framework, I also illustrate in broad strokes some of the differences between multicultural teacher education theory, on the one hand, and teacher education practice, on the other, as well as some of the range and variation among actual examples of policy and programs.

It is important to note that the conceptual framework offered in this chapter is *not* "a model" for teacher education programs to follow nor a set of assertions about which policies and practices are most desirable, although my views on teacher education are presented in many previous publications and are clearly stated throughout this book. Rather the elements of the framework are intended to provide a conceptual structure for interrogating the *multiple* meanings of multicultural teacher education—first simply to reveal them and suggest their complexities, but then also to chart their origins and implications as they both shape and are shaped by local and larger political, economic, and social contexts.

UNDERSTANDING THE MULTIPLE MEANINGS OF MULTICULTURAL TEACHER EDUCATION: A CONCEPTUAL FRAMEWORK

There are a number of conceptual frameworks already available for understanding general variations in teacher education, including Feiman-Nemser's (1990) "structural and conceptual alternatives," Liston and Zeichner's (1991b) "traditions of practice," and Cochran-Smith and Lytle's (1999) "relationships of knowledge and practice in teacher learning communities." In addition, there are several conceptions and typologies of multicultural education in general that have been applied to teacher education, including Sleeter and Grant's (1987) typology for classifying multicultural education studies, Banks's (1993) typology for approaches to multicultural curricular reform, Lynch's (1986) typology of the ideological orientations to policy options, and Jenks, Lee, and Kanpol's (2001) "versions" of multiculturalism based on differing political agendas. More specific to the preparation of teachers for diversity, Zeichner and Hoeft (1996) have suggested that all teacher education programs take a position on four issues: infusion versus segregation of related issues in the curriculum, culture-specific versus culture-general study and experience, interacting with versus studying about cultures, and whether or not a program itself is a model of what it espouses.

This chapter offers a different kind of conceptual framework, at once narrower and broader than others. The framework is narrower in the sense that it is intended specifically to enhance understanding of multicultural teacher preparation rather than to explore multiculturalism in general or teacher education in general. The framework is broader, however, in that it can be used to examine research and practice as well as policy, and it accounts for forces both internal and external to teacher education per se.

The framework is intended to be useful in examinations of all sorts of research, practices, and policies that in some way are related to or have an impact on the preparation of teachers for a diverse society, regardless of epistemological or methodological paradigms and regardless of whether these policies and practices themselves would be considered "liberal," "conservative," or otherwise. For example, in many states and on a national level, there are major policy disagreements about the advisability of alternate entry routes into teaching, with people on all sides of the debate often linking their arguments to equity issues. The framework described here provides a way to make sense of these differing positions. It helps to uncover the contradictory answers to basic questions about teacher recruitment, knowledge for teaching, and how teachers learn that are implicit in differing policies, practices, and research studies related to multicultural education. The framework also helps to reveal that many of these are connected to two larger agendas for teacher education reform—professionalization and deregulation—that are described in Chapters 6 and 7.

In short, the framework offered here is designed as a conceptual tool for educators, policy makers, researchers, and others to make sense of the many instantiations in research, practice, and policy of what it means to recruit, prepare, support, and assess teachers for a multicultural society. In the remainder of this chapter, each of the following pieces of the framework is presented and discussed with brief examples: eight key questions, three external forces, and the larger historical and social contexts related to preparing teachers for diverse populations.

MULTICULTURAL TEACHER EDUCATION:
EIGHT KEY QUESTIONS

Any instance of research, practice, or policy related to multicultural teacher education implicitly (or explicitly) answers eight key questions: the diversity question, the ideology or social justice question, the knowledge question, the teacher learning question, the practice question, the outcomes question, the recruitment/selection question, and the coherence question. The first seven of these, which are represented in Figure 8.1, are encompassed and surrounded by the eighth, the coherence question.

Figure 8.1. Multicultural Teacher Education: Key Questions

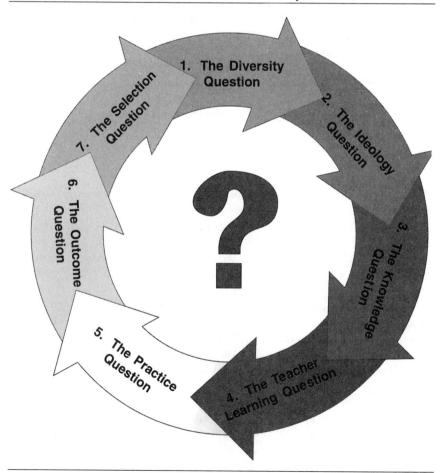

The diversity question asks: How should the increasingly diverse student population in U.S. schools be understood as a challenge or "problem" for teaching and teacher education, and what are the desirable "solutions" to this problem? Many multicultural theorists are critical of traditional teacher education, claiming that historically, the diversity question has been answered from a deficit perspective about the education of poor students, students of color, and students whose first language is not English rather than regarded as a valuable resource to be extended and preserved. Ladson-Billings (1999) calls this the "perversity of diversity" (p. 216) in teacher education where White is normative and diversity is equated with depravity, disadvantage, and deficiency. With the problem of diversity regarded as a deficit, it has also been historically assumed that the "inevitable" solution to the problem is assimilation, wherein differences are expected largely to disappear, and a "one-size-fits-all" approach to curriculum, instruction, and assessment is assumed to equate with equity for all.

Any teacher education policy, program, or research study related in any way to multicultural issues includes a stance or a working answer to the diversity question, which is sometimes made explicit but more often remains implicit. One explicit and early example from policy that challenged traditional views was AACTE's first Commission on Multicultural Education in 1972. This commission explicitly argued that teacher education should regard diversity as a valuable resource to be preserved and extended rather than merely tolerated or expected to "melt away" (Baptiste & Baptiste, 1980). On the other hand, many recent federal policies such as the "No Child Left Behind Act" and Secretary of Education Rod Paige's annual report to Congress on teaching quality (U.S. Department of Education, 2002) use the language of equity and high standards, but implicitly answer the diversity question very differently. Underlying these policies is the assumption that assimilation is the answer to the diversity question and that preparing all K–12 students to enter America's workforce is the ultimate purpose of producing high-quality teachers.

The ideology, or, *social justice question*, is closely related to the diversity question and has to do with ideas, ideals, values, and assumptions. The ideology question asks: What is the purpose of schooling, what is the role of public education in a democratic society, and what historically has been the role of schooling in maintaining or changing the economic and social structure of society? In particular, this set of questions has to do with what images of society in the United States (from meritocratic to hegemonic) as well as what notions of social justice (from everybody learning more and achieving to higher standards to redistributing resources) are assumed in policies, practices, and research. Theorists and researchers who are critical of traditional teacher education have argued that a "seamless ideological web" (Weiner, 2000, p. 381) threads through most traditional programs, taking for granted "the seamless tale of triumph, conquest, and the inevitability of America as a great nation" (Ladson-Billings, 1998, p. 224). Theorists suggest that this ideological web weaves together several key (although faulty) assumptions: American schooling (and indeed most of American life) is meritocratic and thus subtly reinforces the idea that failure for certain individuals or groups is "normal" (Goodwin, 2001); racism and sexism (and other forms of oppression) are old problems that have for the most part been solved (Gay & Howard, 2000); the purpose of schooling is to help all students assimilate into the mainstream and thus produce workers who can help maintain America's dominance in the global economy (Apple, 2001); and high-stakes tests and other standard measures are neutral and objective means of assessing merit.

An answer to the ideology question that challenges traditional practices is sometimes explicitly stated in a multicultural policy or in a position statement about teacher preparation, such as King and Castenell's (2001) position paper on racism and teacher education. They argue that antiracism must be "front and center" (p. 9) in the teacher education reform agenda. Likewise, a few teacher preparation programs, such as the UCLA's Center X urban teacher education program, are rhetorically as well as conceptually and practically committed to social justice at the program and institutional levels (Oakes, Franke, Quartz, & Rogers, 2002). More often, however, the answer to the ideology question that underlies policy, practice, or research in multicultural teacher preparation is unstated, with the continuation of the status quo more or less presumed either by design or by default.

The knowledge question asks: What knowledge, interpretive frameworks, beliefs, and attitudes are necessary to teach diverse populations effectively, particularly knowledge and beliefs about culture and its role in schooling? In multicultural teacher education theory, discussion of the knowledge question is *not* about whether teachers ought to know what is typically included in "the knowledge base" for teacher education. Most of this knowledge, especially deep knowledge of subject matter and of how people learn, is assumed to be essential by multicultural theorists. The theory goes beyond this, however, to ask and answer this question: What do teachers need to know *about* the knowledge base and *what else* do they need to know, including attitudes, knowledge, and beliefs needed to teach diverse groups? Along these lines, a number of multicultural theorists have pointed out that the traditional knowledge base for teacher education concentrates on the Western canon, omits most of what Luis Moll (1992) refers to as cultural "funds of knowledge," and thus limits what can be known (Grant & Wieczorek, 2000; Haberman, 1996; Sleeter, 2001).

In theory, one of the most important aspects of the knowledge question is what it is assumed teachers need to know about culture itself. Many multicultural theorists and some practitioners argue that teachers need to know the meaning of culture, the impact of culture on learning and schooling, the ways in which schools and classrooms function as "cultures," the nature of ethnic, racial, and urban cultures different from their own, and the role of culture in patterns of socialization, interaction, and communication. They also argue that prospective teachers need to learn about their own cultures and think of themselves as cultural beings at the same time they learn positive attitudes toward students with different cultural backgrounds by developing "critical cultural consciousness" (Gay & Howard, 2000) or "sociocultural consciousness" (Villegas & Lucas, 2002).

As noted above, however, multicultural theory and actual programs and policies are often two quite different things. Some recent teacher preparation policies, for example, such as state-level teacher tests or program approval policies in certain states, explicitly eschew the idea that understandings of culture are needed. These imply an answer to the knowledge question that disregards knowledge of culture. In Colorado, for example, the word "diversity" was removed from state guidelines for teacher education program approval, and in Massachusetts, teacher certification tests were designed to cover only communication/literacy skills and subject matter knowledge while omitting attention to educational foundations, pedagogy, culture, and learning theories (see Cochran-Smith, 2002b, for further discussion of these examples). Pinpointing how the knowledge question is being answered can help to sort out some otherwise confusing differences and similarities among policies and practices supposedly intended to provide quality teachers to all students.

The teacher learning question has to do with general assumptions about how, when, and where adults learn to teach. The teacher learning question asks: How do teachers learn to teach diverse populations, and what, in particular, are the pedagogies of teacher preparation (e.g., coursework assignments, readings, field experiences) that make this learning possible? Cochran-Smith and Lytle (1993, 1999) and many others have conceptualized teacher learning in terms of inquiry within learning communities, rather than "training" or other transmission models of teacher education that traditionally prevailed. These theorists suggest that some of the most promising answers to the teacher learning question include conceptualizing inquiry as a way to prepare teachers to be lifelong learners who can work effectively in diverse settings.

In practice, a growing number of teacher education programs are answering the teacher learning question along the lines of inquiry, arranging for prospective teachers to learn in the company of others engaged in learning communities. On the other hand, some alternate routes to certification, such as Teach for America and Troops to Teachers, which received special commendation in Paige's report to Congress (U.S. Department of Education, 2002), answer the teacher learning question differently. They assume that learning to teach is a matter of learning on the job or learning through trial-and-error experience, explicitly rejecting the value of supervised student teaching as well as courses in pedagogy. These contrasts suggest enormous differences in the way the teacher learning question is answered in actual policy and practice.

The practice question is closely related to (and in a certain sense, a subset of) the teacher learning question above. This question asks: What are the competencies and pedagogical skills teachers need to teach diverse populations effectively? This includes teachers' roles as members of school communities, as school leaders, and as theorizers of practice as well as their responsibilities to families and students.

Questions about how experienced teachers work successfully with diverse groups of students are among the most well conceptualized and well researched in the field, with culturally responsive teaching and many related conceptions now well known (see, for example, Gay, 2000; Irvine & Armento, 2001; Ladson-Billings, 1994, 1995b; Villegas, 1991). These theories suggest that prospective teachers need to develop cultural competence to work effectively with parents and families, draw on community and family resources, and know how to learn about the cultures of their students (Gay, 1993; Goodwin, 2000; Zeichner, 1993).

There are many variations in how the practice question is answered in actual policies and practices. Some teacher preparation programs, such as the University of Wisconsin's Teach for Diversity Program (Ladson-Billings, 2001) and teacher education programs at Emory University (Irvine & Armento, 2001), for example, were designed explicitly to prepare teachers to construct culturally responsive curriculum and pedagogy. On the other hand, as noted above, the practices called for in recent government reports on teacher quality explicitly stipulate that teachers do not need knowledge about pedagogy or pedagogical alternatives.

The outcomes question asks: What should the consequences or outcomes of teacher preparation be, and how, by whom, and for what purposes should these outcomes be assessed? In the recent theoretical research on multicultural teacher education, it is clear that high expectations, high standards, and high levels of achievement for all K–12 students ought to be explicit outcomes of teacher preparation. This perspective is in keeping with the general shift in the field away from focusing primarily on curriculum- or program-oriented standards to emphasizing instead performance-based standards and the long-term impacts of teacher preparation on K–12 students' learning. However, there is also a strong theme in the theoretical literature that narrow conceptions of outcomes should be rejected. The fear is that defining achievement *only* as higher test scores perpetuates the cycle of failure for students of color, poor students, and students from linguistic minorities while also having a negative impact on cultural identity.

In practice, there are many variations in how the outcomes question is answered. A few programs are designed to prepare teachers to work against the grain of common practice, to be agents for social change, and to teach to change the world by raising questions about the ways schooling has systematically failed to serve many students from diverse backgrounds (Cochran-Smith, 1991; Ladson-Billings, 1995a; Oakes & Lipton, 1999). The assumption in these programs is that social justice outcomes are important goals in and of themselves because they are fundamental to a democratic society. On the other hand, many current policies and initiatives related to teacher quality—both governmental and those funded by private foundations—answer the outcomes question by focusing almost entirely on K–12 students' increased achievement on standardized tests. Although this kind of outcome is often advocated in the name of equity, the consequences are quite different from those above.

The recruitment/selection question asks: What candidates should be recruited and selected for America's teaching force? For some time now, two theoretical arguments have been made about recruiting teachers to meet the needs of diverse populations. One has to do with the value of diversifying the teaching force—to give children of color the opportunity to work with teachers who are like them in terms of cultural, racial, or linguistic background, to provide role models, and to enrich the learning opportunities of all students. The second has to do with the value of recruiting teachers who are more likely to succeed in high-need areas, particularly in urban centers, because of their previous experiences and/or their maturity.

Some teacher educators work from a very clear answer to the recruitment question. Haberman (1991, 1996), for example, argues that the critical determinant of reform in urban and other high-need areas is the recruitment of teachers who are more likely to succeed—and stay—in urban schools rather than revising curriculum and instruction for young middle-class White women. Haberman's programs in Milwaukee and elsewhere thus jettison the traditional selection criteria associated with a universal approach to teacher preparation and instead recruit older adults who already have the traits and experiences associated with urban success. Recruitment and retention programs sponsored by the Ford Foundation and the Wallace-Reader's Digest Fund answer the recruitment/selection question in a similar way, recruiting from nontraditional pools of minority members and paraprofessionals with the assumption that these teachers enhance the education of all participants and are more likely to stay in the most difficult schools (Clewell & Villegas, 2001; Villegas et al., 1995). Along very different lines, however, teacher recruitment programs such as Teach for America recruit liberal arts graduates as teachers for urban and other understaffed schools regardless of the fact that many of them leave teaching after the required

2 years (Raymond, Fletcher, & Luque, 2001). The assumption here is that experience makes little difference in teaching quality, and subject matter knowledge trumps life experiences and commitments. These contrasting approaches reflect not only different answers to the recruitment/selection question, but also very different goals and notions of equity.

The coherence question, which circles and thus encompasses the seven questions discussed so far, asks: To what degree are the answers to the first seven questions connected to and coherent with one another in particular policies or programs and how are diversity issues positioned in relation to other issues? As with the previous questions, there are stark differences in the answers to the coherence question suggested by theorists, on the one hand, and instantiated in practice, on the other. Multicultural theorists argue that diversity issues must be central, not peripheral, to the rest of the curriculum; mandatory rather than optional for all prospective teachers; and infused throughout courses and fieldwork experiences rather than contained in a single course (Nieto, 2000; Villegas & Lucas, 2001; Zeichner, 1993). These advocates of coherent multicultural teacher preparation caution that when one or two courses (often optional) are added on to the curriculum, many students and faculty assume they are not responsible for the issues, and a multicultural focus is ultimately undermined. At many teacher education institutions across the country, however, what the multiculturalists eschew is exactly what is most likely to be the case. In fact, teacher education program surveys indicate that "diversity" is often relegated to a single optional course (Fuller, 1994), and faculty committed to social justice feel like lone rangers in a larger struggle (Gallavan, 2000). In addition, faculty members within the same teacher preparation programs tend to have quite different ideas about what "multicultural" perspectives on teaching and teacher education are and how important they are, so even when these diversity perspectives are infused through a curriculum (by fiat or otherwise), they may not be coherent.

MULTICULTURAL TEACHER EDUCATION: EXTERNAL FORCES

In addition to taking a stance on each of the key questions discussed above, any particular teacher preparation policy or practice is shaped by several forces that are somewhat more external but heavily influential: institutional capacity and mission, relationships with local communities, and governmental/nongovernmental regulations. Figure 8.2 represents these forces.

Institutional capacity and mission have to do with the nature of the institutions or organizations that sponsor various approaches to teacher preparation and/or various entry routes into the profession in terms of their

Figure 8.2. Multicultural Teacher Education: External Forces

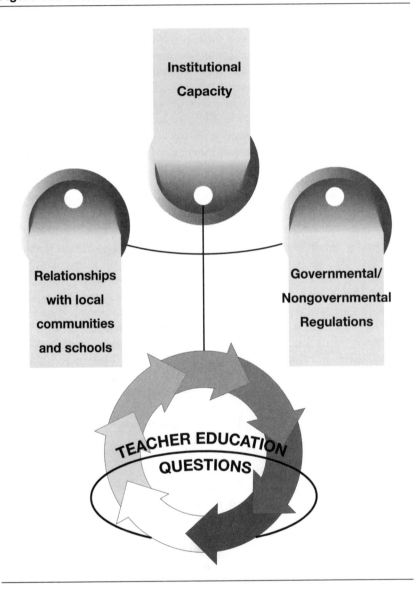

broader missions or purposes. This includes the institutional/organizational factors that either constrain or support attention to issues of culture and diversity, the ways these issues are defined, and the relationships of projects to larger missions and goals. A number of multicultural theorists and practitioners directly discuss the impact of institutional environment on multicultural teacher education (Melnick & Zeichner, 1997; Villegas & Lucas, 2002; Zeichner & Hoeft, 1996), particularly the need to examine programs in light of larger policies on race and affirmative action as well as larger institutional agendas and missions. Specifically with regard to collegiate teacher education, Villegas and Lucas (2002) and Cochran-Smith (2003b) suggest that department, school, and institutional approaches to faculty development are also part of institutional capacity.

Like the other elements of teacher education that have been discussed so far, there are various ways that institutional capacity supports or constrains actual diversity practice. A few collegiate teacher preparation programs committed to preparing teachers for urban schools or for social justice, for example, build into their programs a process of ongoing faculty development intended to enhance the capacity of their institutions to carry out their goals. For example, faculty at the Center for Urban Educators of the School of Education at Long Island University, Brooklyn Campus, use a process of descriptive inquiry to interrogate their own work as urban teacher educators (Traugh, 2002). Similarly faculty at Boston College engaged in a 2-year self-study referred to as "seeking social justice" to examine their mission as a teacher education program (Cochran-Smith et al., 1999). On the other hand, at many institutions, there is enormous inconsistency in faculty members' knowledge, information, and depth of understanding about issues related to culture and teaching underserved populations (Kitano, Lewis, Lynch, & Graves, 1996), and no built-in structures for addressing faculty development along these lines.

Relationships with local communities has to do with the interactions and relationships between a given teacher preparation program or project and local families, neighborhoods, schools, communities, and community agencies, including operating perspectives about the value of community contributions. A number of teacher education reformers have critiqued the lack of connection between teacher preparation programs and their immediate communities, a failing that reflects the universal rather than contextual approach that is dominant in teacher preparation. Increasingly, multicultural advocates argue that community-based experiences are critical but often missing from teacher preparation (Murrell, 2001; Sleeter, 2001; Zeichner & Hoeft, 1996). On the other hand, a few teacher preparation programs, such as the program in the Wai'anae community at the University of Hawaii, are located directly within a local community and intended to prepare students for that community (Au, 2002).

Governmental/nongovernmental regulations refers to the requirements regarding teacher preparation stipulated by the agencies that govern and evaluate programs and approaches, either nonvoluntarily or voluntarily. As Gollnick (1992, 1995) points out, different approaches to multicultural teacher education are related to the differing larger ideological orientations that legitimize particular governmental and nongovernmental regulations at the national and international levels. Governmental and nongovernmental regulations are closely linked to larger social, historical, and economic contexts and to various political agendas for educational reform.

Larger contexts refers to the conditions of schools and the larger social, historical, economic, and political contexts in which all of the above are embedded, including the multiple—sometimes competing—agendas for educational reform that are related to particular political positions. The eight key aspects of teacher education described above, as well as the external forces that influence how these are played out in research, practice, and policy, are embedded within and influenced by these larger contexts and conditions. A number of scholars have examined teacher preparation in relation to larger historical contexts, linking research, practice, and policy in teacher education to broader social and political movements, and to the conditions of schooling (Liston & Zeichner, 1991a; Weiner, 1993, 2000). Along these lines, the future of multicultural teacher education has been analyzed vis-à-vis market-based educational reform agendas that support the privatization of education (Apple, 2001) and at the same time often undermine the goals of social justice (Cochran-Smith, 2001b).

U.S. Secretary of Education Rod Paige's Annual Report on Teaching Quality (U.S. Department of Education, 2002) is the best recent example of policy for teacher preparation that shows the intimate relationships of governmental regulations and the larger political context. The report claims to be based on scientific research evidence about the relationship between teaching quality and teacher qualifications. In fact, however, the report draws heavily on the arguments that have been made by conservative private foundations such as the Fordham Foundation, which favors the deregulation of teacher education, while at the same time ignoring empirical evidence contrary to that position.

CONCLUSION: SORTING OUT THE MULTIPLE MEANINGS

Analyzed together, the key questions, external forces, and the larger contexts within which these are embedded, constitute a framework for understanding the multiple meanings of multicultural teacher preparation policy, research, and practice. The complete framework is represented in Figure 8.3.

Figure 8.3. The Multiple Meanings of Multicultural Teacher Education:
A Conceptual Framework

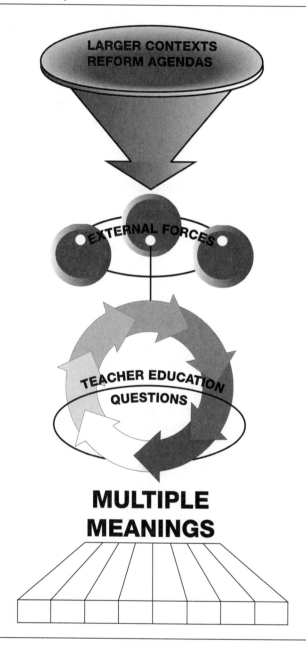

It is reasonable to ask where a framework of this kind gets us as an educational community. What does it help us see besides the tremendous complexity of multicultural teacher education policy, research, and practice, and the enormous difficulties inherent in making genuine change? As I have shown with the brief examples mentioned throughout this chapter, the framework can be used to examine and sort out existing or envisioned teacher preparation approaches by examining the stance taken on the key issues and the way these are influenced by external forces. The framework can also be used as an organizational tool for analyzing the theoretical and/or empirical research related to multicultural teacher education. Further, the framework can provide a structure for analyzing governmental and nongovernmental policies related to the preparation of teachers for culturally and linguistically diverse populations. A significant contribution of the framework, then, is that it lets us see not simply *that* there are deep complexities and multiple meanings involved in understanding multicultural teacher education, but also at what critical junctures the major differences and similarities exist as well as which aspects are emphasized and ignored.

Space limitations prevent an in-depth discussion of applications, but a few preliminary comments are warranted. Applying the framework to multicultural teacher education theory (Cochran-Smith, 2003b) reveals that although there is some divergence in viewpoints, the last decade has seen a fairly consistent call for a "new multicultural teacher education," which would not add on to existing structures and paradigms, but fundamentally reinvent them by challenging traditional ideological underpinnings, placing knowledge about culture and racism front and center, including teaching for social justice as a major outcome, and valuing the cultural knowledge of local communities.

There are certainly some exemplary local programs along these lines, and a number of individual teacher educators strongly committed to preparing teachers for a diverse society. However, the "new multicultural teacher education" envisioned by the theorists does not seem to be in place, at least if we judge by the research about the practice of teacher education. A framework that uncovers differences between theory and practice helps to explain *why* teacher education programs report they have integrated multicultural perspectives and external reviews conclude little has changed.

There are, of course, many teacher preparation programs and practices that have not been researched, so it is difficult to evaluate the actual state of practice. Any program, however, can be examined using the framework to interrogate underlying assumptions and local practices. In a number of places, such as the Department of Early Childhood Education at Georgia State University and the Center for Urban Education at Long Island University, teacher education faculty are using the framework to examine how their programs answer the key teacher education questions and how external forces influence these. When groups of faculty examine how they are implicitly or explicitly answering the key questions, they are able to pinpoint the strengths in their programs and also see inconsistencies, unintended omissions, and where resources are needed. The framework can also be used for assessing planned but not yet implemented initiatives.

Finally, if we use the framework to look across theory and practice, it is possible to see which elements of multicultural teacher education have not been addressed much at all. Using the framework as an organizing structure, for example, our recent comprehensive analysis of the research (Cochran-Smith, Davis, & Fries 2003) indicated that one element that had received very little attention either theoretically or empirically was the outcomes question. In fact, we argued that a missing program of research in multicultural teacher education was a program designed to explore empirically to what extent and in what ways teacher preparation programs, policies, and practices designed to address issues of diversity and equity are related to evidence about quality teaching and students' learning.

At the beginning of the 21st century, there are major debates about teaching quality, teacher preparation, high standards, and high-stakes testing. Carried on in the media, the academy, and local and national policy arenas, these debates are highly visible, often contentious, and enormously consequential for schoolchildren in the United States. Some of these debaters invoke versions of the "all children can learn" or "leaving no child behind" slogan, emphasizing that all schoolchildren need to have basic skills in literacy and numeracy so they can enter the workforce. Others focus on the quality of academic instruction, emphasizing the importance of high standards-based curriculum and instruction aligned with the newest research and understandings in each disciplinary area. Still others talk about redistributing resources and preparing all citizens to participate in civic discourse and contribute to a democratic society.

Despite their differing positions, it is often the case that the debaters use some of the same language and rhetorical strategies, and nearly all of them claim to be advocates of educational equity. This confirms the fact that the meanings associated with education, particularly with "multicultural," "social justice," or "equity" education are multiple and contested. The framework presented in this chapter is designed to interrogate these multiple meanings, probing beneath similarities in language in order to get at fundamentally different answers to critical questions and explore how these both shape and are shaped by larger contexts. At the end of the first few years of the 21st century, interrogating the multiple meanings of multicultural teacher education is a challenge we cannot afford *not* to address.

CHAPTER 9

Teacher Education at the Crossroads: A Call to Action

The final chapter in this book is both an epilogue and a call to action. It makes one essential point that builds on the previous chapters and locates the project of teacher education for social justice squarely in the first few years of the 21st century. These years are dominated by a relentless focus on high-stakes tests, a growing underclass that many fear will be permanent, and a convergence of factors that places the least well-qualified teachers in schools with students in the greatest peril. These years *cannot* be adequately characterized as a challenging time or a complicated context for the project of teaching and teacher education for social justice. The situation is far more serious. Teacher education for social justice—as an idea and a reality—stands at a crossroads where there are multiple paths. If the project is to move forward, we will need more than the efforts of individual teacher educators who urge prospective teachers and colleagues to rethink beliefs and attitudes about difference, privilege, diversity, and culture. We will need more than a handful of exceptional programs around the country in which prospective teachers are genuinely prepared for—and then supported, so they stay—in high-need schools and communities where they challenge inequities at the same time that they provide rich learning opportunities for all students. And we will need more than provocative conference sessions and inspiring books that explore the complex issues related to social justice, equity, and diversity in teacher education.

I am in no way suggesting that we do *not* need these individual and collaborative efforts to build teacher education programs and partnerships for social justice and to study these efforts from a variety of incisive perspectives. We surely do. But we also need many more school- and university-based educators willing to take a stand as public intellectuals in order to expose the far-reaching consequences of the prevailing political agenda and challenge the co-optation of the language of "equity," "high standards," "pluralism," and "leaving no child behind" by those who ignore the brutal inequities of opportunity, resources, and possibility in our society. And we need educators and activists who see it as part of the job of teaching and teacher education to join with community members and other advocates to demand that learning not be reduced to test scores, teaching not be reduced to scripted lessons, and teacher preparation not be reduced to letting smart people or unemployed professionals from other fields learn on the job. In short, it is my argument that in order for the larger project to move forward, we must conceptualize *and act on* teacher education as both a learning problem and a political problem.

Three specific actions are essential: (1) public critique from a social justice perspective of prevailing policies and agendas related to teacher quality, recruitment, preparation, and certification; (2) development of a diversified and rigorous program of empirical research regarding teacher education that rationalizes and operationalizes social justice as an outcome; and (3) identification and analysis of exemplary and innovative programs, projects, partnerships, and modes of inquiry and assessment that can serve as the building blocks for other teacher preparation efforts with the goal of social justice. Each of these actions is discussed below. However, because it is currently the most imperative, the first of these actions—critique of prevailing policies and agendas—is elaborated in the most detail.

PRODUCING "HIGHLY QUALIFIED TEACHERS": THE NEED FOR PUBLIC POLICY CRITIQUE

In the early years of the 21st century, it appears—on the surface, at least—that questions about the importance of teaching quality have been settled. Despite dramatically different assumptions about the purposes of schooling, the nature of teaching as an enterprise, and appropriate ways to measure teaching effectiveness, there is broad consensus that teaching quality matters in learning and school effectiveness. Indeed, the American public, the education profession, researchers, legal advocates, and policy makers of all stripes seem to agree that teachers make a significant difference in students' learning, their achievement, and their life chances (Cochran-Smith, 2003a).

The *No Child Left Behind Act of 2001* (NCLB) (Pub. Law 107–110) cemented this conclusion into law with its guarantee that all schoolchildren must have "highly qualified teachers" who receive "high-quality professional development." Highly qualified teachers were defined as those with full state certification (including through alternate routes) or passing scores on state teacher exams. High-quality professional development was defined as that which improves subject matter knowledge, aligns with standards, and improves instructional strategies drawing on "scientifically based research." The first annual report to Congress on "Meeting the Highly Qualified Teacher Challenge" (U.S. Department of Education, 2002) by the Secretary of Education, Rod Paige, clarified the meaning of NCLB for teacher education and reported on states' performance. This report, taken together with federal laws, public statements, and the stated funding priorities of the current administration regarding teacher education constitute what I refer to here as the agenda to produce "highly qualified teachers." The secretary's report argues that states' academic standards for teachers are low while the barriers that keep out qualified prospective teachers who have not completed collegiate teacher preparation are high. The report claims that alternate route programs are the "model" policy option, which will simultaneously solve the teacher quality and teacher supply problems. The report is crystal clear about what does and does not lead to high-quality teaching: "In summary, we have found that rigorous research indicates that verbal ability and content knowledge are the most important attributes of highly qualified teachers. In addition, there is little evidence that education school coursework leads to improved student achievement" (p. 19).

It is not an exaggeration to say that the agenda to produce "highly qualified teachers" is hostile to university-based teacher preparation and to schools of education. In addition, it is important to point out that its conclusions differ markedly from many of the major syntheses of research on teacher preparation, including one by Wilson, Floden, and Ferrini-Mundy (2001), which was funded by the U.S. Department of Education; and one by Allen (2003), sponsored by the Education Commission of the States and intended to guide state policy makers. In fact, a number of critiques have soundly refuted the secretary's conclusions on empirical and other grounds (e.g., Cochran-Smith, 2002a; Darling-Hammond & Youngs, 2002; Heap, 2002). The most thorough of the empirical critiques, written by Darling-Hammond and Youngs (2002), points out that the report fails to meet its own standards for the use of scientific research in formulating public policy, instead making unsupported claims with almost no citations to scientific studies. Not surprisingly, Darling-Hammond and Youngs reach conclusions that are diametrically opposed to those in the secretary's report: Paige's recommendations are *not* based on scientific evidence, there *is* evidence that teacher preparation contributes at least as much to effectiveness and retention as do verbal ability and content knowledge, and alternate entry paths that *do not* include the core aspects of teacher preparation lead to ineffective teachers who feel underprepared and leave teaching at high rates.

In addition to accounting for empirical critiques of the agenda to produce "highly qualified teachers," it is also important to critique its conceptualizations of teaching, learning, and the purposes of education.

This agenda is based on the following assumptions: teacher preparation is college education, quality teaching is a college-educated person with verbal ability transmitting knowledge, pupil learning is receiving information and demonstrating it on a standardized test, and a good educational system is a set of structural arrangements that make the former effective and cost-efficient.

Each of the above assumptions is severely impoverished. There is certainly evidence that teachers' content knowledge and verbal ability account for some of the variance in students' achievement (Allen, 2003; Gitomer & Latham, 2000; Wilson, Floden, & Ferrini-Mundy, 2001). However, the agenda to produce "highly qualified teachers" is based on a narrow and reductionist view of teaching and learning in the first place. Many years of research indicate that teaching involves much more than transmitting information, and learning to teach involves much more than accumulating subject matter information and then picking up techniques on the job. In contrast, the conceptions of teaching and learning to teach that underlie the social justice agenda include learning to represent complex knowledge in accessible and culturally responsive ways, learning to ask good questions, use diversified forms of assessment to shape curriculum and instruction, develop relationships with students that support and sustain learning, work with—not against—parents and community members, collaborate with other professionals, interpret multiple data sources in support of pupils' learning, maintain high academic standards for students of all abilities and backgrounds, engage in classroom inquiry in the service of pupil and teacher learning, and join with others in larger movements for educational and social equity. Likewise, the view of learning underlying the social justice agenda is not a matter simply of receiving information. The science of learning has shown that learning is a process of developing usable knowledge (not just isolated facts) by building on previous knowledge and experience, understanding, and organizing information in a conceptual framework, and monitoring progress toward learning goals (National Research Council, 2000). From a social justice perspective, a pupil's learning also involves developing critical habits of mind, understanding and sorting out multiple perspectives, and learning to participate in and contribute to a democratic society by developing both the skill and the inclination for civic engagement.

From a social justice perspective, the purpose of education is understood not simply as constructing a system where pupils' test scores and wise monetary investments are the bottom lines. Rather education is also understood to be about preparing students to engage in satisfying work, function as lifelong learners who can cope with the challenges of a rapidly changing global society, recognize inequities in their everyday contexts, and join with others to challenge them.

The now prevalent and very powerful agenda to produce "highly qualified teachers" draws heavily on the language and rhetoric of high standards
and accountability. It also claims, however, that it will increase diversity and
freedom in the schools, will leave no child without a well-qualified teacher,
and thus will provide for the public good (see Chapter 7). It is critical to
acknowledge, however, that although the agenda to produce "highly qualified teachers" is rhetorically persuasive, it actually co-opts language long used
by advocates for children's rights and for the equitable distribution of resources. Despite some of its language, the agenda to produce "highly qualified teachers" is fundamentally anathematic to the larger project of teaching
and teacher education for social justice. One example helps to make this point.
The report by the Secretary of Education mentioned above rejects the use of
"waivers" and other emergency or temporary suspensions of normal certification requirements that allow unqualified people to take teaching positions.
To its credit, the report notes that "high-poverty school districts [are] more
likely to employ teachers on waivers than more affluent districts" (U.S.
Department of Education, 2002, p. 34). However, the report and the larger
agenda to produce "highly qualified teachers" utterly fail to frame the disparities between the qualifications of teachers in high- and low-poverty
schools as a social justice issue. Instead, based on the new definition of "highly
qualified teachers" enacted into law with NCLB, this agenda instantaneously
transforms many unqualified teachers into qualified ones. In other words,
many teachers who were "unqualified" because of no experience in the
classroom, no knowledge of pedagogy (not to mention culturally responsive pedagogy), no study of the many ways people learn and develop, and
no experience working in communities with people different from themselves were—with the stroke of the pen that institutionalized the new federal definition—transformed into "highly qualified teachers."

It is not surprising that these newly minted "highly qualified teachers"
who have no pedagogical, cultural, or community preparation tend to be hired
in high-poverty, urban, and minority schools and school districts (American
Civil Liberties Union, 2000; Darling-Hammond & Sclan, 1996; Oakes,
Franke, Quartz, & Rogers, 2002). This hiring pattern reinforces and exac-
erbates the status quo and reveals that the agenda to produce "highly qualified teachers" is based in part on sleight of hand (and sleight of language)
regarding issues of equity and educational opportunity. At best, this agenda
obfuscates the acute and chronic problem of unequal distribution of resources
to high-poverty schools. At worst, it defines the problem away, reducing the
disparities in teacher qualifications between low- and high-poverty schools
by half simply by changing a definition.

This and many other examples from current policy and from public statements make it clear that the agenda to produce "highly qualified teachers"

works from the perspective that teacher preparation is a training/testing problem. This view relies on a set of deceptively simple, yet powerful and mutually dependent assumptions: teaching is a technical activity, knowledge is static, good practice is universal, being prepared to teach is knowing subject matter, and pupil learning is equal to higher scores on high-stakes tests. In contrast, the social justice agenda works from the perspective, argued throughout this book, that teacher preparation is a learning problem. Here it is assumed that being prepared to teach is having strong subject matter knowledge but also having professional and pedagogical knowledge and being committed to challenging inequities and working for social change. Teaching is regarded as an intellectual activity, knowledge is regarded as constructed and fluid, good practice is contextual, and pupil learning includes academic achievement as well as developing critical habits of mind and preparation for civic engagement.

Further, the agenda to produce "highly qualified teachers" conceptualizes teacher education as a policy problem, assuming that teacher quality issues can be resolved by large-scale policies that eliminate teacher preparation as an entry requirement and let market forces determine teacher placement and retention. Again, this view relies on several interlocking—and problematic—assumptions: equity is holding all pupils to the same standards regardless of resources and learning opportunities; the goal is to supply college graduates willing to teach for a time (with the market deciding which students get "excellent" and which get "good enough" teachers); policies should be based solely on empirical evidence, which provides conclusive guidelines, and/or on efficiency rather than on ideology or values and need not consider local accountability contexts; and the goal of education *writ large* is to produce workers to keep the U. S. economy globally competitive. The assumptions underlying the social justice agenda stand in stark contrast: equity is the redistribution of resources, including learning opportunities and fully prepared teachers; the goal of teacher preparation is to provide fully prepared teachers for all students regardless of market forces; the conclusions of empirical research are debatable, and because it is impossible to develop policies uninfluenced by values and ideologies or by local accountability contexts, these aspects must be critically scrutinized; and the goal of education *writ large* is to prepare all people for meaningful work and for free and equal civic participation in a democratic society.

It is the former agenda—"producing highly qualified teachers"—and not the latter that is being enacted in local schools and school districts all over the country. Increasingly, on-the-job in-service sessions instruct teachers in how to use closely prescribed lesson formats and highly scripted materials that have (supposedly) been certified as universally effective best practice through scientifically based research. Alternate routes to teacher certification in all but a few states are drastically streamlining or bypassing altogether university-based coursework and professionally supervised community-based and school-based fieldwork experiences. In short, federal control of much of the funding for "high-quality" professional development for teachers along with federally mandated high-stakes tests with adequate yearly progress requirements for pupils and schools have created a system that feeds off itself and, at the same time, either co-opts or discounts all agendas that do not also feed that system.

It will take powerful opposing forces to break into and out of this cycle, including excoriating public critiques. These must demonstrate that competing agendas for teacher education have dramatically different outcomes for educational access, distribution of resources, and the life chances of school-children who are differently positioned from one another in terms of socio-economic status, culture, language background, and race. These critiques must demonstrate persuasively that in the final analysis, the agenda to produce "highly qualified teachers" will leave behind the same children who have long been left behind by the educational system.

STRENGTHENING THE SOCIAL JUSTICE RESEARCH BASE IN TEACHER EDUCATION

The second call to action in support of the larger project of teacher education for social justice is to strengthen its research base. As noted above, policy makers in the early years of the 21st century have become intensely interested in whether or not there is a research basis justifying various educational policies and practices in terms of their bottom-line, value-added impact on teaching quality and pupil achievement. Although the report of the Secretary of Education makes sweeping conclusions about what the research says, many of the major syntheses suggest that the research is inconclusive, with a great need for rigorous research about the impact of various policy options on pupils' achievement (Allen, 2003; Lauer, 2001; Wilson et al., 2001).

Debates about the research base for teacher education broadly construed have important implications for the larger project of teacher education for social justice. Over the last 15 years or so, a relatively large body of theory, policy analysis, and empirical study has been generated about issues related to culturally responsive teaching, multicultural teacher education, teacher education for diversity, prospective teachers' beliefs and attitudes, teacher recruitment and retention, urban teacher preparation, and so on. Despite the contributions of this work, however, teacher education for social justice needs to develop much further as an area of scholarly inquiry. We need more studies linking theory and practice. Particularly, we need to know what is happening to notions of multiculturalism, diversity, equity, and social justice in the face of intense emphasis on standards, high-stakes testing, and narrow views of what counts as research. We need to know more about how teacher educators themselves theorize the practice of teacher education for social justice, including the range and variation across and among teacher educators. We also need to know more about the impact of competing agendas for teacher education reform on the development and revision of programs. For example, in light of simultaneous efforts to professionalize and deregulate teacher education, what is happening to programs, practices, and policies that are intended to promote social justice?

One of the most important needs in strengthening the teacher education for social justice research base is research about the impacts of teacher preparation, entry into teaching, and the conditions that support and constrain teacher effectiveness. Only a tiny portion of the research related to the social justice agenda has examined the effects of teacher preparation, or what prospective teachers actually do with what they learn in teacher preparation courses, fieldwork experiences, and community projects. Only a small number of studies have followed prospective teachers into K–12 schools and classrooms to study systematically the pedagogies they develop, the curricula they construct, the beliefs and attitudes that shape their decisions, the actions they take to challenge inequities or serve as advocates for students, or the ways they interact with parents, families, and communities. Even fewer studies have followed teacher candidates after they complete teacher preparation programs and begin work as full-fledged teachers in K–12 schools. Almost no research has examined the impact of teacher preparation committed to social justice on K–12 students' learning.

The call in this chapter for research that addresses the outcomes and effectiveness of teacher preparation for social justice is not new. Grant and Secada (1990) concluded nearly 15 years ago that we need more information about outcomes, as has every major synthesis of research on teacher education and diversity since 1990. One reason we do not yet have this research base is certainly the historical marginalization and underfunding of research related to diversity and education in general. Another is that the heavy emphasis over the last 15 years on teacher knowledge, teacher thinking, and more recently on teacher learning in communities has overshadowed other topics. But a third reason this research has not yet developed is that it is difficult to do, and particularly difficult to do well. If there is one thing that the research on diversity and teaching has made clear, it is the importance of social and cultural contexts and of local meanings in all aspects of school and schooling. In contrast, many studies that focus on outcomes are intended, almost by definition, to produce evidence of the impact of isolatable variables that are generalizable across variations in contexts. Along these lines, Weiner (2000) has argued that a sign of progress in research on urban teaching and teacher preparation was the gradual move in the 1990s away from reductionist studies of single factors in isolation from one another.

A promising way to develop the missing program of research in teacher education for social justice is through studies that map forward from teacher preparation to pupils' outcomes as well as those that map backward from successful outcomes for pupils to quality and kind of teacher preparation. Studies that map forward from initial teacher preparation would feature longitudinal designs that follow up on the experiences, successes, as well as the problems and failures of new teachers who have been prepared in various ways as they embark (or not) on teaching careers and then track teachers' performance in diverse settings over some part of the professional life span. We need to know a great deal more about the conditions and contexts that sustain teachers' efforts to work for social justice as well as the conditions that constrain them. Studies that map backward from successful teaching in diverse settings would begin with successful classroom practice and trace the connections back to teacher learning experiences and varying modes of teacher preparation (Sleeter, 2001).

The most critical aspect of research that maps either forward or backward is the definition of "good teaching" or "successful practice" or "pupil learning" that guides the research. On the one hand, definitions of successful teaching that rely only on teachers' presumed impact on K–12 students' scores on high-stakes tests will simply exacerbate the historical problems for students of color when competence is conceptualized in this narrow way and will reify the notion that learning equals test scores. This kind of approach is certainly not in keeping with the fundamental tenets of teacher education for social justice. On the other hand, definitions of teaching success that rely on principals' or colleagues' evaluations of teachers and/or on parents' and community nominations while ignoring the outcomes of high-stakes assessments will fail to account for the current political context and risk being dismissed by most of the major power brokers in education. Further, neither of these considers as part of teaching "success" the development of classroom pedagogy that is aligned with curriculum and teaching standards in the various subject matter areas and/or with what we know about culturally responsive pedagogy. These need to be included in notions of "successful teaching." Finally, none of the conceptualizations of outcomes mentioned so far directly includes social activism and/or participation in larger community and professional movements for social change. These are also vital to the larger project of teaching and teacher education for social justice. The major challenge in establishing the missing program of research in support of the social justice agenda is to develop rich and sensitive outcomes measures that take all of these aspects of "successful teaching" for social justice into account and then map forward from, or backward to, teacher preparation.

BUILDING ON WHAT WE HAVE

As detailed above, there are enormous challenges to both the idea and practice of teacher education for social justice in the early years of the 21st century. Even in the face of these considerable challenges, however, there have been promising developments over the last 2 decades, including innovative teacher preparation programs, teacher educators engaged in reinventing and systematically studying their own practice, national initiatives to make assessment an internal practice in teacher education, local and regional studies of variations in programs and practices, and development of a solid body of theory related to teacher education for social justice. My third and final call for action in this chapter is that we need to build on these promising developments in order to move the social justice agenda forward.

In some of the most promising developments in teacher education programs, the explicit thrust of the work is related to social justice. For example, there have been local pockets of dramatic change in teacher education with a number of innovative programs designed specifically to prepare teachers for urban schools (e.g., Cochran-Smith, 1995a; Haberman & Post, 1998; Irvine & Armento, 2001; Ladson-Billings, 1999; Oakes et al., 2002; Quartz & TEP Research Group, 2003) and/or for particular populations traditionally not well served by the schools (e.g., Au, 2002). As descriptions and analyses of these programs are disseminated, they serve as building blocks for other innovative efforts. In addition, there is growing evidence that community-based experiences are a particularly promising practice in teacher education, particularly in preparing prospective teachers to work with school and community populations that are different from their own backgrounds (e.g., Irvine, 2001; Seidl & Friend, 2002; Zeichner & Melnick, 1996). Community experiences seem to have an impact on the complexity of prospective teachers' views of culture, their cultural understandings, their appreciation of family resources, and their ability to contextualize the concepts they are learning in courses. The quality and extent of prospective teachers' learning, however, seems to depend on the quality and extent of reflection and reading that are connected to the community experience, the duration and quality of the experience itself, and the facilitation and support that prospective teachers receive as they make sense of the experiences. Like preparation programs aimed at social justice, exemplary community-based experiences have the potential to serve as building blocks in the social justice agenda.

Another promising trend is that a growing number of teacher educators are involved in reinventing teacher education courses and programs, working to challenge what is taken for granted, and questioning traditional notions of authority and position (Cochran-Smith, 2000; Fecho, 2000; Martin & Van Gunten, 2002; Obidah, 2000). Increasingly, teacher educators are engaged in teacher research, action research, narrative research, self-study, and other forms of practitioner inquiry wherein they take their own professional programs and courses as sites for self-critical reflection and for systematic study of issues related to identity, access, power, and learning. This trend suggests that many teacher educators are not satisfied with the status quo; rather they take their work seriously, self-consciously posing questions and investigating them by gathering and analyzing the data of practice. The focus of much of this work is on what teacher educators and prospective teachers actually learn from courses and program experiences designed to enhance multicultural understandings—how their knowledge, attitudes, and beliefs may change, how they interact with program content, and what kinds of learning opportunities are provided by particular teacher education pedagogies. Along these lines, it appears that opportunities for educators to reflect on their own identities and raise questions within the context of larger communities of learners may be particularly rich sites for the continuing education of teacher educators themselves.

Building on the increasing number of teacher educators engaged in critical studies of their own practice also has the potential to help strengthen the research base regarding teacher education for social justice, as called for above. Although they were not discussing research related to social justice, Wilson, Floden, and Ferrini-Mundy (2001) suggested a number of "strategic investments" in research initiatives in the conclusion of their report on the research base for teacher preparation, including linking individual studies into multi-site research programs. Particularly given the number of teacher educators engaged in inquiry about their own practice and seemingly committed to the tenets of teacher education for social justice, there are very promising possibilities here. Multi-site research programs in this area could capitalize on the natural laboratory of variations in program types, structures, and arrangements and perhaps lead to both findings generalizable beyond the individual site and programs that benefited from cross-pollination and external critique from other practitioners. With appropriate funding, there is great potential in the area of multisite practitioner inquiry about various programs and projects.

Along related lines, there are also some national initiatives such as Teachers for a New Era, funded primarily by the Carnegie Corporation of New York, and Project Delta, sponsored by the Carnegie Foundation for the Advancement of teaching, which are intended to make teacher preparation more internally research-driven and assessment based. It is nothing short of a culture shift to transform teacher education into an enterprise that is grounded in research, that revolves around continuous assessment of learning, and that makes decisions driven by evidence. To forward the social justice agenda, we can build on these and other initiatives if we can ensure that social justice outcomes are built into definitions of the impact of teacher education from the start. Ultimately the success of initiatives like these will depend upon sustainability and dissemination. But we must also insist that as teacher education becomes more driven by internal assessments, we must keep social justice on the agenda and be sure there is evidence that teacher preparation ultimately makes a difference in children's lives.

Another emergent trend in teacher education that we may build on to forward the social justice agenda are regional and local studies of naturally occurring variations in teacher preparation programs, elements, and pathways (e.g., different models of preparation at the same universities, teacher candidates with and without preparation aligned with state standards, different program structures across institutions). These are intended to generate evidence to guide program design decisions but also inform larger policy by connecting teacher preparation with learning and teaching outcomes by examining links among elements and aspects of preparation, on the one hand, and teachers' learning, professional practice, and K–12 students' learning, on the other. Again, to strengthen this trend and forward the social justice agenda, we must be sure that the impacts studied include social justice outcomes: for pupils, rich learning opportunities regardless of background, development of critical thinking and inquiry skills, and preparation for satisfying work and civic engagement; and for teachers, subject matter as well as pedagogical and professional knowledge, development of inquiry skills for learning across the professional life span, and preparation to join with others in larger social movements to challenge inequities and create a more just society.

A final current strength to build on in the larger project of teacher education for social justice is the development over the past decade of a rich and sophisticated body of theoretical and conceptual scholarship related to critical multiculturalism in teacher education. Although there is some divergence in viewpoints, this work has been fairly consistent. I referred to this body of work in Chapter 1 as a "new multicultural teacher education," which does not add on to or supplement existing structures and paradigms in teacher education, but rather fundamentally reinvents them. Radical new ways to theorize the preparation of teachers for a diverse society are intended to interrupt conventional teacher education discourse and tradition which, although not able to meet the challenges of the 21st century, have become ingrained and institutionalized (Gay & Howard, 2000; Ladson-Billings,

1999). Although there is a great divide between theory and practice, the new multicultural teacher education conceptualized in theory provides a framework and a vision for multicultural teacher education as it is carried out in the real world of institutional constraints and political exigencies.

BEYOND THE CROSSROADS

Now more than ever, teacher education for social justice stands at a crossroads. As I have argued throughout this chapter, the early years of the 21st century are dominated by an acutely conservative political climate that has made the development (and endurance) of the project of teacher education for social justice both less likely and more essential than ever before. To move beyond the crossroads—and to keep on walking the road, in the sense in which I have used the metaphor throughout this book—we must acknowledge and build on promising developments in teacher education such as those noted above. But we must also pay much more attention to the current political situation and to the shortcomings of our own previous research and program efforts. Those of us who are committed to teacher education for social justice must launch a research agenda that focuses on the impacts and outcomes of teacher preparation for K–12 students' learning as well as for prospective and experienced teachers' learning. This requires the development of rigorous and multiple measures of both students' and teachers' learning that include scores on high-stakes tests, but which also includes the acquisition of knowledge needed to live and work in a multicultural society, participate in a democracy, and engage in critical discourse about competing ideas.

Those who are committed to multicultural teacher education need to make a compelling argument for the necessity of a social justice agenda in a democratic and increasingly diverse society. Our voices need to be heard much more loudly and articulately in the policy-making arenas that are dominated by conservative, well-funded, and well-organized forces, arenas that have traditionally been avoided by university-based educators who prefer the supposedly more rational and less political discourse of academic debate and scholarship. Finally, we need to conjoin efforts in all our individual spheres of influence, whether these are public, professional, or political. We need to be part of larger movements for social change and demonstrate to others that social justice itself is a valid outcome and an essential purpose of teacher preparation that runs much deeper than traditional measures of achievement but that in the final analysis, deeply undergirds the future of our society.

References

Allen, M. (2003). *Eight questions on teacher preparation: What does the research say?* Denver: Education Commission of the States.

American Association of Colleges for Teacher Education. (1997). *Selected data from the 1995 AACTE/NCTE joint data collection system*, Washington, DC: Author.

American Association of Colleges for Teacher Education. (1999). *Teacher education pipeline IV: Schools, colleges, and departments of education enrollments by race, ethnicity, and gender.* Washington, DC: Author.

American Civil Liberties Union [ACLU]. (2000). *ACSL-Southern California Docket: Williams et al. v. State of California et al.* Available: www.aclu-sc.org/litigation/docket/williams. Retrieved October 2001.

Anyon, J. (1994). Teacher development and reform in an inner-city school. *Teachers College Record, 96*(1), 14–34.

Apple, M. (1986). *Teachers and texts: A political economy of class and gender relations in education.* New York: Routledge and Kegan Paul.

Apple, M. (1996). *Cultural politics in education.* New York: Teachers College Press.

Apple, M. (2000). Can critical pedagogies interrupt rightist policies? *Educational Theory, 50*(2), 229–254.

Apple, M. (2001). Markets, standards, teaching, and teacher education. *Journal of Teacher Education, 52*(3), 182–195.

Aronowitz, S., & Giroux, H. (1985). *Education under siege.* New York: New World Foundation.

Au, K. (2002). Communities of practice: Engagement, imagination, and alignment in research on teacher education. *Journal of Teacher Education, 53*(3), 222–227.

Au, K., & Kawakami, A. (1994). Cultural congruence in instruction. In E. Hollins, J. King, & W. Hayman (Eds.), *Teaching diverse populations: Formulating a knowledge base* (pp. 5–24). Albany: State University of New York Press.

Ball, D. (1996). Teacher learning and mathematics reform: What we think we know and what we need to learn. *Phi Delta Kappan, 77*(7), 500–508.

Ball, D. (2000). Bridging practices: Intertwining content and pedagogy in teaching and learning to teach. *Journal of Teacher Education, 51*(3), 241–247.

Ball, D., & Cohen, D. (1999). Developing practice, developing practitioners: Toward a practice-based theory of professional education. In L. Darling-Hammond & G. Sykes (Eds.), *Teaching as the learning profession: Handbook of policy and practice* (pp. 3–32). San Francisco: Jossey-Bass.

Ballenger, C. (1992). Because you like us: The language of control. *Harvard Educational Review, 62*(2), 199–208.

Ballou, D., & Podgursky, M. (1997). Reforming teacher training and recruitment. *Government Union Review, 14*(4), 1–53.

Ballou, D., & Podgursky, M. (1999). Teacher training and licensure: A layman's guide. In M. Kanstoroom & C. Finn (Eds.), *Better teachers, better schools* (pp. 31–82). Washington, DC: The Thomas Fordham Foundation.

Ballou, D., & Podgursky, M. (2000). Reforming teacher preparation and licensing: What is the evidence? *Teachers College Record, 102*(1), 5–27.

Banks, J. (1993). Multicultural education: Characteristics and goals. In J. Banks & C. Banks (Eds.), *Multicultural education: Issues and perspectives* (2nd ed., pp. 3–28). Boston: Allyn & Bacon.

Banks, J. (1995). Multicultural education: Historical development, dimensions, and practice. In J. Banks & C. Banks (Eds.), *Handbook of research on multicultural education* (pp. 3–24). New York: Macmillan.

Banks, J. (2000). Citizenship education and diversity: Implications for teacher education. *Journal of Teacher Education, 52*(1), 5–16.

Baptiste, H., & Baptiste, M. (1980). Competencies toward multiculturalism. In H. Baptiste, M. Baptiste, & D. Gollnick (Eds.), *Multicultural teacher education: Preparing teacher educators to provide educational equity* (Vol. 1). Washington, DC: American Association of Colleges for Teacher Education.

Barnes, H. (1989). Structuring knowledge for beginning teaching. In M. Reynolds (Ed.), *Knowledge base for the beginning teacher* (pp. 13–22). New York: Pergamon Press.

Beckum, L. C. (1992). Diversity assessment: Always factoring in the reform equation. In M. Dilworth (Ed.), *Diversity in teacher education*. San Francisco: Jossey-Bass.

Bell, B., Gaventa, J., & Peters, J. (Eds.). (1990). *We make the road by walking: Conversations on education and social change, Myles Horton and Paulo Freire*. Philadelphia: Temple University Press.

Berlak, A., & Berlak, H. (1981). *Dilemmas of schooling: Teaching and social change*. London: Methuen.

Berthoff, A. (1987). The teacher as Researcher. In D. Goswami & P. R. Stillman (Eds.), *Reclaiming the classroom: Teacher research as an agency for change* (pp. 28–48). Upper Montclair, NJ: Boynton/Cook.

Beyer, L. (1984). Field experience, ideology, and the development of critical reflectivity. *Journal of Teacher Education, 35*(3), 36–41.

Borrowman, M. (1956). *The liberal and technical in teacher education: A historical survey of American thought*. New York: Teachers College Press.

Borrowman, M. (1965). *Teacher education in America: A documentary history*. New York: Teachers College Press.

Britzman, D. (1991). *Practice makes practice: A critical study of learning to teach*. Albany: State University of New York Press.

Bruner, J. (1996). *The culture of education*. Cambridge, MA: Harvard University Press.

Calderhead, J. (1989). Reflective teaching and teacher education. *Teaching and Teacher Education, 5*(1), 43–52.

Carini, P. (1986). *Prospect's documentary process.* Bennington, VT: Prospect School Center.

Castenell, L., & Pinar, W. (Eds.). (1993). *Understanding curriculum as racial text: Representations of identity and difference in education.* Albany: State University of New York Press.

Cazden, C., & Mehan, H. (1989). Principles from sociology and anthropology: Context, code, classroom, and culture. In C. Reynolds (Ed.), *Knowledge base for the beginning teacher* (pp. 47–58). Oxford: Pergamon Press.

Children's Defense Fund. (2000). *The state of America's children: Yearbook 2000.* Washington, DC: Author.

Clark, C., & Peterson, P. (1986). Teachers' thought processes. In M. Wittrock (Ed.), *Handbook of research on teaching* (3rd ed., pp. 255–296). New York: Macmillan.

Clewell, B.-C., & Villegas, A. M. (2001). *Ahead of the class: A handbook for preparing new teachers from new sources.* Washington, DC: Urban Institute.

Clift, R., Veal, M., Johnson, M., & Holland, P. (1990). Restructuring teacher education through collaborative action research. *Journal of Teacher Education, 41,* 52–62.

Cochran-Smith, M. (1991). Learning to teach against the grain. *Harvard Educational Review, 51*(3), 279–310.

Cochran-Smith, M. (1994). The power of teacher research in teacher education. In S. Hollingsworth & H. Sockett (Eds.), *Teacher research and educational reform* (pp. 142–165). Chicago: University of Chicago Press.

Cochran-Smith, M. (1995a). Color blindness and basket making are not the answers: Confronting the dilemmas of race, culture, and language diversity in teacher education. *American Educational Research Journal, 32*(3), 493–522.

Cochran-Smith, M. (1995b). Uncertain allies: Understanding the boundaries of race and teaching. *Harvard Educational Review, 65*(4), 541–570.

Cochran-Smith, M. (1997). Knowledge, skills, and experiences for teaching culturally diverse learners: A perspective for practicing teachers. In J. Irvine (Ed.), *Critical knowledge for diverse learners and teachers.* Washington, DC: American Association of Colleges for Teacher Education.

Cochran-Smith, M. (1998). Teaching for social change: Toward a grounded theory of teacher education. In A. Hargreaves, A. Lieberman, M. Fullan, & D. Hopkins (Eds.), *The international handbook of educational change* (pp. 916–951). The Netherlands: Kluwer Academic Publishers.

Cochran-Smith, M. (1999). Learning to teach for social justice. In G. Griffin (Ed.), *The education of teachers: Ninety-eighth yearbook of the National Society for the Study of Education* (pp. 114–144). Chicago: University of Chicago Press.

Cochran-Smith, M. (2000). Blind vision: Unlearning racism in teacher education. *Harvard Educational Review, 70*(2), 157–190.

Cochran-Smith, M. (2001a). Constructing outcomes in teacher education: Policy, practice and pitfalls. *Educational Policy Analysis Archives, 9*(11).

Cochran-Smith, M. (2001b). The outcomes question in teacher education. *Teaching & Teacher Education, 17*(5), 527–546.

Cochran-Smith, M. (2002a). Editorial: Reporting on teacher quality: The politics of politics. *Journal of Teacher Education, 53*(5), 379–382.

Cochran-Smith, M. (2002b). Editorial: What's preparation got to do with it? *Journal of Teacher Education, 53*(2), 99–101.

Cochran-Smith, M. (2003a). Editorial: Teaching quality matters. *Journal of Teacher Education, 54*(2), 95–98.

Cochran-Smith, M. (2003b). The multiple meanings of multicultural teacher education. *Teacher Education Quarterly, 30*(2), 7–26.

Cochran-Smith, M., Albert, L., DiMattia, P., Freedman, S., Jackson, R., Mooney, J., et al. (1999). Seeking social justice: A teacher education faculty's self-study. *International Leadership in Education, 2*(3), 229–253.

Cochran-Smith, M., Davis, D., & Fries, K. (2003). Multicultural teacher education: Research, practice and policy. In J. Banks (Ed.), *Handbook of research on multicultural education* (3rd ed., pp. 931–975). San Francisco: Jossey-Bass.

Cochran-Smith, M., & Lytle, S. (1990). Research on teaching and teacher research: The issues that divide. *Educational Researcher, 19*(2), 2–11.

Cochran-Smith, M., & Lytle, S. (1992). Communities for teacher research: Fringe or forefront? *American Journal of Education, 100*(3), 298–324.

Cochran-Smith, M., & Lytle, S. (1993). *Inside/outside: Teacher research and knowledge.* New York: Teachers College Press.

Cochran-Smith, M., & Lytle, S. (1998). Teacher research: The question that persists. *International Journal of Leadership in Education, 1*(1), 19–36.

Cochran-Smith, M., & Lytle, S. (1999). Relationship of knowledge and practice: Teacher learning in communities. In A. Iran-Nejad & C. Pearson (Eds.), *Review of research in education* (Vol. 24, pp. 249–306). Washington, DC: American Educational Research Association.

Cochran-Smith, M., & Lytle, S. (2001). Beyond certainty: Taking an inquiry stance on practice. In A. Lieberman & L. Miller (Eds.), *Teachers caught in the action: Professional development in practice* (pp. 45–60). New York: Teachers College Press.

Cochran-Smith, M., & Lytle, S. L. (in press). Practitioner inquiry, knowledge, and university culture. In J. Loughran, M. L. Hamilton, V. LaBoskey, & T. Russell (Eds.), *International handbook of research of self-study of teaching and teacher education practices.* Amsterdam: Kluwer.

Cohen, D., & Ball, D. (1990). Policy and practice: An overview. *Educational Evaluation and Policy Analysis, 12*(3), 347–353.

Cohen, D., McLaughlin, M., & Talbert, J. (Eds.). (1993). *Teaching for understanding: Challenges for policy and practice.* San Francisco: Jossey-Bass.

Commission on Multicultural Education. (1978). *Directory: Multicultural education programs in teacher education institutions in the United States.* Washington, DC: American Association of Colleges for Teacher Education.

Cone, J. (1990). *Untracking advanced placement English: Creating opportunity is not enough: Research in writing: Working papers of teacher researchers.* Berkeley, CA: Bay Area Writing Project, University of California.

Counts, G. (1926). *The senior high school curriculum*. Chicago: University of Chicago Press.

Counts, G. (1932). *Dare the schools build a new social order?* Chicago: University of Chicago Press.

Curtin, D. (2001, February 2). Report blasts teacher prep: CU, Metro State called too liberal. *Denver Post*, pp. 1B, 3B.

Darling-Hammond, L. (Ed.). (1994). *Professional development schools: Schools for developing a profession*. New York: Teachers College Press.

Darling-Hammond, L. (1995). Inequality and access to knowledge. In J. A. Banks & C.A.M. Banks (Eds.), *Handbook of research on multicultural education*. New York: Macmillan.

Darling-Hammond, L. (1996). Who teaches and why: Dilemmas of building a profession for twenty-first century schools. In J. Sikula, T. Buttery, & E. Guyton (Eds.), *Handbook of research on teacher education* (2nd ed., pp. 67–93). New York: Macmillan.

Darling-Hammond, L. (1998). Teacher learning that supports student learning. *Educational Leadership, 55*(5), 6–11.

Darling-Hammond, L. (2000a). How teacher education matters. *Journal of Teacher Education, 51*(3), 166–173.

Darling-Hammond, L. (2000b). Reforming teacher preparation and licensing: Debating the evidence. *Teachers College Record, 102*(1), 28–56.

Darling-Hammond, L. (Ed.). (2000c). *Studies of excellence in teachers*. Washington, DC: National Commission on Teaching and America's Future.

Darling-Hammond, L. (2000d). Teacher quality and student achievement: A review of state policy evidence. *Education Policy Analysis Archives, 8*(1).

Darling-Hammond, L. (2000e). Teaching for America's future: National commissions and vested interests in an almost profession. *Educational Policy, 14*(1), 162–183.

Darling-Hammond, L., & McLaughlin, M. (1999). Investing in teaching as a learning profession: Policy, problems, and prospects. In L. Darling-Hammond & G. Sykes (Eds.), *Teaching as the learning profession: Handbook of policy and practice* (pp. 376–412). San Francisco: Jossey-Bass.

Darling-Hammond, L., & Sclan, E. M. (1996). Who teaches and why. In J. Sikula (Ed.), *Handbook of research on teacher education* (pp. 67–101). New York: Simon & Schuster Macmillan.

Darling-Hammond, L., & Sykes, G. (Eds.). (1999). *Teaching as the learning profession: Handbook of policy and practice*. San Francisco: Jossey-Bass.

Darling-Hammond, L., & Youngs, P. (2002). Defining 'highly qualified teachers': What does 'scientifically-based research' actually tell us? *Educational Researcher, 31*(9), 13–25.

Delpit, L. (1988). The silenced dialogue: Power and pedagogy in educating other people's children. *Harvard Educational Review, 58*(3), 280–298.

Dewey, J. (1904). The relation of theory to practice in education. In C. McMurray (Ed.), *The third NSSE yearbook*. Chicago: University of Chicago Press.

Diez, M., & Hass, J. (1997). No more piecemeal reform: Using performance-based approaches to rethink teacher education. *Action in teacher education, XIX*(2), 17–26.

Dill, W. (1998). Specialized accreditation: An idea whose time has come? Or gone? *Change, 30*(4),18–25.

Dilworth, M. (1992). *Diversity in teacher education.* San Francisco: Jossey-Bass.

Duckworth, E. (1987). *The having of wonderful ideas and other essays on teaching and learning.* New York: Teachers College Press.

Earley, P. (2000). Finding the culprit: Federal policy and teacher education. *Educational Policy, 14*(1), 25–39.

Edelsky, C., Altwerger, B., & Flories, B. (1991). *Whole language: What's the difference.* Portsmouth, NH: Heinemann.

Edmundsen, P. J. (1990). A normative look at the curriculum in teacher education. *Phi Delta Kappan, 71*(9), 717–722.

Education Commission of the States. (2000). *Two paths to quality teaching—the debate.* Available: www.ecs.org.

Educational Research Service. (1995). *Demographic factors in American education.* Arlington: VA: Educational Research Service.

Eisner, E. (1985). *Learning and teaching the ways of knowing.* Chicago: University of Chicago Press.

Elmore, R. (2002). The testing trap. *Harvard Magazine, 105*(1), 35.

Elmore, R., & Burney, D. (1997). *Investing in teacher learning: Staff development and instructional improvement in Community School District #2, New York City.* New York: National Commission on Teaching & America's Future.

Erickson, F. (1981). Taught cognitive learning in its immediate environments: A neglected topic in the anthropology of education. *Anthropology and Education Quarterly, 13,* 149–180.

Evertson, C. (1990). Bridging knowledge and action through clinical experiences. In D. Dill (Ed.), *What teachers need to know* (pp. 94–109). San Francisco: Jossey-Bass.

Farkas, S., & Johnson, J. (1997). *Different drummers: How teachers of teachers view public education.* New York: Public Agenda.

Fecho, R. (2000). Developing critical mass: Teacher education and critical inquiry pedagogy. *Journal of Teacher Education, 51*(3), 194–199.

Feiman-Nemser, S. (1983). Learning to teach. In L. Shulman & G. Sykes (Eds.), *Handbook of teaching and policy* (pp. 150–170). New York: Longman.

Feiman-Nemser, S. (1990). Teacher preparation: Structural and conceptual alternatives. In W. R. Houston (Ed.), *Handbook of research on teacher education* (pp. 212–233). New York: Macmillan.

Fenstermacher, G. (1990). Some moral considerations on teaching as a profession. In R.S.J. Goodlad & K. A. Sirotnik (Eds.), *The moral dimensions of teaching* (pp. 130–151). San Francisco: Jossey-Bass.

Fine, M. (1994). *Chartering urban school reform: Reflections on pubic high schools in the midst of change.* New York: Teachers College Press.

Flippo, R. (1986). Teacher certification testing: Perspectives and issues. *Journal of Teacher Education, 37*(2), 2–9.

Foster, M. (1994). Effective black teachers: A literature review. In E. Hollins, J. King, & W. Hayman (Eds.), *Teaching diverse populations: Formulating a knowledge base* (pp. 225–242). Albany: State University of New York Press.

Fox, W., & Gay, G. (1995). Integrating multicultural and curriculum principles in teacher education. *Peabody Journal of Education, 70*, 64–82.

Freire, P. (1970). *Pedagogy of the oppressed* (M. B. Ramos, Trans.). New York: Seabury Press.

Fuller, M. (1994). The monocultural graduate in the multicultural environment: A challenge for teacher educators. *Journal of Teacher Education, 45*(4), 269–277.

Gage, N. (1978). Reviewing what we know: The results of recent research. In N. Gage (Ed.), *The scientific basis of the art of teaching*. New York: Teachers College Press.

Gallagher, K., & Bailey, J. (2000). The politics of teacher education reform: Strategic philanthropy and public policy making. *Educational Policy, 14*(1), 11–24.

Gallavan, N. P. (2000). Multicultural education at the academy: Teacher educators' challenges, conflicts and coping skills. *Equity and Excellence in Education, 33*(3), 5–11.

Garcia, P. (1986). The impact of national testing on ethnic minorities: With proposed solutions. *Journal of Negro Education, 55*(3), 347–357.

Gay, G. (1993). Building cultural bridges: A bold proposal for teacher education. *Education and Urban Society, 25*(3), 285–289.

Gay, G. (2000). *Culturally responsive teaching: Theory, research and practice*. New York: Teachers College Press.

Gay, G., & Howard, T. C. (2000). Multicultural teacher education for the 21st century. *The Teacher Educator, 36*(1), 1–16.

Gee, J. (1996). *Social linguistics and literacies: Ideology in discourses*. London: Taylor & Francis.

Ginsburg, M. (1988). *Contradictions in teacher education and society: A critical analysis*. Philadelphia: Falmer.

Ginsburg, M., & Clift, R. (1990). The hidden curriculum of preservice teacher education. In R. Houston (Ed.), *Handbook of research on teacher education* (pp. 450–465). New York: MacWilliams Publishing.

Ginsburg, M., & Lindsay, B. (1995a). *Comparative perspectives on policy formation, socialization, and society*. Philadelphia: Falmer Press.

Ginsburg, M., & Lindsay, B. (1995b). The political dimension in teacher education. In M. Ginsburg & B. Lindsay (Eds.), *Comparative perspectives on policy formation, socialization, and society*. London: Falmer Press.

Giroux, H. (1984). Rethinking the language of schooling. *Language Arts, 61*, 33–40.

Giroux, H. (1988). *Teachers as intellectuals*. Westport, CT: Bergin & Harvey.

Gitlin, A. (Ed.). (1994). *Power and method: Political activism and educational research*. New York: Routledge.

Gitlin, A., & Teitelbaum, K. (1983). Linking theory and practice: The use of ethnographic methodology by prospective teachers. *Journal of Education for Teaching, 9*, 225–234.

Gitomer, D., & Latham, A. (2000). Generalizations in teacher education: Seductive and misleading. *Journal of Teacher Education*, *51*(3), 215–220.

Glazer, N. (1997). A new word for an old problem: Multicultural 'school wars' date to the 1840s. In D. Flinders & S. Thornton (Eds.), *The curriculum studies reader* (pp. 274–278). New York: Routledge.

Gollnick, D. (1992). Understanding the dynamics of race, class, and gender. In M. Dilworth (Ed.), *Diversity in teacher education*. San Francisco: American Association of Colleges for Teacher Education/Jossey-Bass.

Gollnick, D. (1995). National and state initiatives for multicultural education. In J. A. Banks (Ed.), *Handbook of research on multicultural education*. New York: Macmillan.

Goodlad, J. (1984). *A place called school*. New York: McGraw-Hill.

Goodlad, J. (1990a). Studying the education of educators: From conception to findings. *Phi Delta Kappan*, *71*(9), 698–701.

Goodlad, J. (1990b). *Teachers for our nation's schools*. San Francisco: Jossey-Bass.

Goodman, J. (1986a). Making early field experience meaningful: A critical approach. *Journal of Education for Teachers*, *12*(2), 109–125.

Goodman, J. (1986b). University education course and descriptive analysis. *Teaching and Teacher Education*, *2*, 341–353.

Goodman, K. S. (1988). *Report card on basal readers*. New York: Richard C. Owen Publishers.

Goodwin, A. L. (2000). Teachers as (multi)cultural agents in schools. In R. Carter (Ed.), *Addressing cultural issues in organizations: Beyond the corporate context* (pp. 104–114). Thousand Oaks, CA: Sage.

Goodwin, A. L. (2001). Seeing with different eyes: Reexamining teachers' expectations through racial lenses. In S. King & L. Castenell (Eds.), *Racism and racial inequality: Implications for teacher education*. Washington, DC: American Association of Colleges for Teacher Education.

Gore, J., & Zeichner, K. (1991). Action research and reflective teaching in preservice teacher education. *Teaching and Teacher Education*, *7*, 119–136.

Graham, P., Lyman, R., & Trow, M. (1998). *Accountability of colleges and universities: An essay*. New York: Columbia University Press.

Gramsci, A. (1977). Indifference. In Q. Hoare (Ed.), *Antonio Gramsci: Selections from political writings 1910–1920*. London: Lawrence & Wishart. Original work published 1916.

Grant, C., & Secada, W. (1990). Preparing teachers for diversity. In W. R. Houston, M. Haberman, & J. Sikula (Eds.), *Handbook of research on teacher education* (pp. 403–422). New York: Macmillan.

Grant, C., Sleeter, C., & Anderson, J. (1986). The literature on multicultural education: Review and analysis. *Educational Studies*, *12*(1), 47–71.

Grant, C., & Wieczorek, K. (2000). Teacher education and knowledge in "the knowledge society": The need for social moorings in our multicultural schools. *Teachers College Record*, *102*(5), 913–935.

Grimmett, P. P., & Neufeld, J. (1994). *Teacher development and the struggle for authenticity: Professional growth and restructuring in the context of change*. New York: Teachers College Press.

Gutman, A. (1999). *Democratic education (with a new preface and epilogue).* Princeton, NJ: Princeton University Press.

Haberman, M. (1991). Rationale for training adults as teachers. In C. Sleeter (Ed.), *Empowerment through multicultural education* (pp. 275–286). Albany: State University of New York Press.

Haberman, M. (1996). Selecting and preparing culturally competent teachers for urban schools. In J. Sikula, T. Buttery, & E. Guyton (Eds.), *Handbook of research on teacher education* (2nd ed., pp. 747–760). New York: Macmillan.

Haberman, M., & Post, L. (1998). Teachers for multicultural schools: The power of selection. *Theory into Practice, 37*(2), 96–104.

Hardy, B. (1978). Towards a poetics of fiction: An approach through narrative. In M. Meek & G. Barton (Eds.), *The cool web* (pp. 12–23). New York: Atheneum.

Harris, S. (1986). Evaluation of a curriculum to support literacy growth in young children. *Early Childhood Research Quarterly, 1*(4), 333–348.

Hawley, W., & Valli, L. (1999). The essentials of effective professional development: A new consensus. In L. Darling-Hammond & G. Sykes (Eds.), *Teaching as the learning profession: handbook of policy and practice* (pp. 127–150). San Francisco: Jossey–Bass.

Heap, J. (2002). The DOE Secretary's report: Meeting the highly qualified teachers challenge. Governor's Commission on Teaching Success, Athens, Ohio.

Heath, S. (1983). *Ways with words: Language, life, and work in communities and classrooms.* Cambridge, MA: Harvard University Press.

Hodgkinson, H. (2001). Educational demographics: What teachers should know. *Educational Leadership, 58*(4), 6–11.

Hodgkinson, H. (2002). Demographics and teacher education. *Journal of Teacher Education, 53*(2), 102–105.

Hollins, E., King, J., & Hayman, W. (Eds.). (1994). *Teaching diverse populations: Formulating a knowledge base.* Albany: State University of New York Press.

hooks, b. (1994). *Teaching to transgress: Education as the practice of freedom.* New York: Routledge.

Howey, K., Arends, R., Yarger, S., & Zimpher, N. (1994). *RATE VI: The context of reform of teacher education.* Washington, DC: American Association of Colleges of Teacher Education.

Hursh, D. (1988). *Liberal discourse and organizational structure as barriers to reflective teaching.* Unpublished manuscript, Swarthmore College.

Irvine, J. (1990). *Black students and school failure: Policies, practice and prescriptions.* New York: Greenwood Press.

Irvine, J. (Ed.). (1997). *Constructing the knowledge base for urban teacher education.* Washington, DC: American Association of Colleges for Teacher Education.

Irvine, J. (2000, April). *Seeing with the cultural eye: Different perspectives of African American teachers and researchers.* Paper presented at the annual meeting of the American Educational Research Association, New Orleans.

Irvine, J. (2001, February). *Caring, competent teachers in complex classrooms.* Paper presented at the Charles W. Hunt Memorial Lecture for the American Association of Colleges for Teacher Education, Dallas, TX.

Irvine, J., & Armento, B. (2001). *Culturally responsive teaching: Lesson planning for elementary and middle schools.* Boston: McGraw-Hill.

Irvine, J., & Fraser, J. (1998, May 13). Warm demanders. *Education Week,* p. 35.

Irvine, J., & York, D. (1995). Learning styles and culturally diverse students: A literature review. In J. A. Banks & C.A.M. Banks (Eds.), *Handbook of research on multicultural education.* New York: Macmillan.

Jenks, C., Lee, J.-O., & Kanpol, B. (2001). Approaches to multicultural education in preservice teacher education: Philosophical frameworks and models for teaching. *The Urban Review, 33*(2), 87–105.

Kanstoroom, M. (1999). *Boosting teacher quality: A common sense proposal. Testimony prepared for delivery to the Subcommittee on Postsecondary Education of the Committee on Education and the Workforce, U.S. House of Representatives.* Washington, DC: Thomas B. Fordham Foundation.

Kanstoroom, M., & Finn, C. (1999). *Better teachers, better schools.* Washington, DC: Thomas B. Fordham Foundation.

Kilborn, P. T. (1996, November 30). The welfare overhaul: A special report. *The New York Times,* pp. 1, 10.

King, J. (1994). The purpose of schooling for African American children: Including cultural knowledge. In E. Hollins, J. King, & W. Hayman (Eds.), *Teaching diverse populations: Formulating a knowledge base* (pp. 25–60). Albany: State University of New York Press.

King, J., Hollins, E., & Hayman, W. (Eds.). (1997). *Preparing teachers for cultural diversity.* New York: Teachers College Press.

King, S., & Castenell, L. (Eds.). (2001). *Racism and racial identity: Implications for teacher education.* Washington, DC: American Association of Colleges for Teacher Education.

Kitano, M. K., Lewis, R., Lynch, E., & Graves, A. (1996). Teaching in a multicultural classroom: Teacher educators' perspectives. *Equity and Excellence in Education, 29*(3), 70–77.

Kozol, J. (1991). *Savage inequalities: Children in America's schools.* New York: Harper & Row.

Labaree, D. (1997). Public good, private goods: The American struggle over educational goals. *American Educational Research Journal, 34*(1), 39–81.

Ladson-Billings, G. (1994). *The dreamkeepers: Successful teachers of African-American children.* San Francisco: Jossey-Bass.

Ladson-Billings, G. (1995a). Multicultural teacher education: Research, practice, and policy. In J. A. Banks & C. A. Banks (Eds.), *Handbook of research on multicultural education* (pp. 747–761). New York: Macmillan.

Ladson-Billings, G. (1995b). Toward a theory of culturally relevant pedagogy. *American Educational Research Journal, 32*(3), 465–491.

Ladson-Billings, G. (1998). Teaching in dangerous times: Culturally relevant approaches to teacher assessment. *Journal of Negro Education, 67*(3), 255–267.

Ladson-Billings, G. (1999). Preparing teachers for diverse student populations: A critical race theory perspective. In A. Iran-Nejad & D. Pearson (Eds.), *Review of research in education* (Vol. 24, pp. 211–248). Washington, DC: American Educational Research Association.

Ladson-Billings, G. (2001). *Crossing over to Canaan*. San Francisco: Jossey-Bass.

Lakoff, G., & Johnson, M. (1980). *Metaphors we live by*. Chicago: University of Chicago Press.

Lampert, M. (1985). How do teachers manage to teach? Perspectives on problems in practice. *Harvard Educational Review, 55*, 178–194.

Lampert, M. (1990). When the problem is not the question and the solution is not the answer: Mathematical knowing and teaching. *American Educational Research Journal, 27*(1), 29–63.

Lampert, M., & Ball, D. (1998). *Teaching, multimedia, and mathematics: Investigations of real practice*. New York: Teachers College Press.

Lampert, M., & Ball, D. (1999). Aligning teacher education with contemporary K–12 reform visions. In L. Darling-Hammond & G. Sykes (Eds.), *Teaching as the learning profession: A handbook of policy and practice* (pp. 33–53). San Francisco: Jossey-Bass.

Lather, P. (1986). Research as praxis. *Harvard Educational Review, 56*(3), 257–277.

Lauer, P. (2001). *A secondary analysis of a review of teacher preparation research*. Denver, CO: Education Commission of the States.

Lawrence, S., & Tatum, B. (1997). Teachers in transition: The impact of antiracist professional development on classroom practice. *Teachers College Record, 99*(1), 162–178.

Leistyna, P., Woodrum, A., & Sherblo, S. A. (Eds.). (1996). *Breaking free: The transformative power of critical pedagogy*. Cambridge, MA: Harvard Educational Review.

Lieberman, A., & Miller, J. (1991). *Staff development for education in the '90s*. New York: Teachers College Press.

Lieberman, A., & Miller, L. (1994). Problems and possibilities of institutionalizing teacher research. In S. Hollingsworth & H. Socket (Eds.), *Teacher research and educational reform* (pp. 204–220). Chicago: University of Chicago Press.

Liston, D., & Zeichner, K. (1991a). *Teacher education and the social conditions of schooling*. New York: Routledge.

Liston, D., & Zeichner, K. (1991b). Traditions of reform in U.S. teacher education. In D. Liston & K. Zeichner (Eds.), *Teacher education and the social conditions of schooling* (pp. 1–37). New York: Routledge.

Little, J. (1987). Teachers as colleagues. In V. Richardson-Koehler (Ed.), *Educators' handbook*. New York: Longman.

Little, J. (1993a). Professional community in comprehensive high schools: The two worlds of academic and vocational teachers. In J. Little & M. McLaughlin (Eds.), *Teacher's work: Individuals, colleagues, and contexts* (pp. 137–163). New York: Teachers College Press.

Little, J. (1993b). Teachers' professional development in a climate of educational reform. *Educational Evaluation and Policy Analysis, 15*(2), 129–151.

Loucks-Horsley, S. (1995). Professional development and the learner centered school. *Theory into Practice, 34*(4), 265–271.

Luna, C., Solsken, J., & Kutz, E. (2000). Defining literacy: Lessons from high-stakes teacher testing. *Journal of Teacher Education, 51*(4), 276–288.

Lynch, J. (1986). *Multicultural education: Principles and practice.* London: Routledge.

Lytle, S., & Cochran-Smith, M. (1995, March). *Teacher research and the constructive disruption of university culture.* Paper presented at the Ethnography and Education Forum, Philadelphia.

MacCann, D. (1993). Native Americans in books for the young. In V. Harris (Ed.), *Teaching multicultural literature in grades K-8.* Norwood, MA: Christopher-Gordon Publishers.

Madaus, G., & O'Dwyer, L. (1999). A short history of performance assessment: Lessons learned. *Phi Delta Kappan, 80*(9), 688–695.

Maggio, R. (Ed.). (1997). *Quotations on education.* Paramus, NJ: Prentice-Hall.

Maimon, G. (1996). *Little pigs, big ideas.* Unpublished paper, University of Pennsylvania Graduate School of Education, Philadelphia.

Martin, R., & Van Gunten, D. (2002). Reflected identities: Applying positionality and multicultural social reconstructionism in teacher education. *Journal of Teacher Education, 53*(1), 44–54.

McCarthy, C. (1993). Multicultural approaches to racial inequality in the United States. In L. Castenell & W. Pinar (Eds.), *Understanding curriculum as racial text.* Albany: State University of New York Press.

McDonald, J. (1992). *Teaching: Making sense of an uncertain craft.* New York: Teachers College Press.

McIntosh, P. (1989, July/August). White privilege: Unpacking the invisible knapsack. *Peace and Freedom,* pp. 10–12.

McLaughlin, M. (1993). What matters most in teachers' workplace context? In J. W. Little & M. McLaughlin (Eds.), *Teachers' work* (pp. 79–103). New York: Teachers College Press.

McNergney, R., Lloyd, J., Mintz, S., & Moore, J. (1988). Training for pedagogical decision making. *Journal of Teacher Education, 39*(5), 37–43.

Melnick, S., & Pullin, D. (2000). "Can you take dictation?" Prescribing teacher quality through testing. *Journal of Teacher Education, 51*(4), 262–275.

Melnick, S., & Zeichner, K. (1997). Enhancing the capacity of teacher education institutions to address diversity issues. In J. King, E. Hollins, & W. Hayman (Eds.), *Preparing teachers for cultural diversity* (pp. 23–39). New York: Teachers College Press.

Metzger, D. (1986). Circles of stories. *Parabola, 4*(4), 1–4.

Moll, L. (1992). Funds of knowledge for teaching: Using a qualitative approach to connect homes and classrooms. *Theory into Practice, 31*(1), 32–41.

Murrell, P. (2001). *The community teacher.* New York: Teachers College Press.

National Center for Education Statistics. (1997a). *Digest of educational statistics.* Washington DC: U.S. Government Printing Office.

National Center for Education Statistics. (1997b). *NAEP 1996 mathematics report card for the nation and the states.* Washington, DC: U.S. Government Printing Office.

National Center for Education Statistics. (1998). *1998 data file: 1996–1997 common core of data public elementary and secondary school universe.* Washington, DC: U.S. Government Printing Office.

National Center for Education Statistics. (1999). *NAEP 1998 reading report card for the nation.* Washington, DC: U.S. Government Printing Office.

National Commission on Teaching and America's Future. (1996). *What matters most: Teaching for America's future.* New York: Teachers College, Columbia University.

National Commission on Teaching and America's Future. (1997). *Doing what matters most: Investing in quality teaching.* New York: Author.

National Council for Accreditation of Teacher Education. (1999). *Proposed NCATE 2000 unit standards.* Washington, DC: Author.

National Education Goals Panel. (1994). *Data volume for the National Education Goals Report: Volume 1—National data.* Washington, DC: U.S. Government Printing Office.

National Research Council. (2000). *How people learn: Brain, mind, experience and school.* Washington, DC: National Academy Press.

Nieto, S. (2000). Placing equity front and center: Some thoughts on transforming teacher education for a new century. *Journal of Teacher Education, 51*(3), 180–187.

No Child Left Behind Act of 2001, P.L. 107–110.

Noffke, S. (1997). Professional, personal, and political dimensions of action research. In M. Apple (Ed.), *Review of research in education* (Vol. 22, pp. 305–343).

Oakes, J. (1988). *Keeping track: How high schools structure inequality.* New Haven, CT: Yale University Press.

Oakes, J., Franke, M., Quartz, K., & Rogers, J. (2002). Research for high-quality urban teaching: Defining it, developing it, assessing it. *Journal of Teacher Education, 53*(3), 228–234.

Oakes, J., & Lipton, M. (1999). *Teaching to change the world.* Boston: McGraw-Hill.

Oakes, J., Quartz, K. H., Ryan, S., & Lipton, M. (2000). *Becoming good American schools: The struggle for civic virtue in education reform.* San Francisco: Jossey-Bass.

Obidah, J. (2000). Mediating boundaries of race, class, and professional authority as a critical multiculturalist. *Teachers College Record, 102*(5), 1035–1060.

Pinar, W., Reynolds, W., Slattery, P., & Taubman, P. (Eds.). (2002). *Understanding curriculum: An introduction to the study of historical and contemporary curriculum discourses.* New York: Peter Lang.

Public Agenda. (2001). *What is public agenda?* Available: www.publicagenda.org/aboutpa/aboutpa.htm.

Quartz, K., & TEP Research Group. (2003). Too angry to leave: Supporting new teachers' commitment to transform urban schools. *Journal of Teacher Education, 54*(2), 99–111.

Ravitch, D. (2000). *Left back: A century of failed school reforms.* New York: Simon & Schuster.

Raymond, M., Fletcher, S. H., & Luque, J. (2001). *Teach for America: An evaluation of teacher differences and student outcomes.* Houston: Thomas B. Fordham Foundation.

Richardson-Koehler, V. (1988). Barriers to the effective supervision of students: A field of study. *Journal of Teacher Education, 39,* 28–34.

Robertson, H. (1998). Public education in a corporate-dominated culture. In A. Hargreaves, A. Lieberman, M. Fullan, & D. Hopkins (Eds.), *International handbook of educational change* (pp. 396–417). Boston: Kluwer Academic Publishers.

Rochester City Schools/University of Rochester Ford Foundation Report. (1988–89). *Professional development site: A community of learners (Part A).* Rochester, NY: Author.

Rosenberg, P. (1996). Underground discourses: Exploring whiteness in teacher education. In M. Fine, L. Powell, L. Weis, & M. Wong (Eds.), *Offwhite: Readings on race, power, and society* (pp. 79–89). New York: Routledge.

Rosenshine, B., & Stevens, R. (1986). Teaching functions. In M. Wittrock (Ed.), *Handbook of research on teaching* (3rd ed., pp. 376–391). New York: Macmillan.

Ross, D. (1987). Action research for preservice teachers: A description of why and how. *Peabody Journal of Education, 64,* 131–150.

Sanders, D., & McCutcheon, G. (1986). The development of practical theories of teaching. *Journal of Curriculum and Supervision, 2*(1), 50–67.

Sanders, W., & Horn, S. (1998). Research findings from the Tennessee Value-Added Assessment System (TVAAS) database: Implications for educational evaluation and research. *Journal of Personnel Evaluation in Education, 12*(3), 247–256.

Schalock, D., & Imig, D. (2000). *Shulman's union of insufficiencies +7: New dimensions of accountability for teachers and teacher educators.* Washington, DC: American Association of Colleges for Teacher Education.

Schalock, D., & Myton, D. (1988). A new paradigm for teacher licensure: Oregon's demand for evidence of success in fostering learning. *Journal of Teacher Education, 39*(6), 27–32.

Schalock, D., Schalock, M., & Girod, G. (1997). Teacher work sample methodology as used at Western Oregon State College. In J. Millman (Ed.), *Grading teachers, grading schools* (pp. 15–45). Thousand Oaks, CA: Corwin Press.

Schalock, D., Schalock, M., & Myton, D. (1998). Effectiveness—along with quality—should be the focus. *Phi Delta Kappan, 79*(6), 468–470.

Schön, D. (1983a). The crisis of confidence in professional knowledge. In D. Schön (Ed.), *Educating the reflective practitioner* (pp. 3–19). San Francisco: Jossey-Bass.

Schön, D. (1983b). *The reflective practitioner: How professionals think in action.* San Francisco: Jossey-Bass.

Schön, D. (1987). *Educating the reflective practitioner.* San Francisco: Jossey-Bass.

Seidl, B., & Friend, G. (2002). The unification of church and state: Working together to prepare teachers for diverse classrooms. *Journal of Teacher Education, 53*(2), 142–152.

Shannon, P. (1988). *Merging literacy: Reading instruction in 20th century America.* South Hadley, MA: Bergin & Garvey.

Shulman, L. (1987). Knowledge and teaching: Foundations of the new reform. *Harvard Educational Review, 51,* 1–22. Original work published 1983.

Silverman, D. (2000). Analyzing talk and text. In D. Denzin & Y. Lincoln (Eds.), *Handbook of qualitative research* (2nd ed., pp. 821–834). Thousand Oaks, CA: Sage Publications.

Slapin, B., & Seale, B. (1992). *Through Indian eyes: The native experience in books for children.* Philadelphia: New Society Publishers.

Sleeter, C. (1992). Restructuring schools for multicultural education. *Journal of Teacher Education, 43*(2), 141–148.

Sleeter, C. (1995). Reflections on my use of multicultural and critical pedagogy when students are white. In C. Sleeter & P. McLaren (Eds.), *Multicultural education, critical pedagogy: The politics of difference.* Albany: State University of New York Press.

Sleeter, C. (1996). *Multicultural education as social activism.* Albany: State University of New York Press.

Sleeter, C. (2001). Epistemological diversity in research on preservice teacher preparation for historically underserved children. In W. Secada (Ed.), *Review of research in education* (Vol. 25, pp. 209–250). Washington, DC: American Educational Research Association.

Sleeter, C., & Grant, C. (1987). An analysis of multicultural education in the United States. *Harvard Educational Review, 57*(4), 421–444.

Smith, G. (1984). The critical issue of excellence and equity in competency testing. *Journal of Teacher Education, 35*(2), 6–9.

Smith, M., Heinecke, W., & Noble, A. (1999). Assessment policy and political spectacle. *Teachers College Record, 101*(2), 157–191.

Stein, M., Smith, M., & Silver, E. (1999). The development of professional developers: Learning to assist teachers in new settings in new ways. *Harvard Educational Review, 69*(3), 237–269.

Stotsky, S. (1999). *Losing our language: How multicultural classroom instruction is undermining our children's ability to read, write, and reason.* New York: Free Press.

Su, Z. (1990). The function of the peer group in teacher socialization. *Phi Delta Kappan, 71,* 723–727.

Tabachnick, B. R., & Zeichner, K. (1984). The impact of the student teaching experience on the development of teacher perspectives. *Journal of Teacher Education, 35*(6), 28–36.

Tabachnick, B. R., & Zeichner, K. (1991). *Issues and practices in inquiry-oriented teacher education.* London: Falmer Press.

Tatum, B. (1992). Talking about race, learning about racism. The applications of racial identity development theory. *Harvard Educational Review, 62*(1), 1–24.

Taxel, J. (1993). The politics of children's literature: Reflections on multiculturalism and Christopher Columbus. In V. Harris (Ed.), *Teaching multicultural literature in grades K–8* (pp. 1–36). Norwood, MA: Christopher-Gordon Publishers.

Teitelbaum, K., & Britzman, D. (1991). Reading and doing ethnography: Teacher education and reflective practice. In B. R. Tabachnick & K. Zeichner (Eds.), *Issues and practices in inquiry-oriented teacher education*. London: Falmer Press.

Thiessen, D. (2000). Developing knowledge for preparing teachers: Redefining the role of schools of education. *Educational Policy, 14*(1), 129–144.

Thomas B. Fordham Foundation. (1999a). *The quest for better teachers: Grading the states*. Washington, DC: Author.

Thomas B. Fordham Foundation. (1999b). The teachers we need and how to get more of them: A manifesto. In M. Kanstoroom & C. Finn (Eds.), *Better teachers, better schools* (pp. 1–18). Washington, DC: Author.

Tom, A. R. (1985). Inquiring into inquiry-oriented teacher education. *Journal of Teacher Education, 36*(5), 35–44.

Traugh, C. (2002). Inquiry as a mode of renewal: Imagining the possibilities of circumstance. *CUE Point of View, 1*(1), 1–7.

U.S. Department of Education. (1996). *Reforms in preservice preparation programs and teacher certification standards*. Available: http://www.ed.gov. Retrieved February 2000.

U.S. Department of Education. (1998). *Promising practices: New ways to improve teacher quality*. Washington, DC: Author.

U.S. Department of Education. (2000). *President's summit on teacher quality*. Washington, DC: Author.

U.S. Department of Education. (2002, June). *Meeting the highly qualified teachers challenge: The Secretary's annual report on teacher quality*. Washington, DC: U.S. Department of Education, Office of Postsecondary Education.

Valenzuela, A. (2002). Reflections on the subtractive underpinnings of education research and policy. *Journal of Teacher Education, 53*(3), 235–241.

Villegas, A. (1991). *Culturally responsive pedagogy for the 1990's and beyond*. Princeton, NJ: Educational Testing Service.

Villegas, A., Clewell, B., Anderson, M., Goertz, M., Joy, F., Bruschi, B., et al. (1995). *Teaching for diversity: Models for expanding the supply of minority teachers*. Princeton, NJ: Educational Testing Service.

Villegas, A., & Lucas, T. (2001). *Preparing culturally responsive teachers: A coherent approach*. Albany: State University of New York Press.

Villegas, A., & Lucas, T. (2002). Preparing culturally responsive techers: Rethinking the curriculum. *Journal of Teacher Education, 53*(1), 20–32.

Weiner, L. (1990). Preparing the brightest for urban schools. *Urban Education, 25*(3), 258–273.

Weiner, L. (1993). *Preparing teachers for urban schools, lessons from 30 years of school reform*. New York: Teachers College Press.

Weiner, L. (2000). Research in the 90s: Implications for urban teacher preparation. *Review of Educational Research, 70*(3), 369–406.

Whitty, G., Power, S., & Halpin, D. (1998). *Devolution and choice in education: The school, the state, and the market*. Melbourne: Australian Council for Educational Research.

Wilcox, D., & Finn, C. (1999, August 9). Education: Board games; Business backs a losing education strategy. *National Review*, p. L1.

Willis, P. E. (1978). *Learning to labour*. Hampshire, England: Gower.

Wilson, S., Floden, R., & Ferrini-Mundy, J. (2001). *Teacher preparation research: Current knowledge, gaps, and recommendations*. Washington, DC: Center for the Study of Teaching and Policy.

Wise, A. (1988). *Impacts of teacher testing: State educational governance through standard-setting* (ERIC Document No. NIE-G-83-0023). Santa Monica, CA: Rand Corporation.

Wise, A. (1996, November). Building a system of quality assurance for the teaching profession: Moving towards the 21st century. *Phi Delta Kappan, 78*(3), 191–192.

Wise, A. (1998). *NCATE: Assuring quality for the nation's teachers. Testimony of Arthur E. Wise at the Senate committee on labor and human resources hearing on "Better teachers for today's classroom: How to make it happen."* Available: http://www.ncate.org/specfoc/arttest.html. Retrieved February 2000.

Wise, A. (1999). *Standards or no standards? Teacher quality in the 21st century.* Available: http://www.ncate.org/specfoc/preparation.htm. Retrieved February 2000.

Yeo, F. L. (1997). Teacher preparation and inner-city schools: Sustaining educational failure. *The Urban Review, 29*, 127–143.

Yinger, R. (1999). The role of standards in teaching and teacher education. In G. Griffin (Ed.), *The education of teachers: The 98th yearbook of the NSSE* (pp. 85–113). Chicago: University of Chicago Press.

Yinger, R., & Hendricks-Lee, M. (2000). The language of standards and teacher education reform. *Educational Policy, 14*(1), 94–106.

Zeichner, K. (1986). Preparing reflective teachers: An overview of instructional strategies which have been employed in preservice teacher education. *International Journal of Educational Research, 7*(5), 565–575.

Zeichner, K. (1993). *Educating teachers for cultural diversity* (National Center for Research on Teacher Learning Special Report). East Lansing, MI: Michigan State University. (ERIC Document No. ED 359 167)

Zeichner, K., & Hoeft, K. (1996). Teacher socialization for cultural diversity. In J. Sikula, T. J. Buttery, & E. Guyton (Eds.), *Handbook of research on teacher education* (2nd ed., pp. 525–547). New York: Macmillan.

Zeichner, K., & Liston, D. (1985). Varieties of supervisory discourse. *Teaching & Teacher Education, 1*, 155–174.

Zeichner, K., & Liston, D. (1987). Teaching student teachers to reflect. *Harvard Educational Review, 57*, 1–22.

Zeichner, K., Liston, D., Mahlios, M., & Gomez, M. (1988). The structure and goals of a student teaching program and the character and quality of supervisory discourse. *Teaching and Teacher Education, 4*, 349–362.

Zeichner, K., & Melnick, S. (1996). The role of community field experiences in preparing teachers for cultural diversity. In K. Zeichner, S. Melnick, & M.

Gomez (Eds.), *Currents of reform in preservice teacher education* (pp. 176–198). New York: Teachers College Press.

Zeichner, K., Tabachnick, B. R., & Densmore, K. (1987). Individual, institutional, and cultural influences on the development of teachers' craft knowledge. In J. Calderhead (Ed.), *Exploring teachers' thinking* (pp. 21–59). London: Cassell.

Zumwalt, K. (1989). Beginning professional teachers: The need for a curricular vision of teaching. In M. Reynolds (Ed.), *Knowledge base for the beginning teacher* (pp. 173–184). New York: Pergamon Press.

Index

About the Author

Marilyn Cochran-Smith is professor of education and the director of doctoral studies in curriculum and instruction at the Lynch School of Education at Boston College, where she teaches courses and directs numerous doctoral dissertations. An active researcher and participant in the national and international teacher education communities, Cochran-Smith is president of the American Educational Research Association (AERA) for 2004–2005. She served as AERA vice president for Division K (Teaching and Teacher Education) from 1998 to 2000 and chair of publications from 2001 to 2003. Dr. Cochran-Smith is also the editor of *The Journal of Teacher Education*, coeditor of the Teachers College Press series on *Practitioner Inquiry*, coeditor of the forthcoming *Handbook of Research on Teacher Education* (3rd *edition*), and cochair of AERA's National Panel on Research and Teacher Education. She is also a member of the National Academy of Education's Committee on Teacher Education, a member of the advisory board for the Carnegie Foundation's K–12 CASTL project, and senior mentor for UCLA's Center X Urban Teacher Educators Network.

Dr. Cochran-Smith has written award-winning articles and books on diversity in teaching and teacher education as well as on teacher research, teacher learning, and policy issues in teacher education. She is a frequent presenter and keynote speaker nationally and internationally. In 1999, Dr. Cochran-Smith received the Margaret Lindsey Award for Outstanding Research in Teacher Education from AACTE, and in 2000, she received the Boston College Senior Research Award. She has also received research and writing awards from AERA's Division K, the Association of Teacher Educators (ATE), the American Association for Colleges of Teacher Education (AACTE), and the National Council of Teachers of English (NCTE). Her well-known book about teacher research, *Inside/Outside: Teacher Research and Knowledge*, coauthored with Susan L. Lytle, was published by Teachers College Press in 1993. Earlier books on young children's literacy development include *The Making of a Reader* (Ablex Publishing, 1983) and *Learning to Write Differently: Young Children and Word Processing*, which she coauthored with Cynthia Paris and Jessica Kahn (Ablex Publishing, 1994).